Garfield
bigger and better

BY: JIM DAVIS

Ballantine Books • New York

Copyright © 1996 by PAWS, Incorporated.

All rights reserved under International and Pan-American Copyright
Conventions. Published in the United States by Ballantine Books, a
division of Random House, Inc., New York, and simultaneously in
Canada by Random House of Canada Limited, Toronto.

http://www.randomhouse.com

Library of Congress Catalog Card Number: 96-96531

ISBN: 0-345-40770-9

Manufactured in the United States of America

First Edition: October 1996

10 9 8 7 6 5 4 3 2 1

"You've done worse!"

GARFIELDin '96 FOR PRESIDENT

IF GARFIELD WERE PRESIDENT, HE WOULD...

- Abolish Mondays!
- Put a sweat tax on gyms and health clubs
- Give federal subsidies for napping
- Pour millions into the fight against dog breath
- Establish The President's Council on Snacking!
- Put a dessert bar in every school cafeteria!

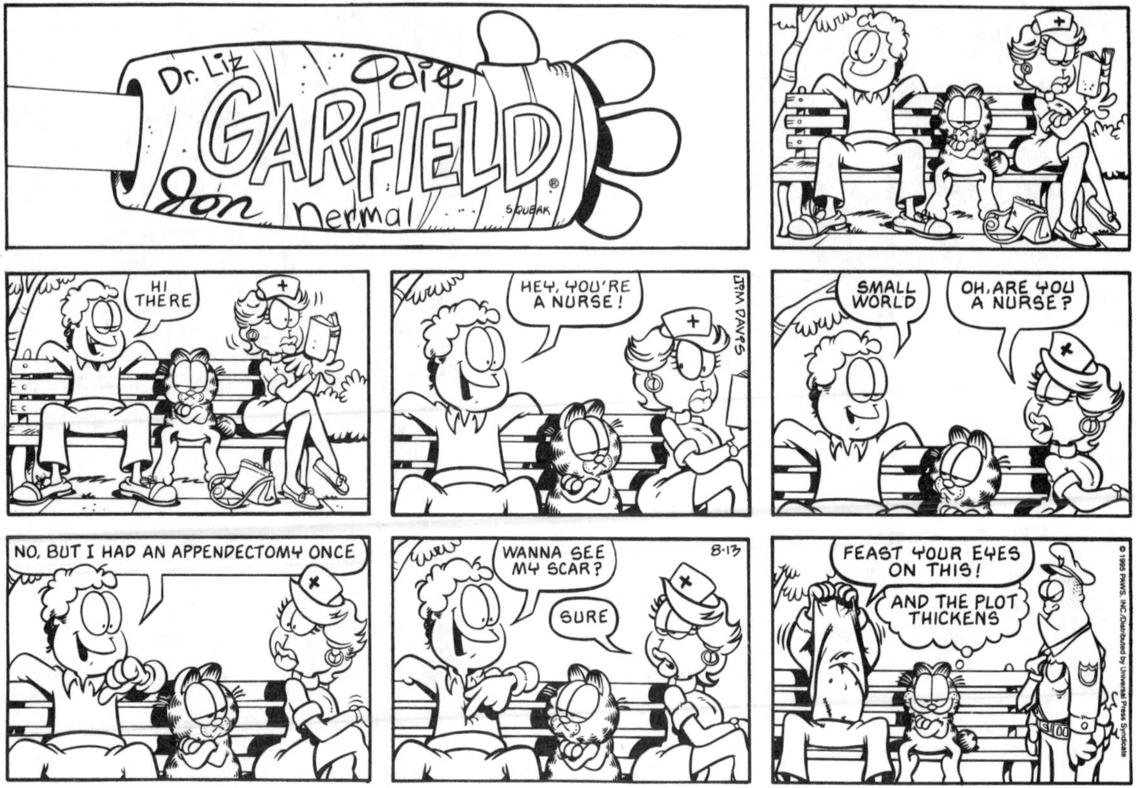
Dr. Liz
Odie
GARFIELD®
Jon
Nermal
HI THERE
HEY, YOU'RE A NURSE!
JIM DAVIS
SMALL WORLD
OH, ARE YOU A NURSE?
NO, BUT I HAD AN APPENDECTOMY ONCE
WANNA SEE MY SCAR?
8-13
SURE
FEAST YOUR EYES ON THIS!
AND THE PLOT THICKENS
© 1995 PAWS, INC./Distributed by Universal Press Syndicate

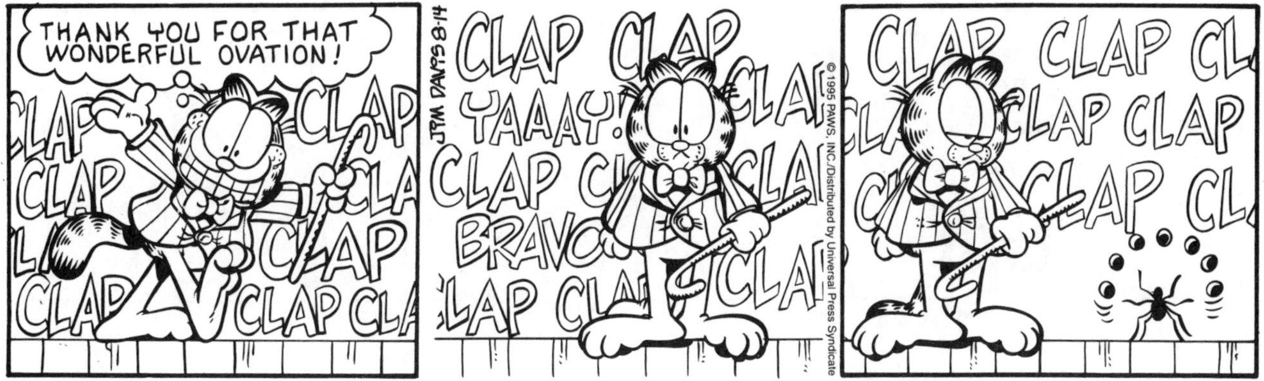
THANK YOU FOR THAT WONDERFUL OVATION!
CLAP CLAP CLAP CLAP CLAP CLAP
JIM DAVIS 8-14
CLAP CLAP
YAAAY!
CLAP
BRAVO
CLAP
© 1995 PAWS, INC./Distributed by Universal Press Syndicate
CLAP CLAP CLAP CLAP CLAP CLAP

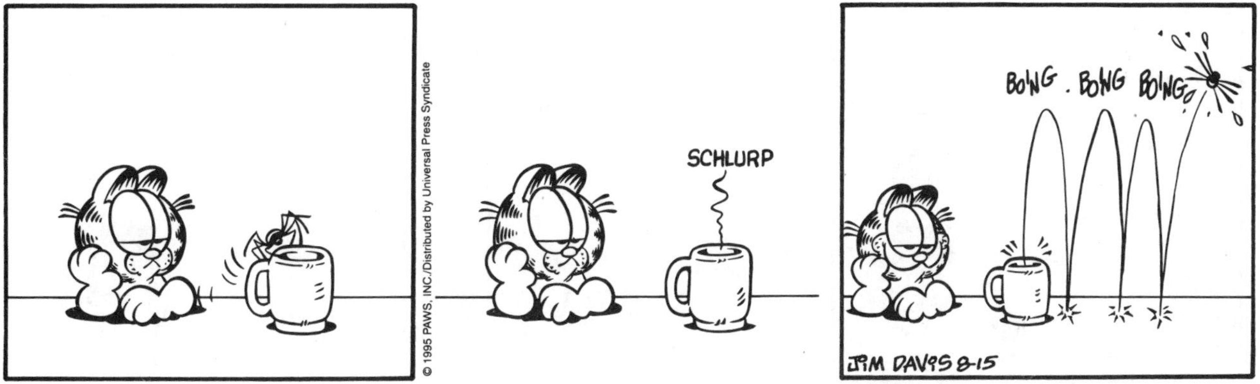
© 1995 PAWS, INC./Distributed by Universal Press Syndicate
SCHLURP
BOING BOING BOING
JIM DAVIS 8-15

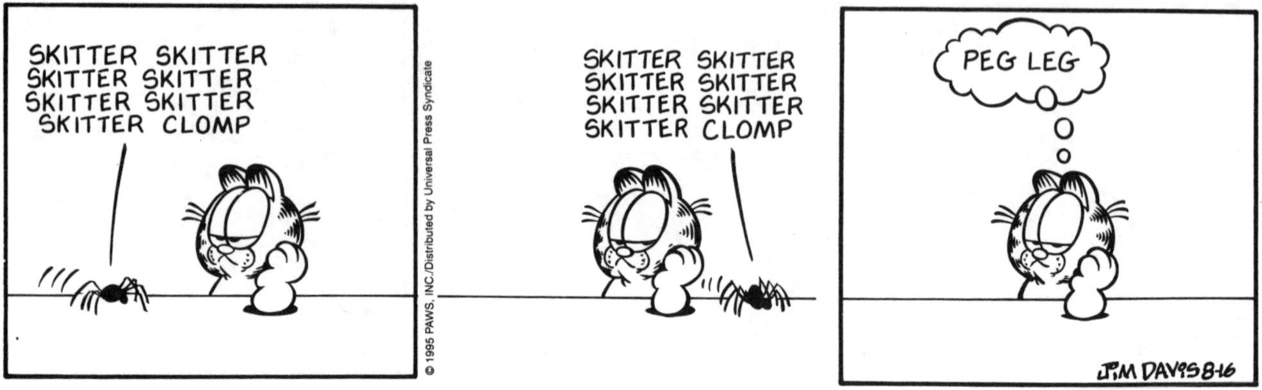
SKITTER SKITTER SKITTER SKITTER SKITTER SKITTER SKITTER CLOMP
SKITTER SKITTER SKITTER SKITTER SKITTER SKITTER SKITTER CLOMP
PEG LEG
JIM DAVIS 8-16

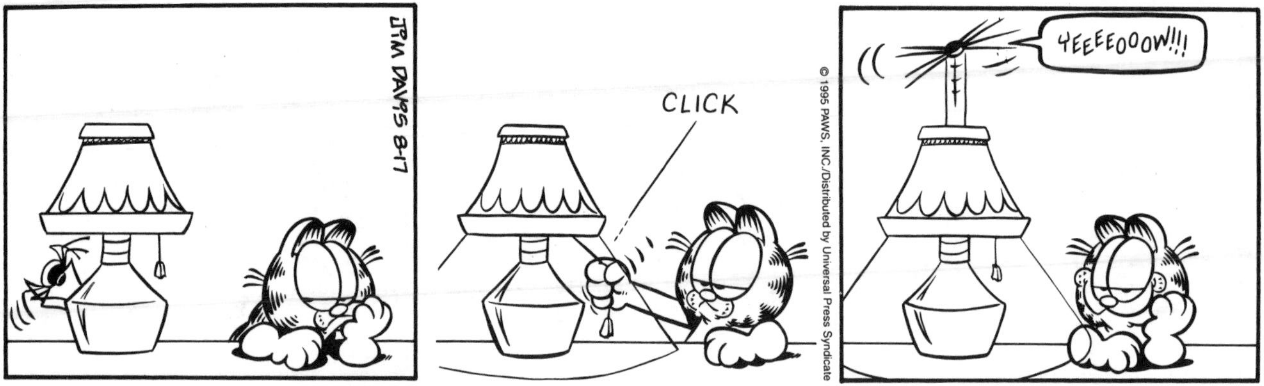
JIM DAVIS 8-17
CLICK
YEEEEOOOW!!!

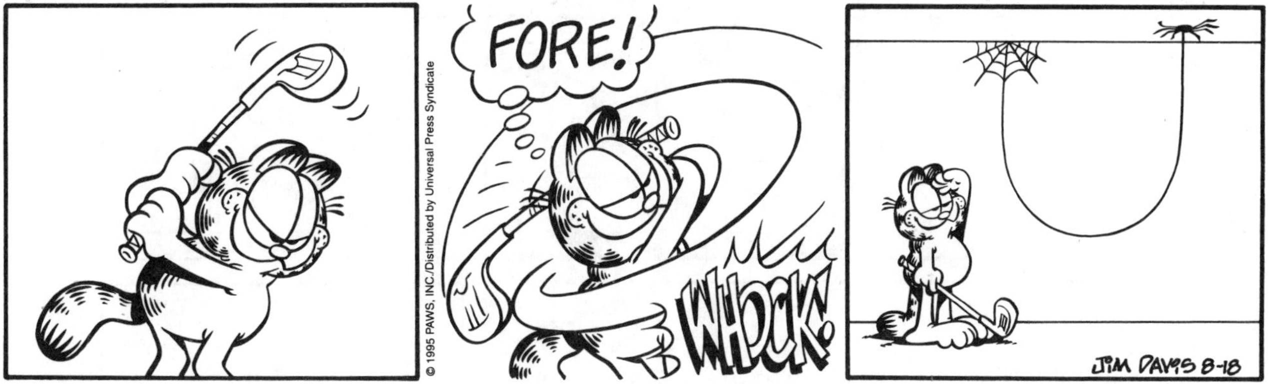
FORE!
WHOCK!
© 1995 PAWS, INC./Distributed by Universal Press Syndicate
JIM DAVIS 8-18

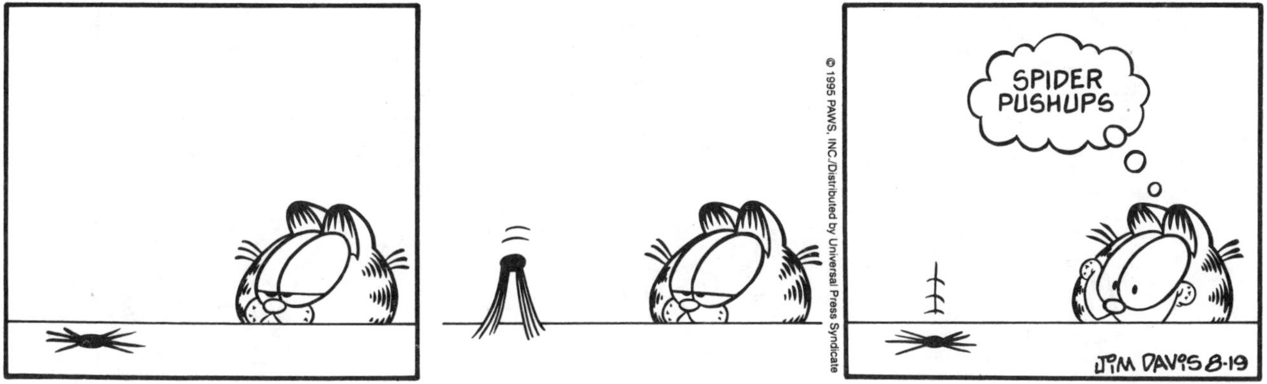
© 1995 PAWS, INC./Distributed by Universal Press Syndicate
SPIDER PUSHUPS
JIM DAVIS 8-19

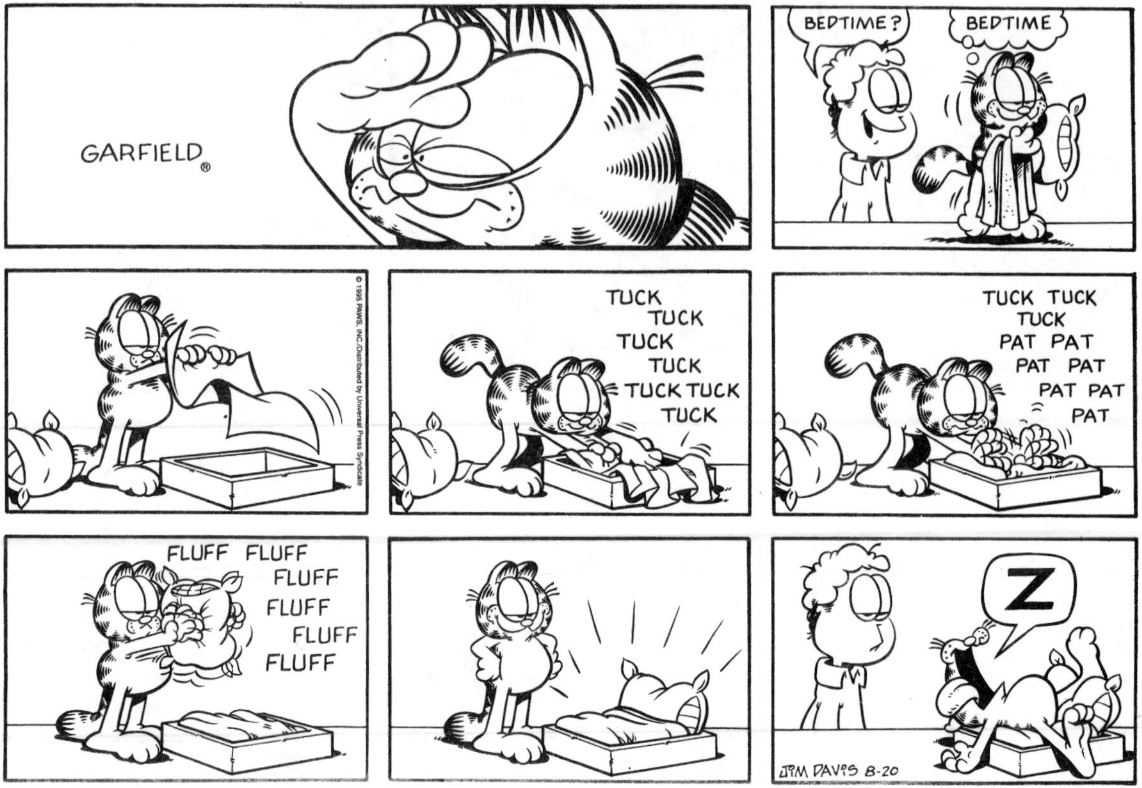

GARFIELD®
BEDTIME?
BEDTIME
© 1995 PAWS, INC./Distributed by Universal Press Syndicate
TUCK TUCK TUCK TUCK TUCK TUCK TUCK
TUCK TUCK TUCK PAT PAT PAT PAT PAT PAT PAT
FLUFF FLUFF FLUFF FLUFF FLUFF FLUFF
Z
JIM DAVIS 8-20

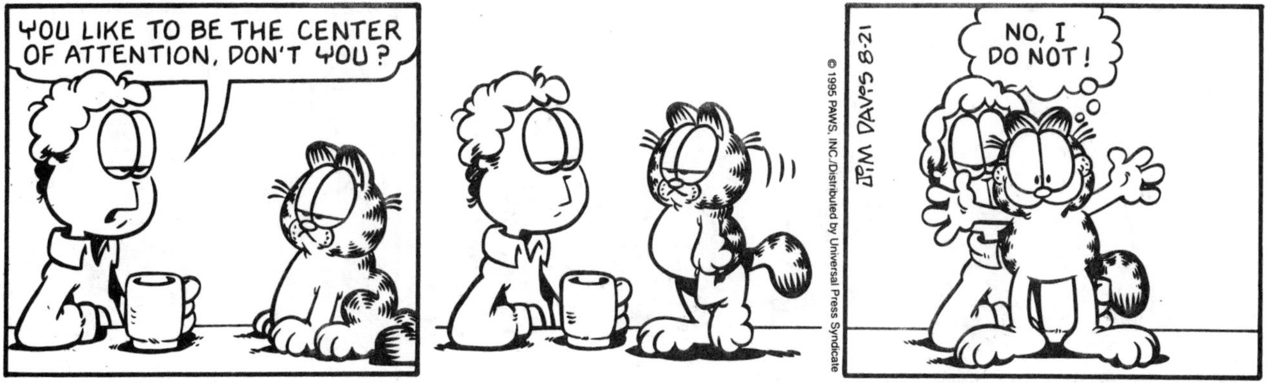
YOU LIKE TO BE THE CENTER OF ATTENTION, DON'T YOU?
© 1995 PAWS, INC./Distributed by Universal Press Syndicate
JIM DAVIS 8-21
NO, I DO NOT!

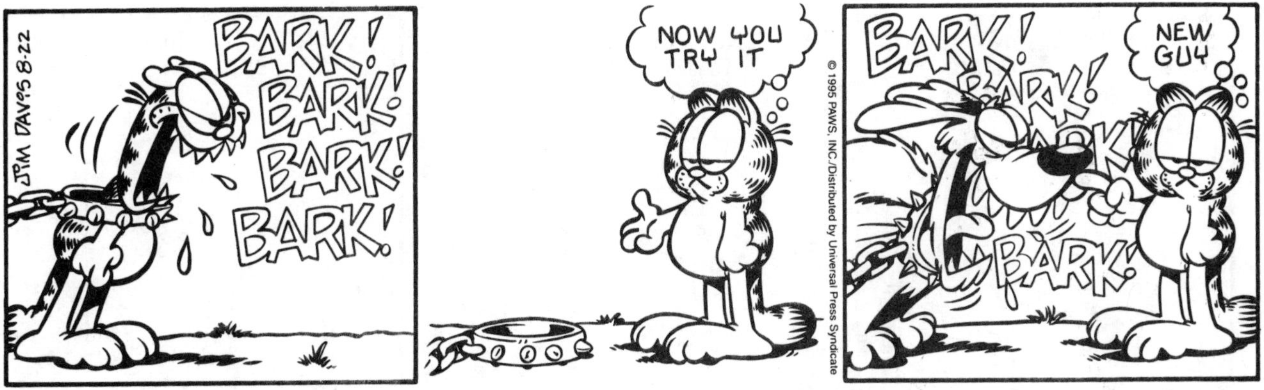
JIM DAVIS 8-22
BARK! BARK! BARK! BARK!
NOW YOU TRY IT
© 1995 PAWS, INC./Distributed by Universal Press Syndicate
BARK! BARK! BARK! BARK!
NEW GUY

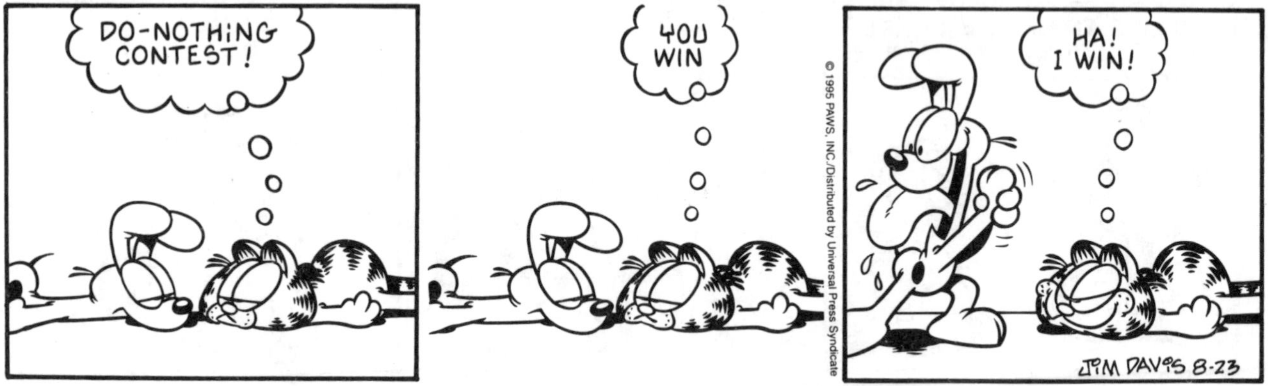
DO-NOTHING CONTEST!
YOU WIN
HA! I WIN!
© 1995 PAWS, INC./Distributed by Universal Press Syndicate
JIM DAVIS 8-23

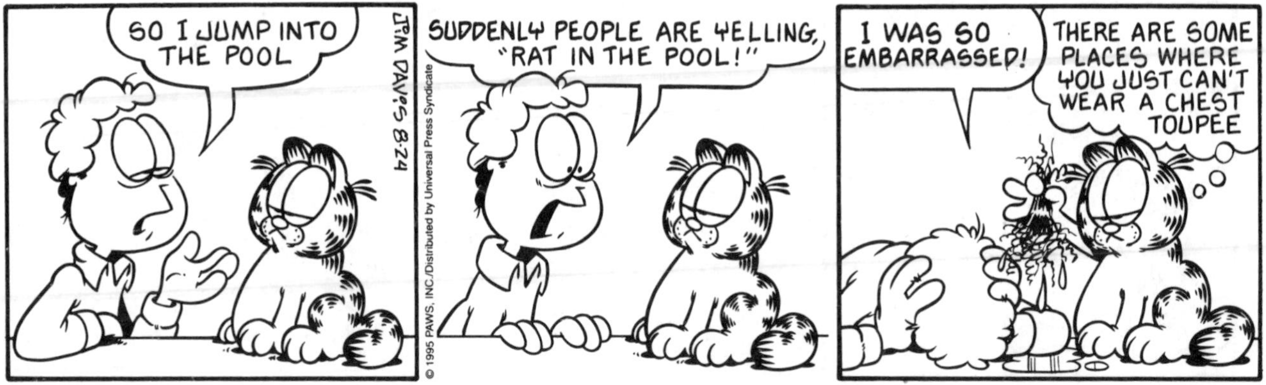
SO I JUMP INTO THE POOL
JIM DAVIS 8-24
© 1995 PAWS, INC./Distributed by Universal Press Syndicate
SUDDENLY PEOPLE ARE YELLING, "RAT IN THE POOL!"
I WAS SO EMBARRASSED!
THERE ARE SOME PLACES WHERE YOU JUST CAN'T WEAR A CHEST TOUPEE

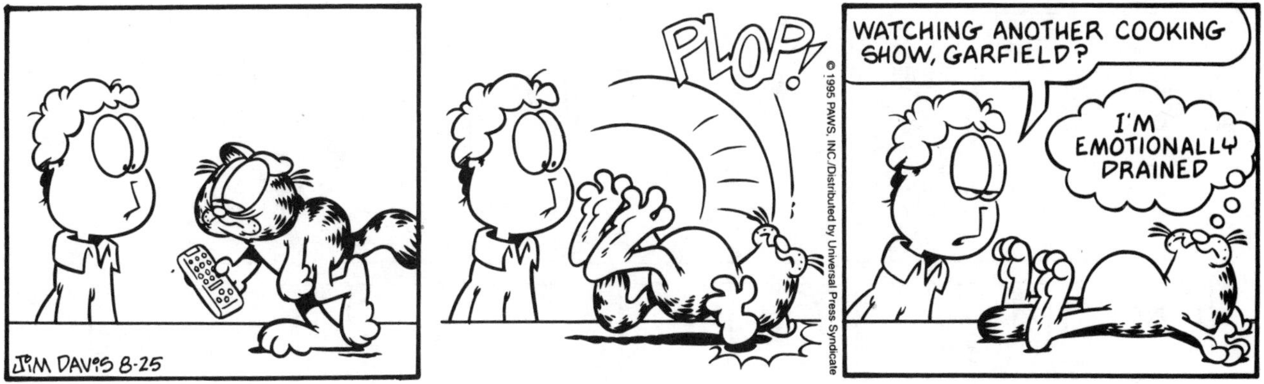
JIM DAVIS 8-25
PLOP!
© 1995 PAWS, INC./Distributed by Universal Press Syndicate
WATCHING ANOTHER COOKING SHOW, GARFIELD?
I'M EMOTIONALLY DRAINED

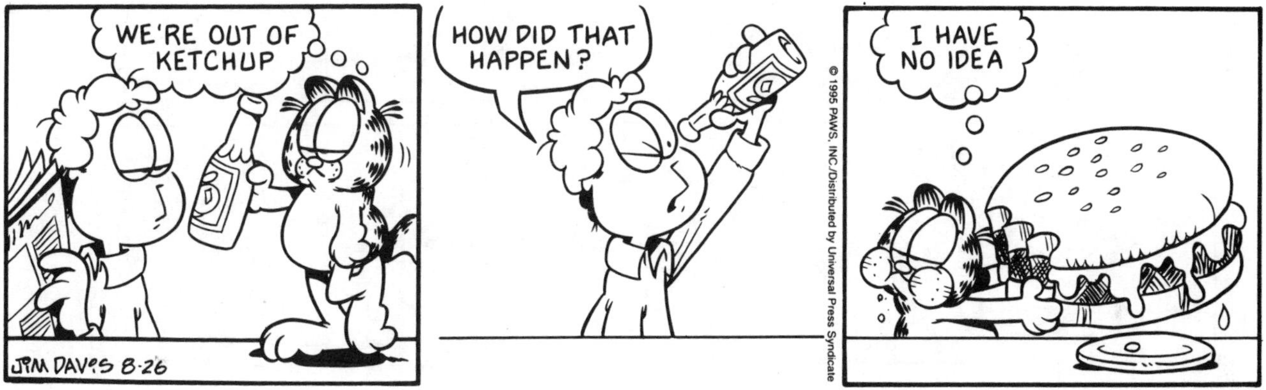
WE'RE OUT OF KETCHUP
JIM DAVIS 8-26
HOW DID THAT HAPPEN?
© 1995 PAWS, INC./Distributed by Universal Press Syndicate
I HAVE NO IDEA

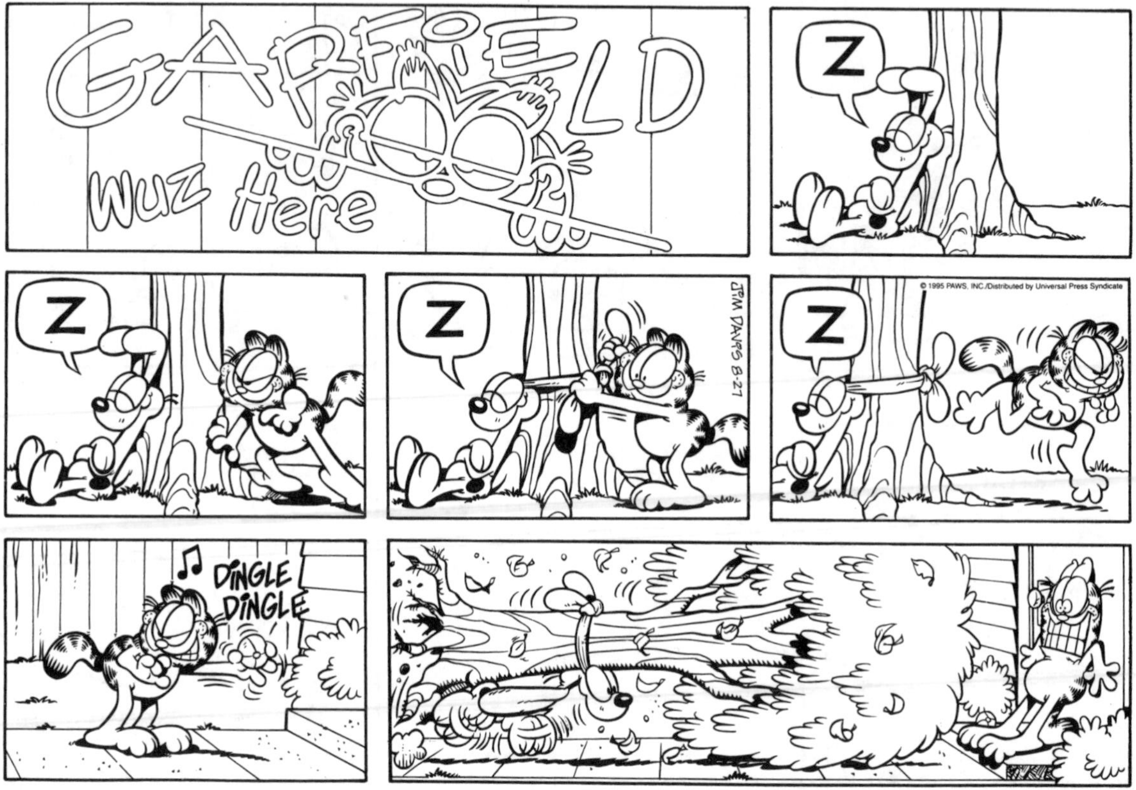
GARFIELD
Wuz Here
Z
Z
Z
JIM DAVIS 8-27
© 1995 PAWS, INC./Distributed by Universal Press Syndicate
Z
DINGLE
DINGLE

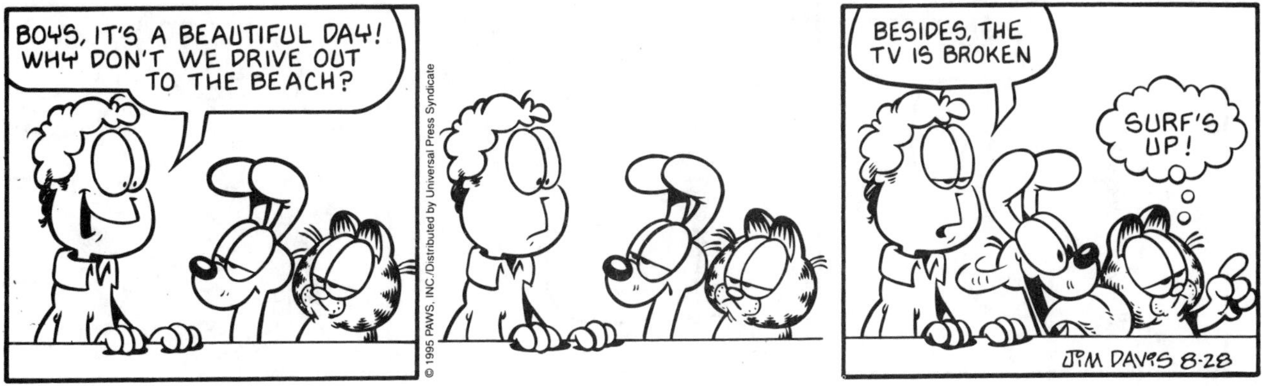
BOYS, IT'S A BEAUTIFUL DAY! WHY DON'T WE DRIVE OUT TO THE BEACH?
BESIDES, THE TV IS BROKEN
SURF'S UP!
JIM DAVIS 8-28

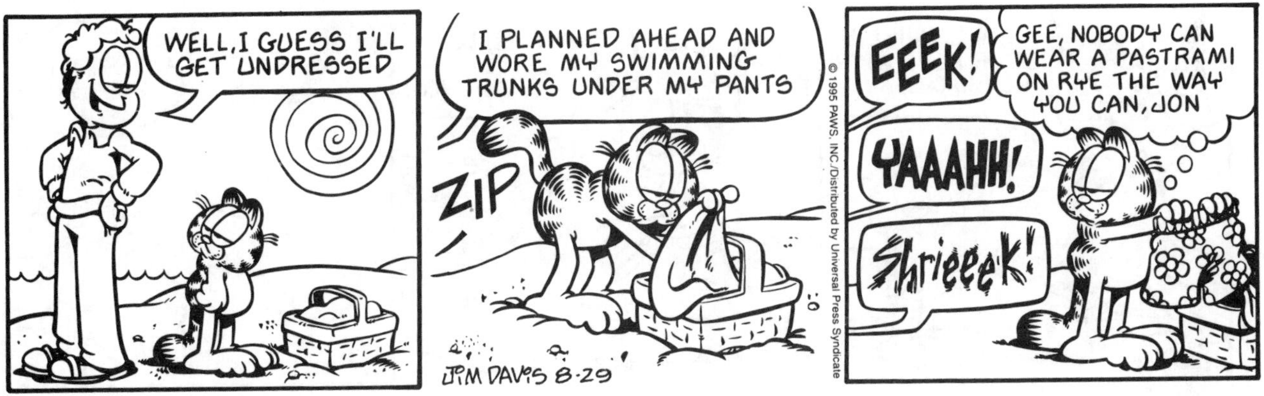
WELL, I GUESS I'LL GET UNDRESSED
I PLANNED AHEAD AND WORE MY SWIMMING TRUNKS UNDER MY PANTS
ZIP
JIM DAVIS 8-29
EEEK!
YAAAHH!
Shrieeek!
GEE, NOBODY CAN WEAR A PASTRAMI ON RYE THE WAY YOU CAN, JON

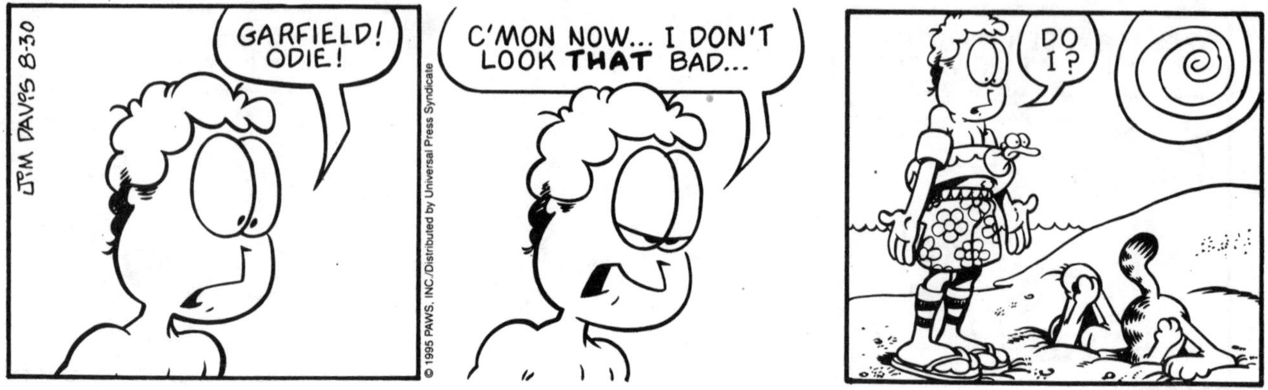
JIM DAVIS 8-30
GARFIELD! ODIE!
© 1995 PAWS, INC./Distributed by Universal Press Syndicate
C'MON NOW... I DON'T LOOK **THAT** BAD...
DO I?

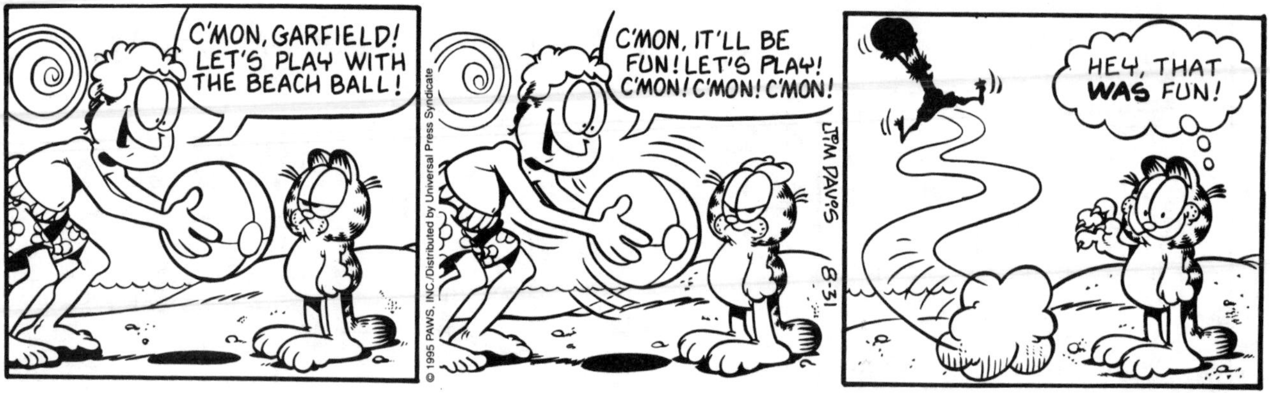
C'MON, GARFIELD! LET'S PLAY WITH THE BEACH BALL!
© 1995 PAWS, INC./Distributed by Universal Press Syndicate
C'MON, IT'LL BE FUN! LET'S PLAY! C'MON! C'MON! C'MON!
JIM DAVIS 8-31
HEY, THAT **WAS** FUN!

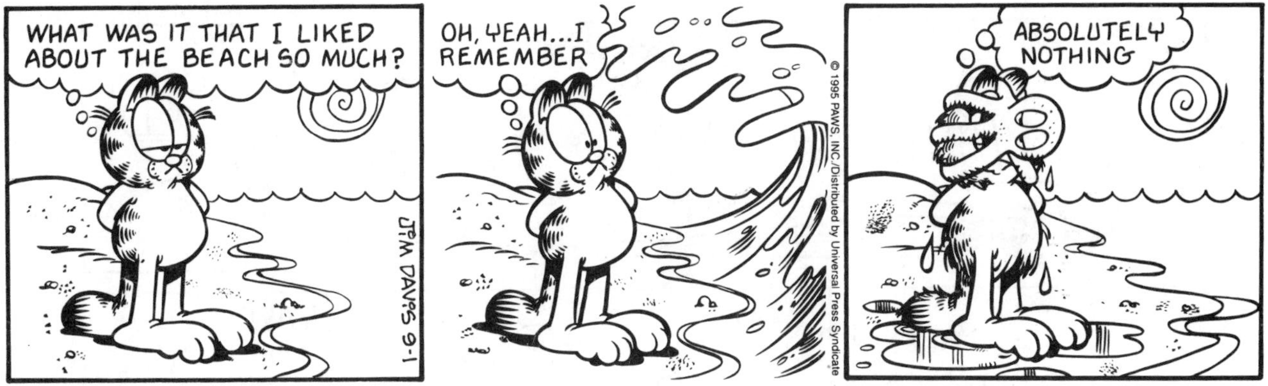
WHAT WAS IT THAT I LIKED ABOUT THE BEACH SO MUCH?
JIM DAVIS 9-1
OH, YEAH...I REMEMBER
© 1995 PAWS, INC./Distributed by Universal Press Syndicate
ABSOLUTELY NOTHING

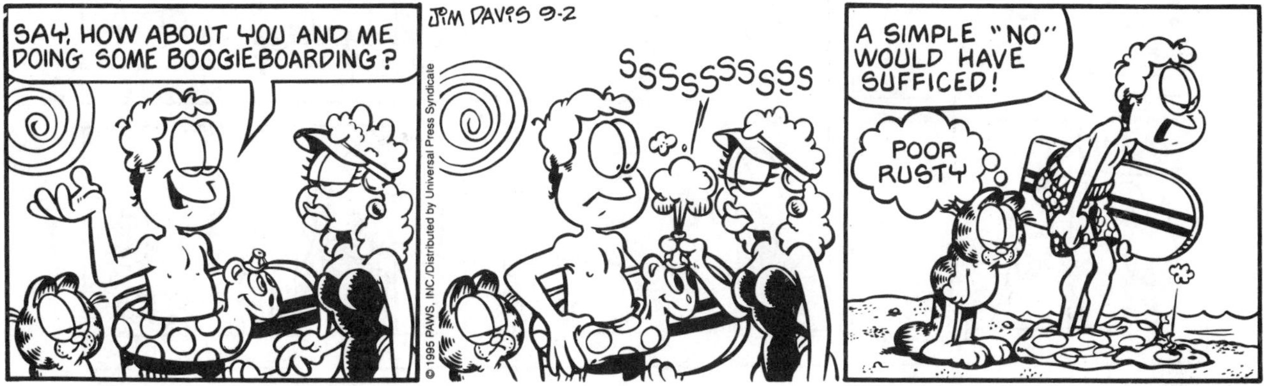
SAY, HOW ABOUT YOU AND ME DOING SOME BOOGIEBOARDING?
© 1995 PAWS, INC./Distributed by Universal Press Syndicate
JIM DAVIS 9-2
SSSSSSSSSSS
A SIMPLE "NO" WOULD HAVE SUFFICED!
POOR RUSTY

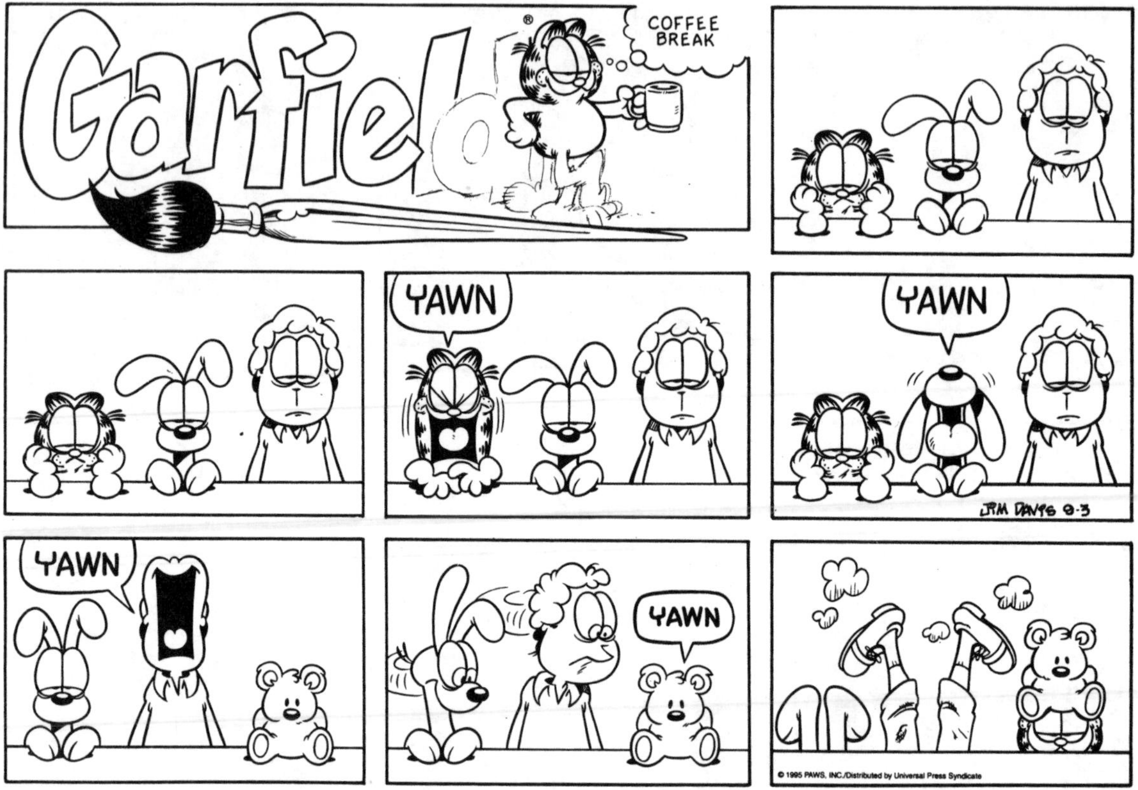
Garfield®
COFFEE BREAK
YAWN
YAWN
JIM DAVIS 9-3
YAWN
YAWN
© 1995 PAWS, INC./Distributed by Universal Press Syndicate

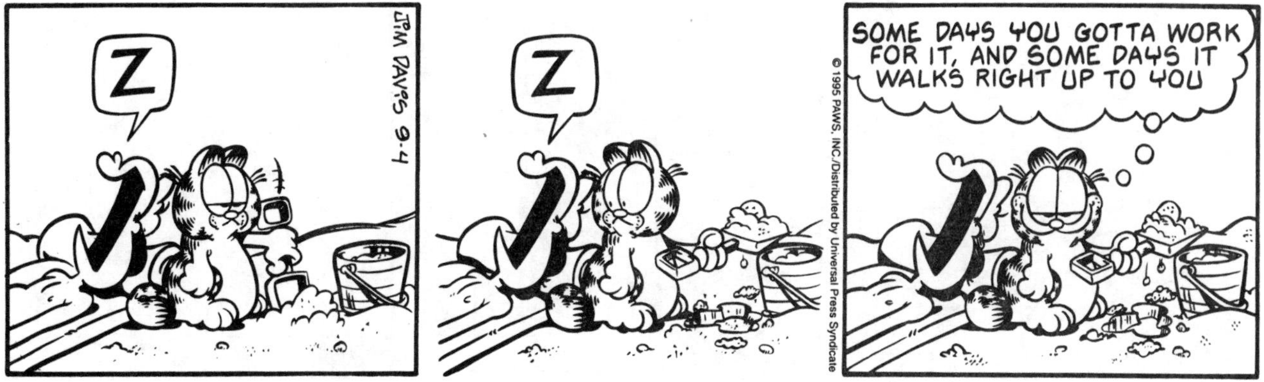

JIM DAVIS 9-4
Z
Z
SOME DAYS YOU GOTTA WORK FOR IT, AND SOME DAYS IT WALKS RIGHT UP TO YOU
© 1995 PAWS, INC./Distributed by Universal Press Syndicate

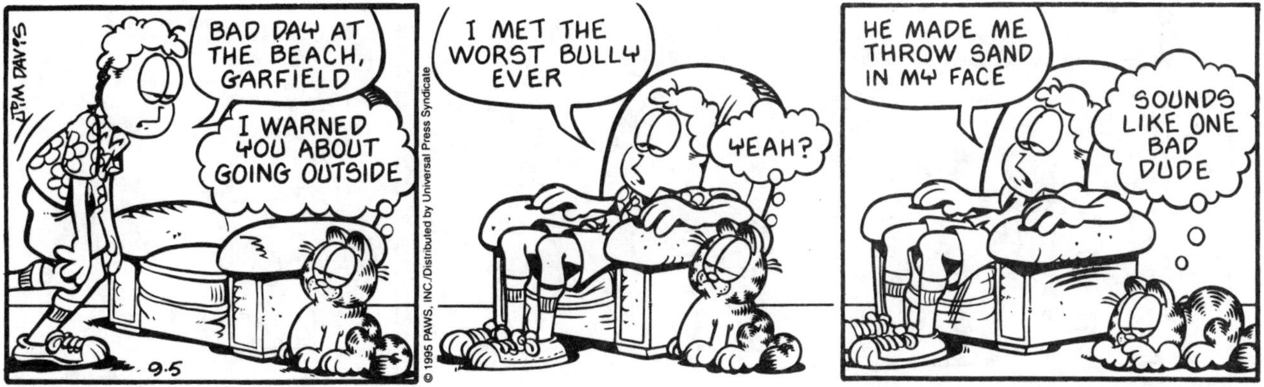

JIM DAVIS 9-5
BAD DAY AT THE BEACH, GARFIELD
I WARNED YOU ABOUT GOING OUTSIDE
© 1995 PAWS, INC./Distributed by Universal Press Syndicate
I MET THE WORST BULLY EVER
YEAH?
HE MADE ME THROW SAND IN MY FACE
SOUNDS LIKE ONE BAD DUDE

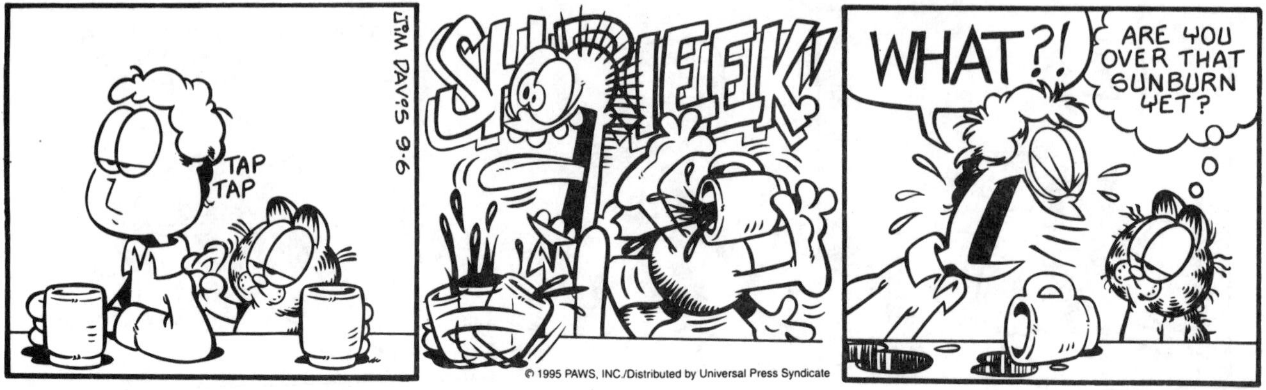
JIM DAVIS 9-6
TAP
TAP
SHRIEEK!
© 1995 PAWS, INC./Distributed by Universal Press Syndicate
WHAT?!
ARE YOU OVER THAT SUNBURN YET?

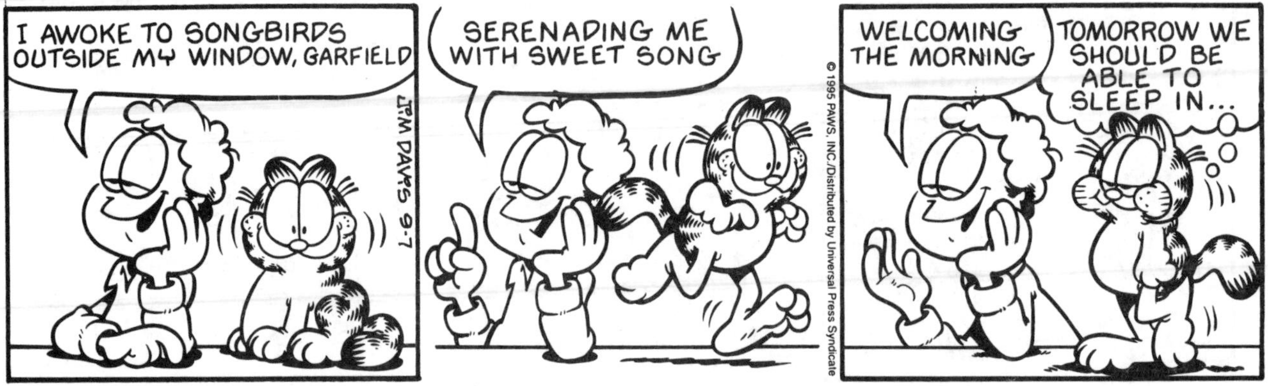
I AWOKE TO SONGBIRDS OUTSIDE MY WINDOW, GARFIELD
JIM DAVIS 9-7
SERENADING ME WITH SWEET SONG
© 1995 PAWS, INC./Distributed by Universal Press Syndicate
WELCOMING THE MORNING
TOMORROW WE SHOULD BE ABLE TO SLEEP IN...

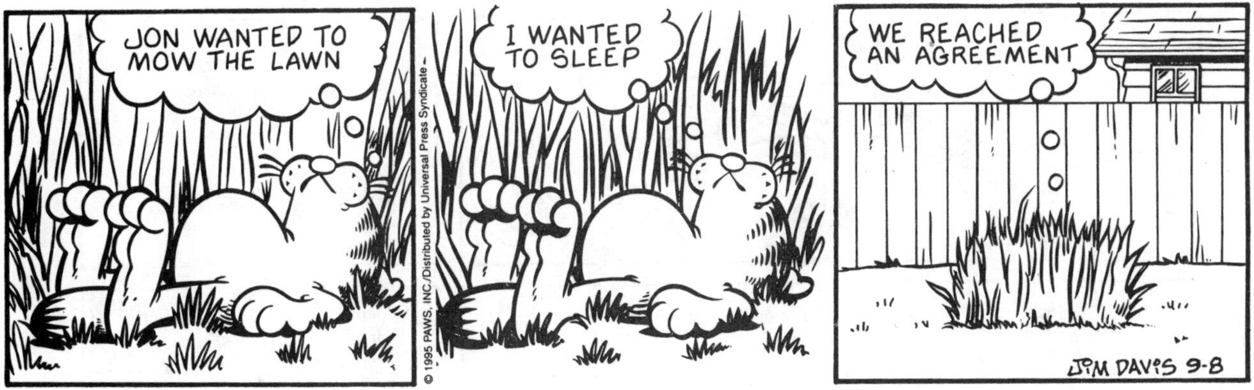
JON WANTED TO MOW THE LAWN
© 1995 PAWS, INC./Distributed by Universal Press Syndicate
I WANTED TO SLEEP
WE REACHED AN AGREEMENT
JIM DAVIS 9-8

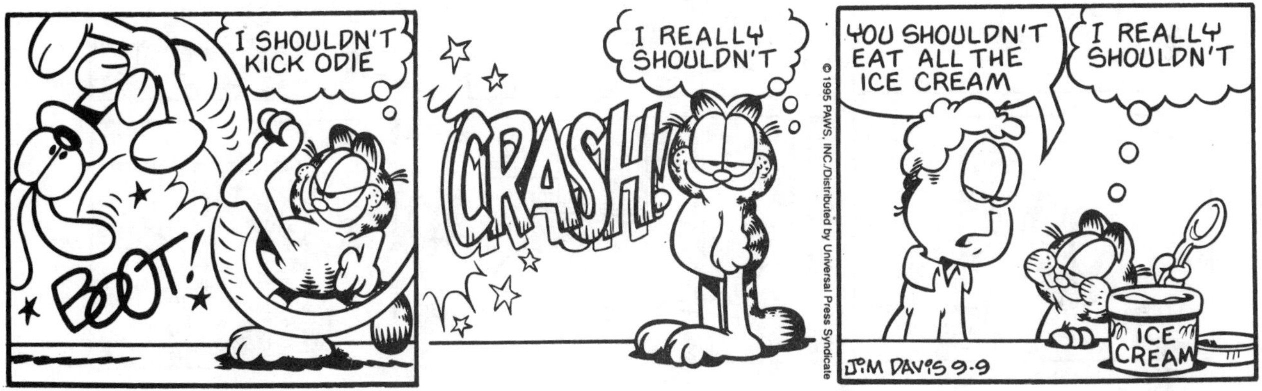
I SHOULDN'T KICK ODIE
BOOT!
CRASH
I REALLY SHOULDN'T
© 1995 PAWS, INC./Distributed by Universal Press Syndicate
YOU SHOULDN'T EAT ALL THE ICE CREAM
I REALLY SHOULDN'T
ICE CREAM
JIM DAVIS 9-9

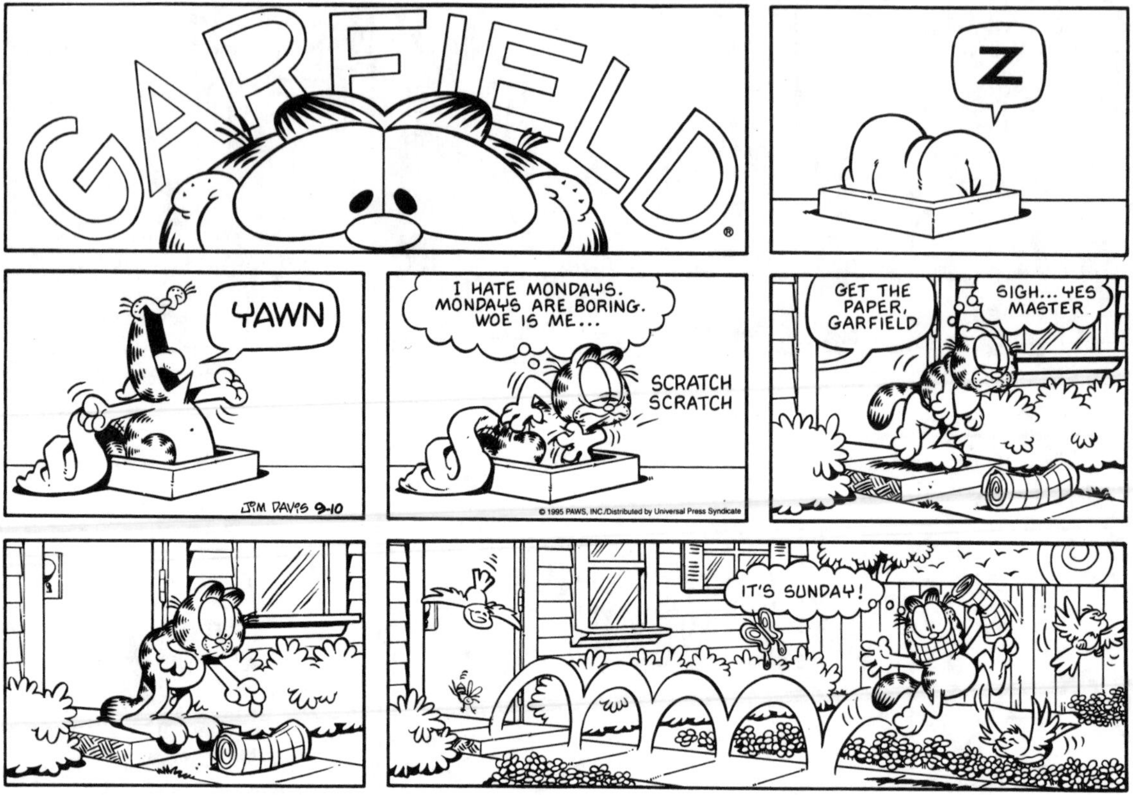
GARFIELD
Z
YAWN
JIM DAVIS 9-10
I HATE MONDAYS. MONDAYS ARE BORING. WOE IS ME...
SCRATCH SCRATCH
© 1995 PAWS, INC./Distributed by Universal Press Syndicate
GET THE PAPER, GARFIELD
SIGH... YES MASTER
IT'S SUNDAY!

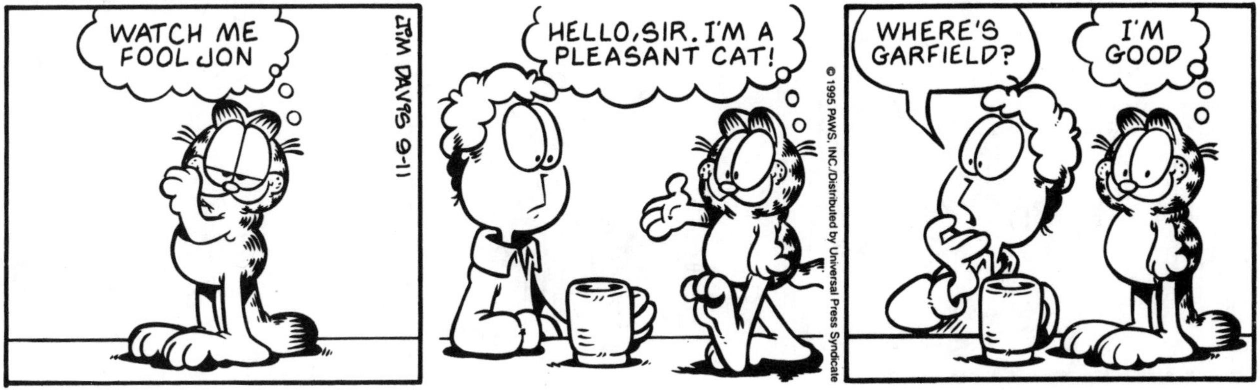
WATCH ME FOOL JON
JIM DAVIS 9-11
HELLO, SIR. I'M A PLEASANT CAT!
© 1995 PAWS, INC./Distributed by Universal Press Syndicate
WHERE'S GARFIELD?
I'M GOOD

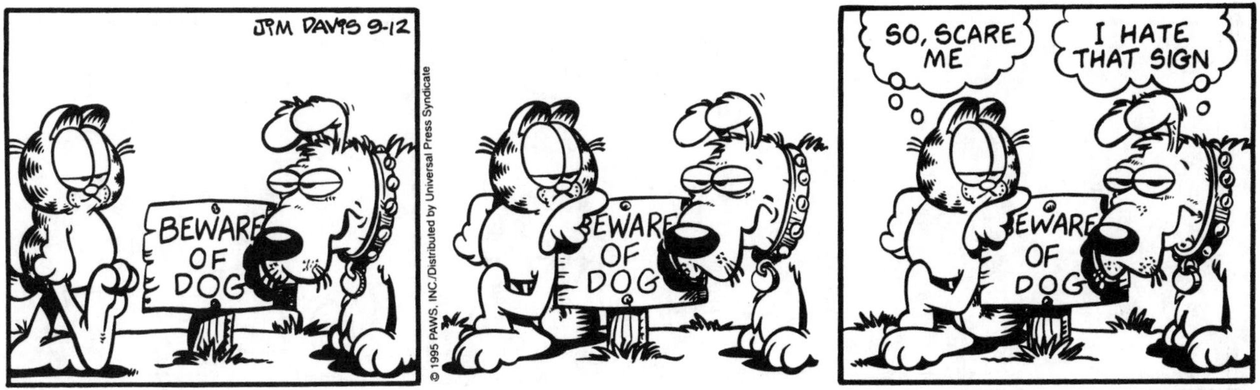
JIM DAVIS 9-12
BEWARE OF DOG
© 1995 PAWS, INC./Distributed by Universal Press Syndicate
BEWARE OF DOG
SO, SCARE ME
I HATE THAT SIGN
BEWARE OF DOG

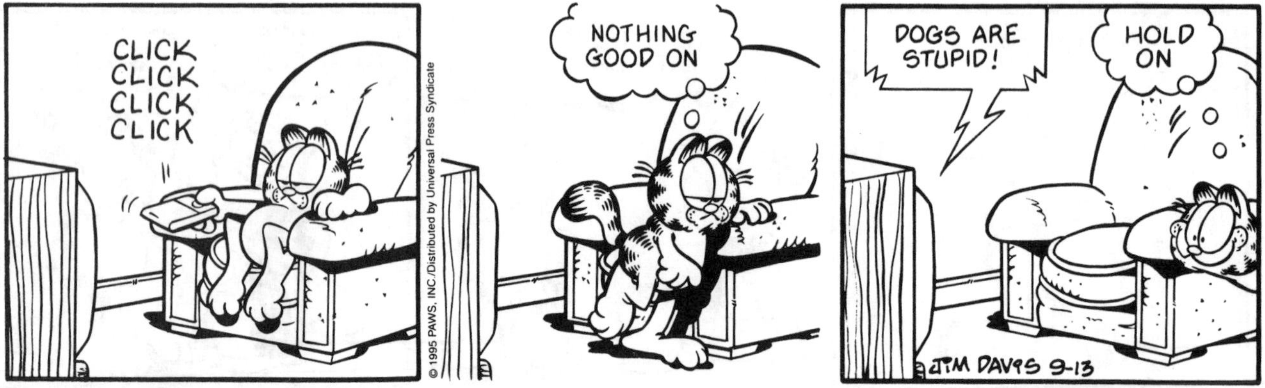
CLICK
CLICK
CLICK
CLICK
© 1995 PAWS, INC./Distributed by Universal Press Syndicate
NOTHING GOOD ON
DOGS ARE STUPID!
HOLD ON
JIM DAVIS 9-13

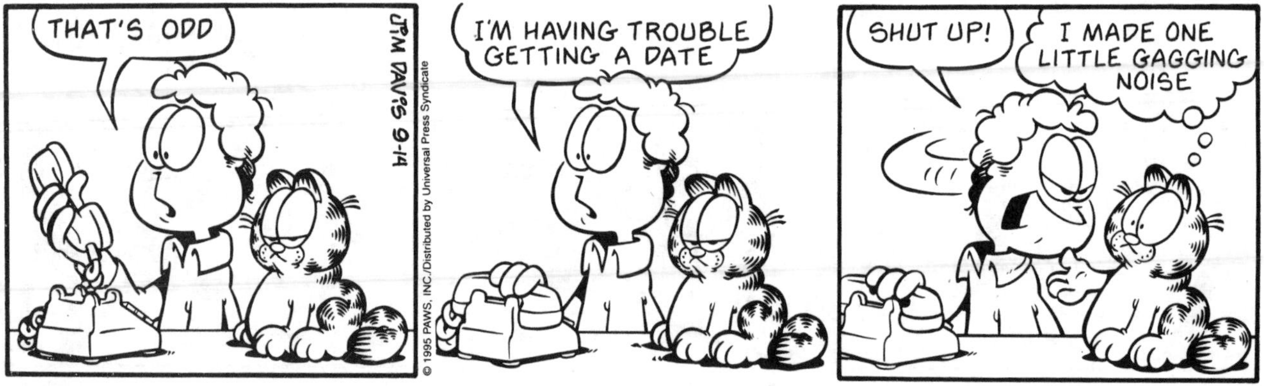
THAT'S ODD
JIM DAVIS 9-14
© 1995 PAWS, INC./Distributed by Universal Press Syndicate
I'M HAVING TROUBLE GETTING A DATE
SHUT UP!
I MADE ONE LITTLE GAGGING NOISE

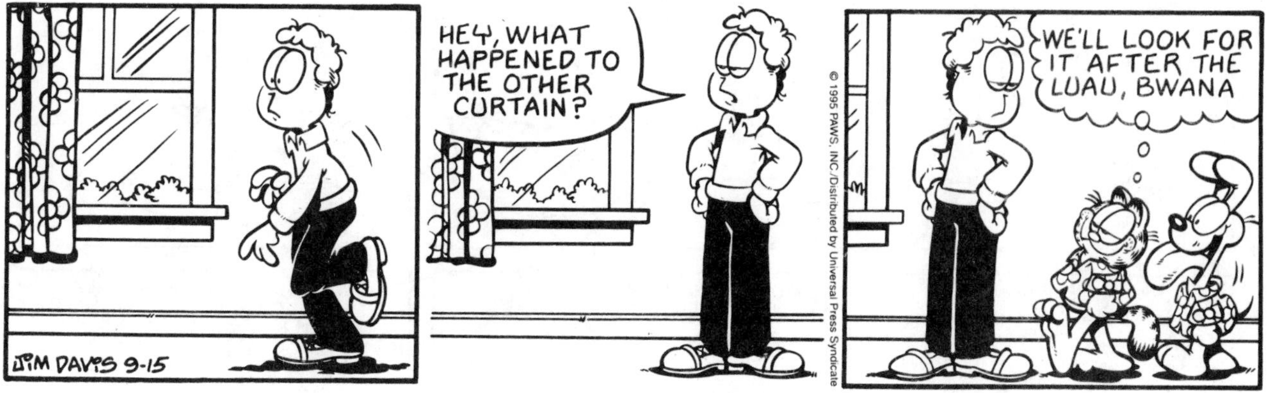
JIM DAVIS 9-15
HEY, WHAT HAPPENED TO THE OTHER CURTAIN?
© 1995 PAWS, INC./Distributed by Universal Press Syndicate
WE'LL LOOK FOR IT AFTER THE LUAU, BWANA

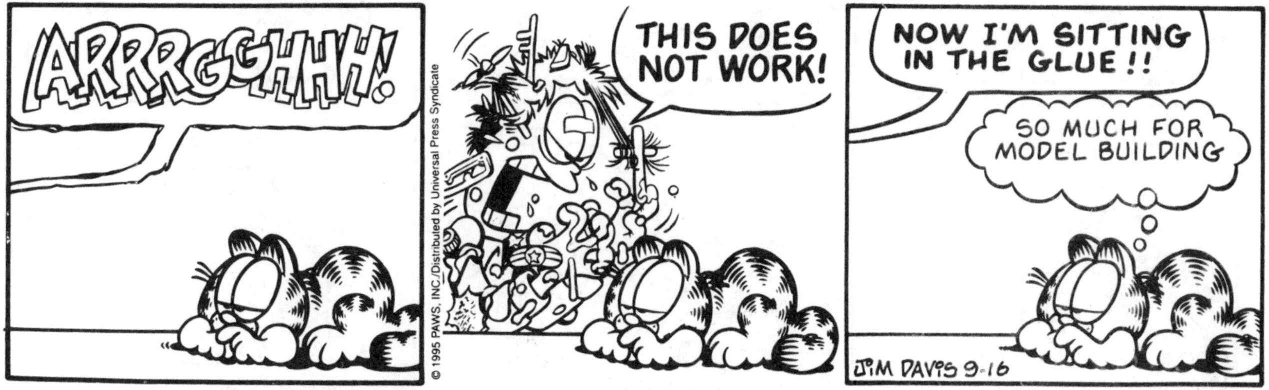
ARRRGGHHH!
© 1995 PAWS, INC./Distributed by Universal Press Syndicate
THIS DOES NOT WORK!
NOW I'M SITTING IN THE GLUE!!
SO MUCH FOR MODEL BUILDING
JIM DAVIS 9-16

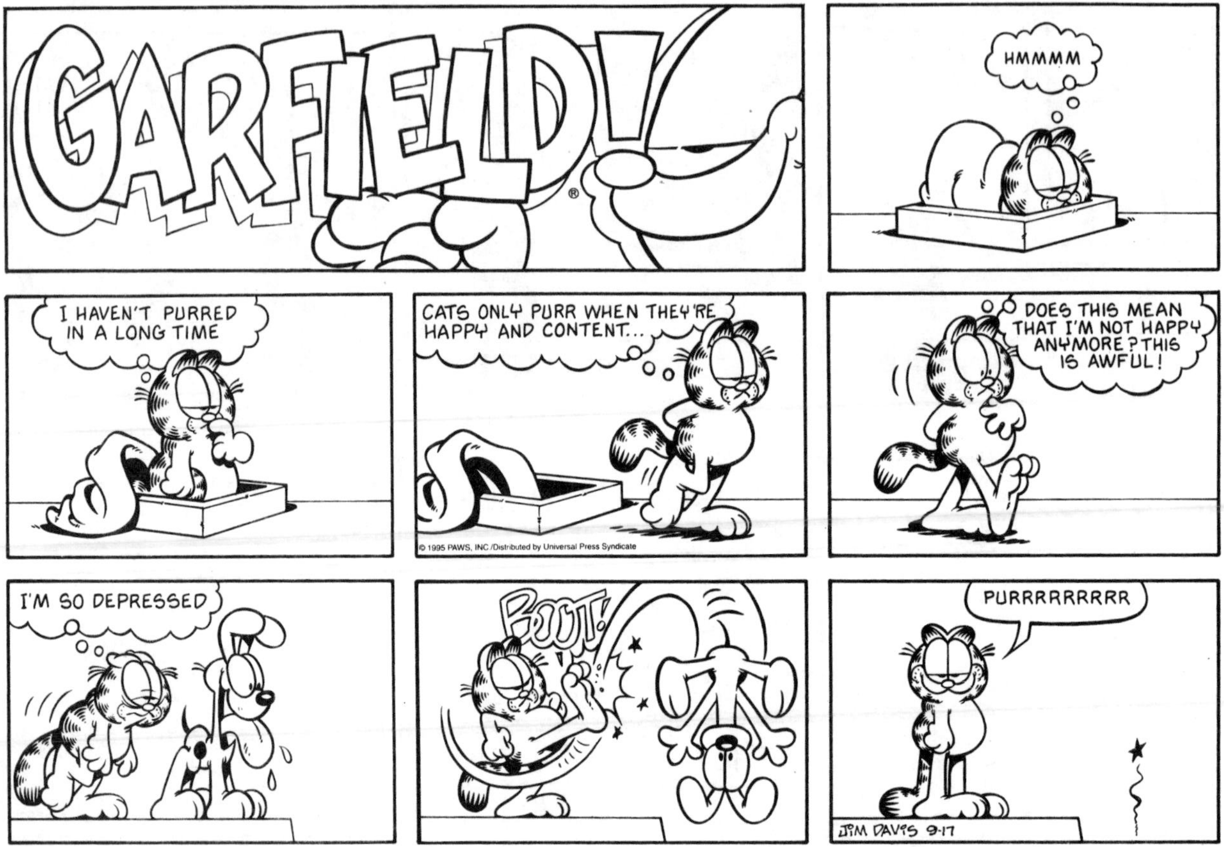
GARFIELD!
HMMMM
I HAVEN'T PURRED IN A LONG TIME
CATS ONLY PURR WHEN THEY'RE HAPPY AND CONTENT...
© 1995 PAWS, INC./Distributed by Universal Press Syndicate
DOES THIS MEAN THAT I'M NOT HAPPY ANYMORE? THIS IS AWFUL!
I'M SO DEPRESSED
BOOT!
PURRRRRRRRR
JIM DAVIS 9-17

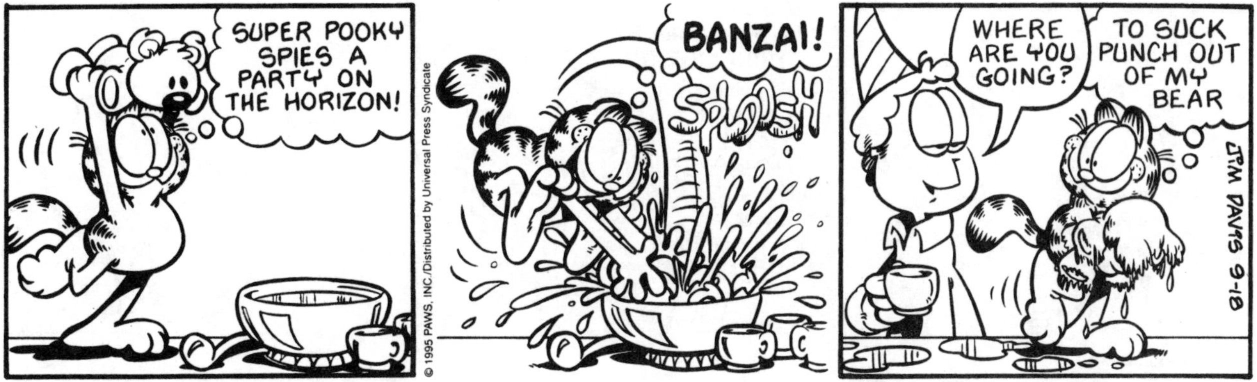
SUPER POOKY SPIES A PARTY ON THE HORIZON!
© 1995 PAWS, INC./Distributed by Universal Press Syndicate
BANZAI!
SPLOOSH
WHERE ARE YOU GOING?
TO SUCK PUNCH OUT OF MY BEAR
JIM DAVIS 9-18

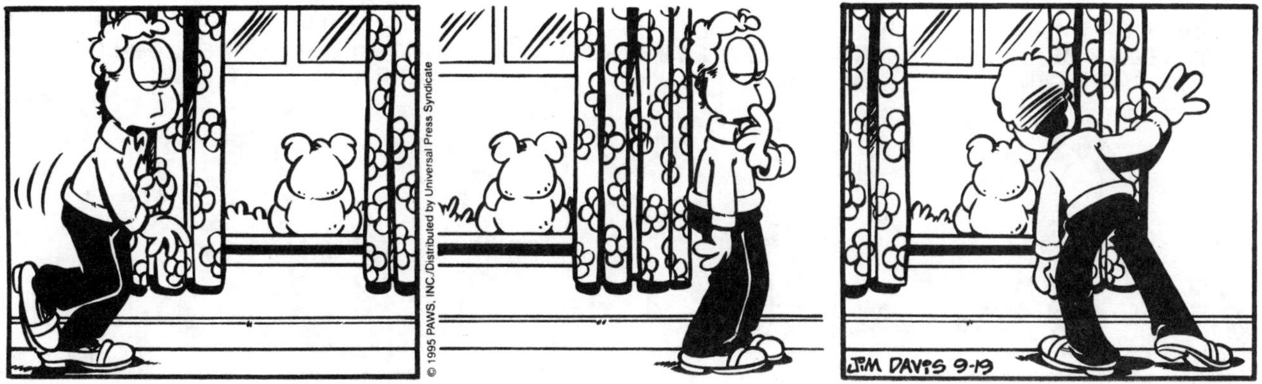
© 1995 PAWS, INC./Distributed by Universal Press Syndicate
JIM DAVIS 9-19

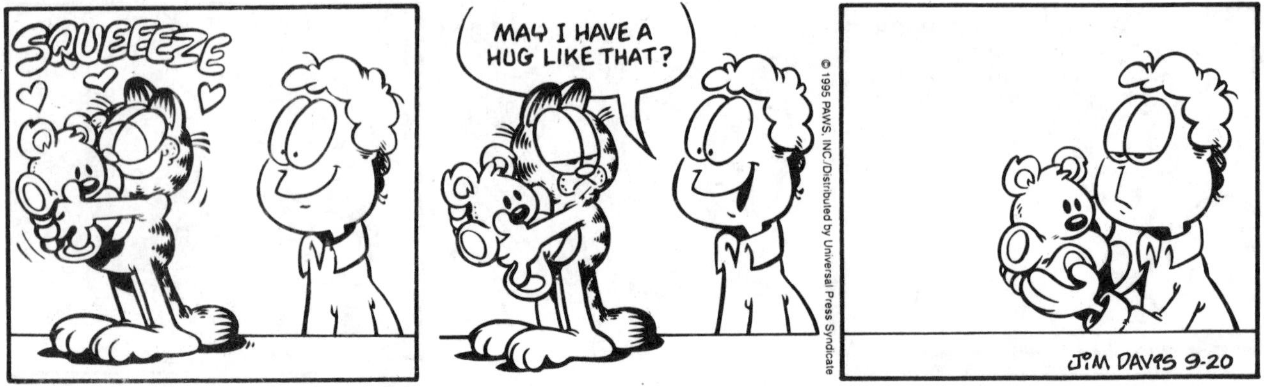
SQUEEEEZE
MAY I HAVE A HUG LIKE THAT?
© 1995 PAWS, INC./Distributed by Universal Press Syndicate
JIM DAVIS 9-20

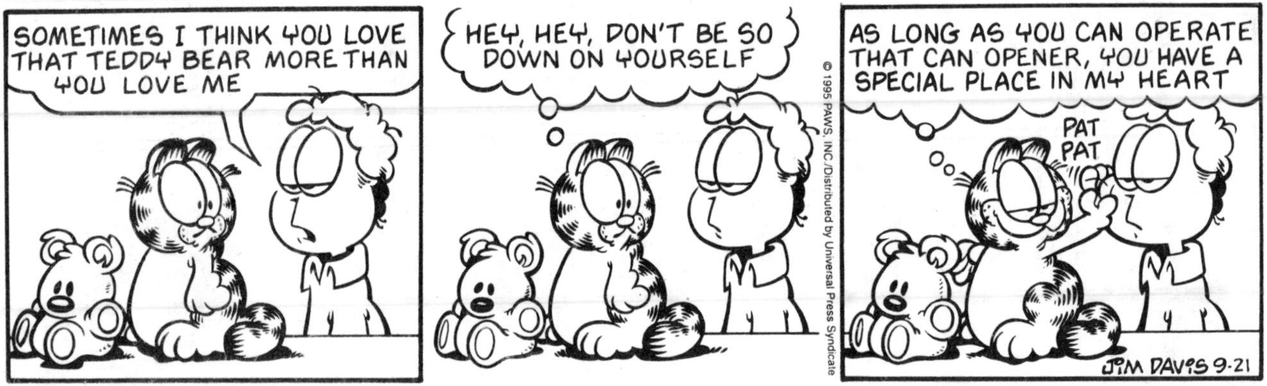
SOMETIMES I THINK YOU LOVE THAT TEDDY BEAR MORE THAN YOU LOVE ME
HEY, HEY, DON'T BE SO DOWN ON YOURSELF
© 1995 PAWS, INC./Distributed by Universal Press Syndicate
AS LONG AS YOU CAN OPERATE THAT CAN OPENER, YOU HAVE A SPECIAL PLACE IN MY HEART
PAT PAT
JIM DAVIS 9-21

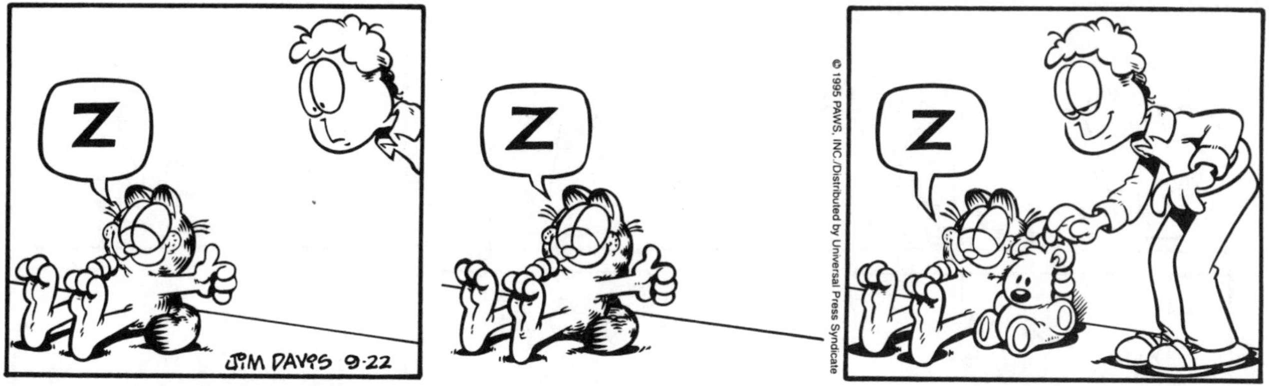
Z
Z
Z
JIM DAVIS 9-22
© 1995 PAWS, INC./Distributed by Universal Press Syndicate

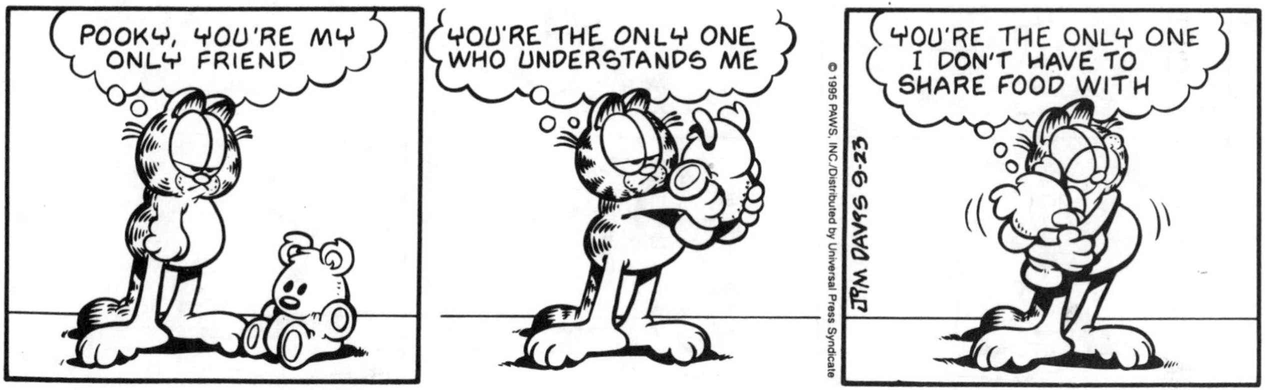
POOKY, YOU'RE MY ONLY FRIEND
YOU'RE THE ONLY ONE WHO UNDERSTANDS ME
YOU'RE THE ONLY ONE I DON'T HAVE TO SHARE FOOD WITH
JIM DAVIS 9-23
© 1995 PAWS, INC./Distributed by Universal Press Syndicate

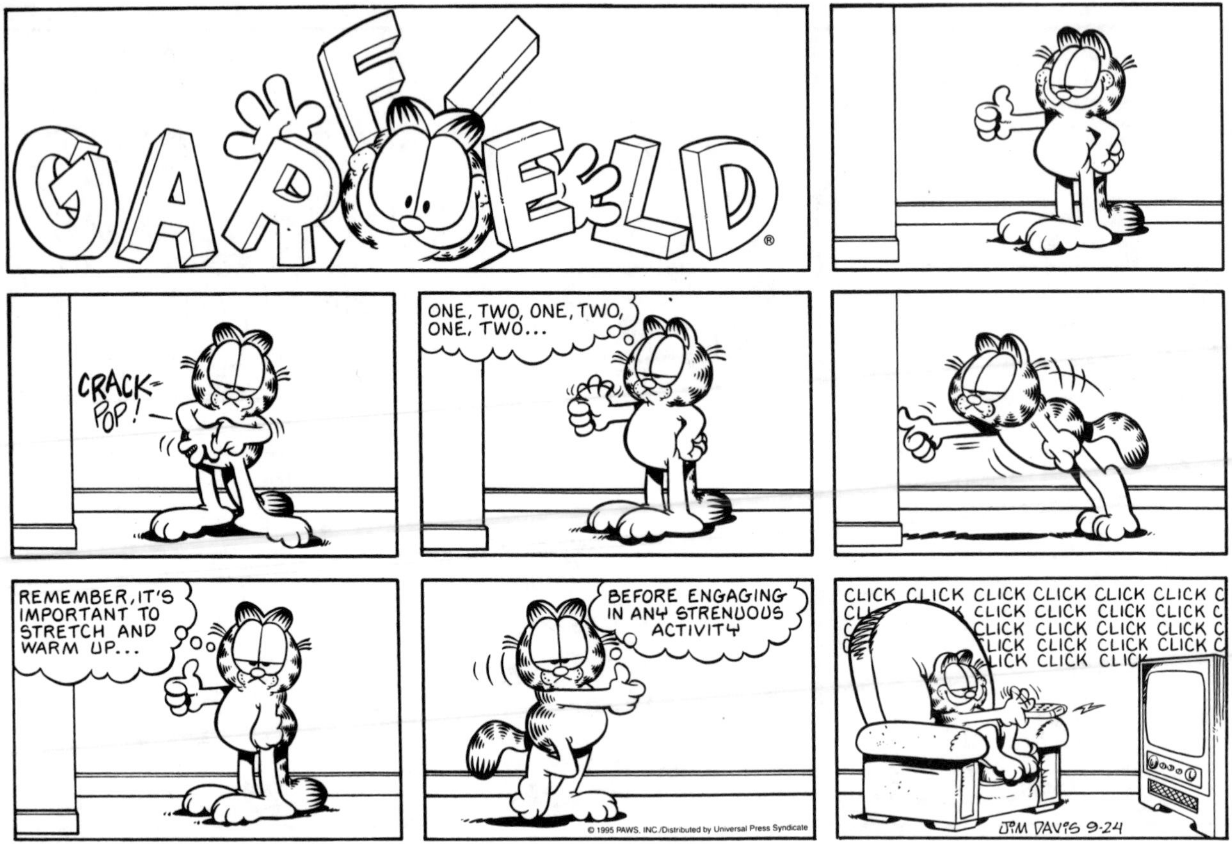
GARFIELD ®
CRACK-POP!
ONE, TWO, ONE, TWO, ONE, TWO...
REMEMBER, IT'S IMPORTANT TO STRETCH AND WARM UP...
BEFORE ENGAGING IN ANY STRENUOUS ACTIVITY
© 1995 PAWS, INC./Distributed by Universal Press Syndicate
CLICK CLICK CLICK CLICK CLICK CLICK
CLICK CLICK CLICK CLICK
CLICK CLICK CLICK CLICK
CLICK CLICK CLICK
CLICK CLICK CLICK
JIM DAVIS 9-24

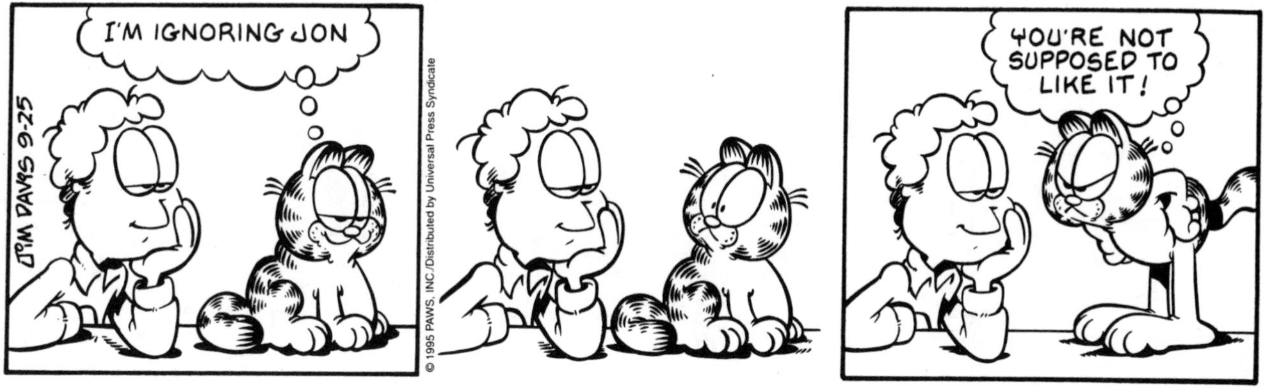
I'M IGNORING JON
YOU'RE NOT SUPPOSED TO LIKE IT!
JIM DAVIS 9-25
© 1995 PAWS, INC./Distributed by Universal Press Syndicate

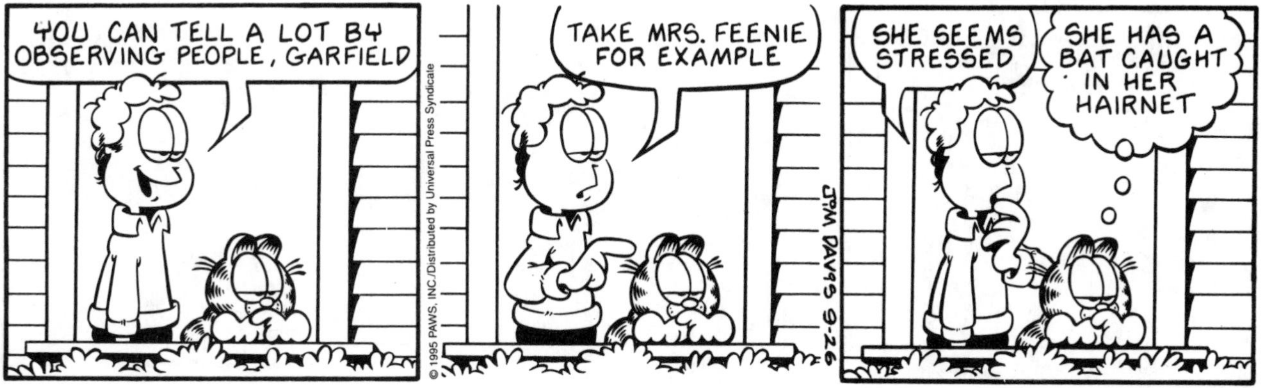
YOU CAN TELL A LOT BY OBSERVING PEOPLE, GARFIELD
TAKE MRS. FEENIE FOR EXAMPLE
SHE SEEMS STRESSED
SHE HAS A BAT CAUGHT IN HER HAIRNET
JIM DAVIS 9-26
© 1995 PAWS, INC./Distributed by Universal Press Syndicate

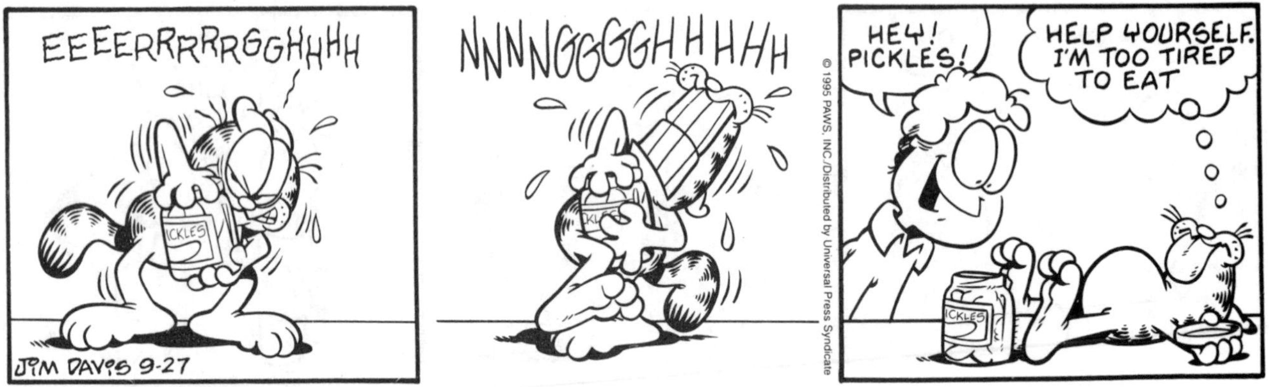
EEEERRRRRGGHHHH
NNNNGGGGHHHHH
HEY! PICKLES!
HELP YOURSELF. I'M TOO TIRED TO EAT
PICKLES
JIM DAVIS 9-27
© 1995 PAWS, INC./Distributed by Universal Press Syndicate

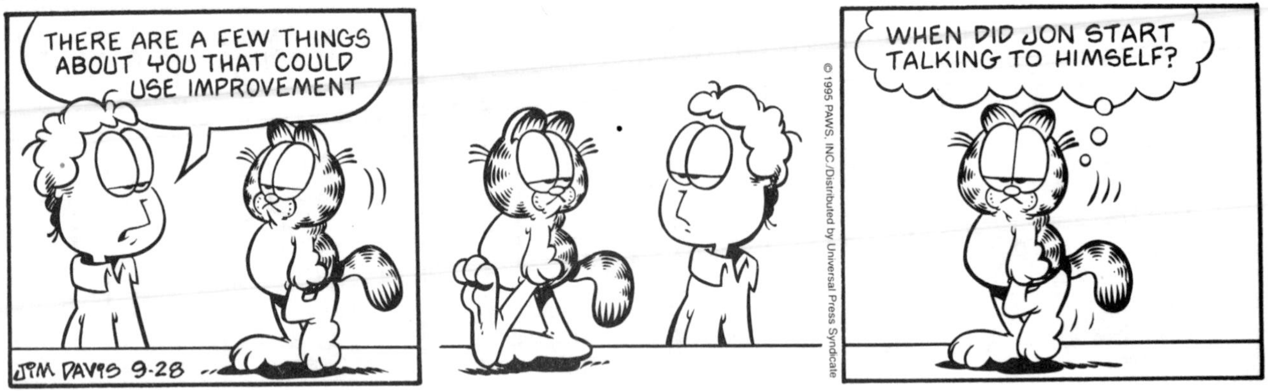
THERE ARE A FEW THINGS ABOUT YOU THAT COULD USE IMPROVEMENT
WHEN DID JON START TALKING TO HIMSELF?
JIM DAVIS 9-28
© 1995 PAWS, INC./Distributed by Universal Press Syndicate

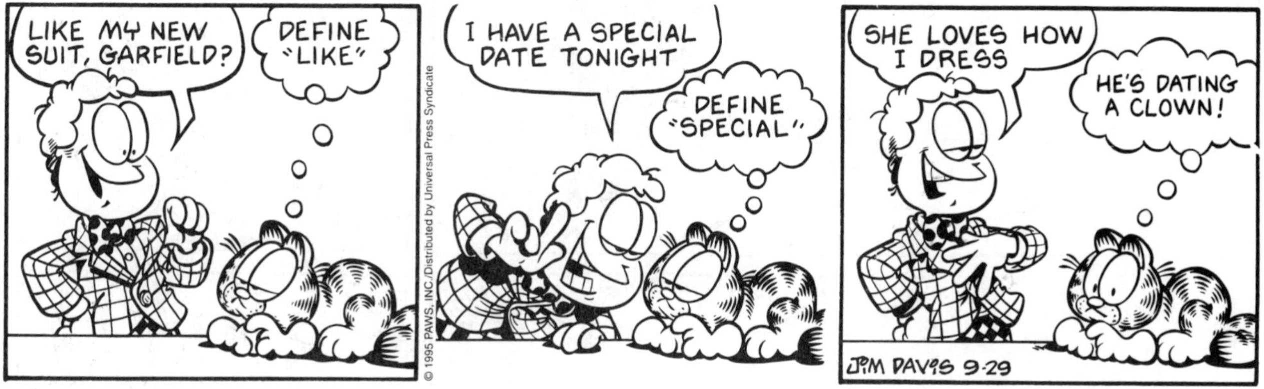
LIKE MY NEW SUIT, GARFIELD?
DEFINE "LIKE"
I HAVE A SPECIAL DATE TONIGHT
DEFINE "SPECIAL"
SHE LOVES HOW I DRESS
HE'S DATING A CLOWN!
© 1995 PAWS, INC./Distributed by Universal Press Syndicate
JIM DAVIS 9-29

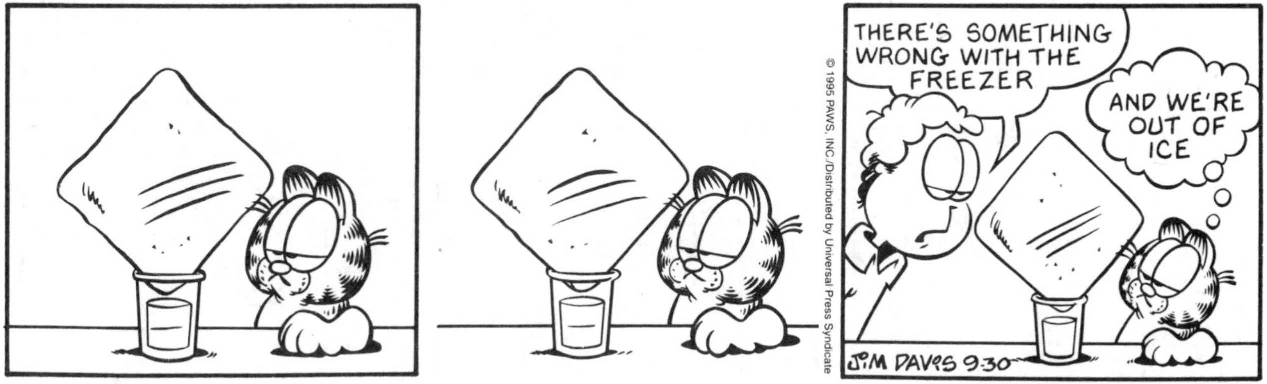
THERE'S SOMETHING WRONG WITH THE FREEZER
AND WE'RE OUT OF ICE
© 1995 PAWS, INC./Distributed by Universal Press Syndicate
JIM DAVIS 9-30

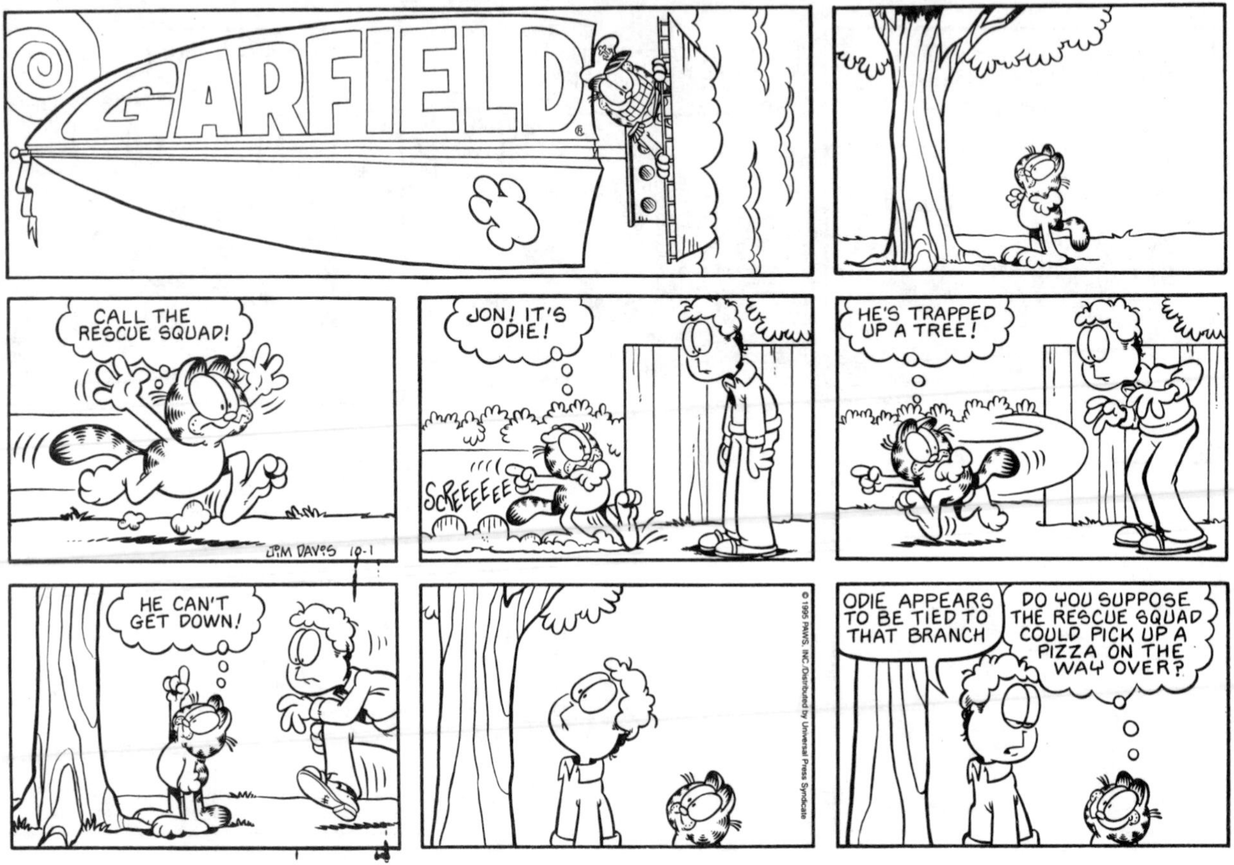
GARFIELD
CALL THE RESCUE SQUAD!
JIM DAVIS 10-1
JON! IT'S ODIE!
SCREEEEEE
HE'S TRAPPED UP A TREE!
HE CAN'T GET DOWN!
© 1995 PAWS, INC./Distributed by Universal Press Syndicate
ODIE APPEARS TO BE TIED TO THAT BRANCH
DO YOU SUPPOSE THE RESCUE SQUAD COULD PICK UP A PIZZA ON THE WAY OVER?

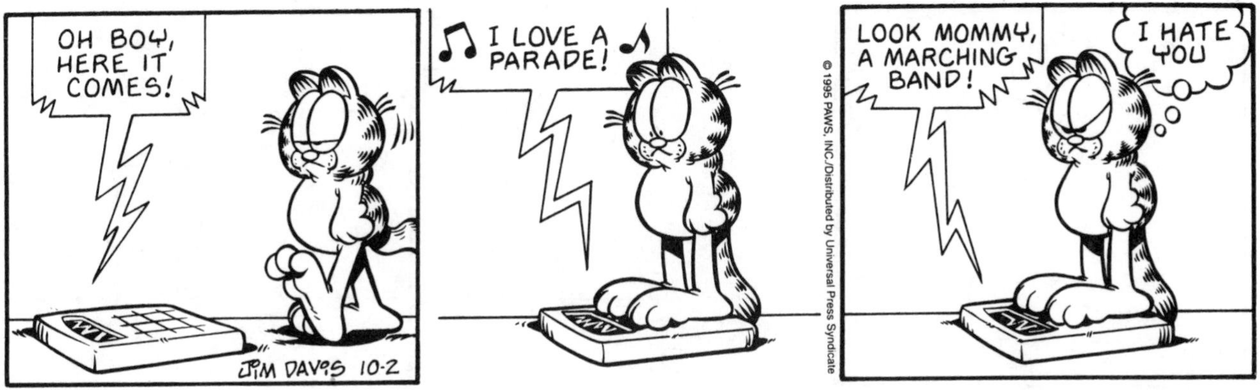
OH BOY, HERE IT COMES!
I LOVE A PARADE!
LOOK MOMMY, A MARCHING BAND!
I HATE YOU
JIM DAVIS 10-2
© 1995 PAWS, INC./Distributed by Universal Press Syndicate

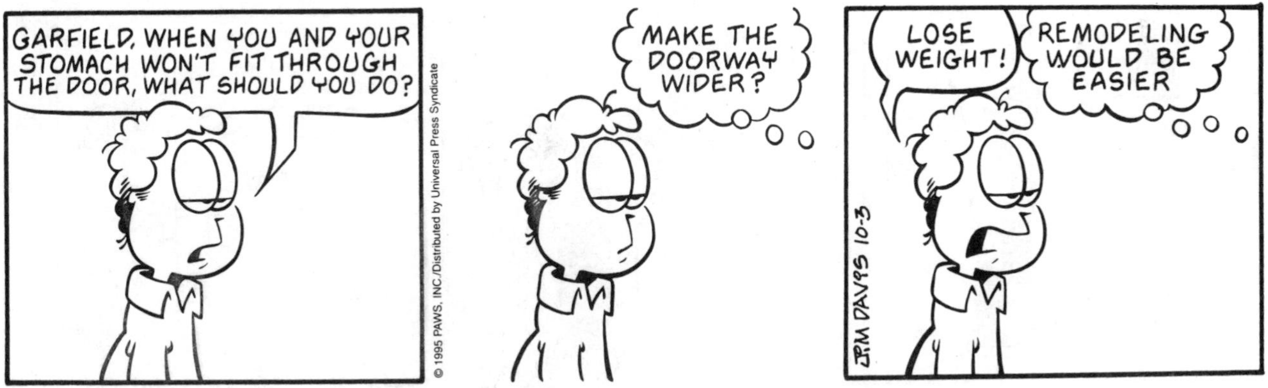
GARFIELD, WHEN YOU AND YOUR STOMACH WON'T FIT THROUGH THE DOOR, WHAT SHOULD YOU DO?
MAKE THE DOORWAY WIDER?
LOSE WEIGHT!
REMODELING WOULD BE EASIER
JIM DAVIS 10-3
© 1995 PAWS, INC./Distributed by Universal Press Syndicate

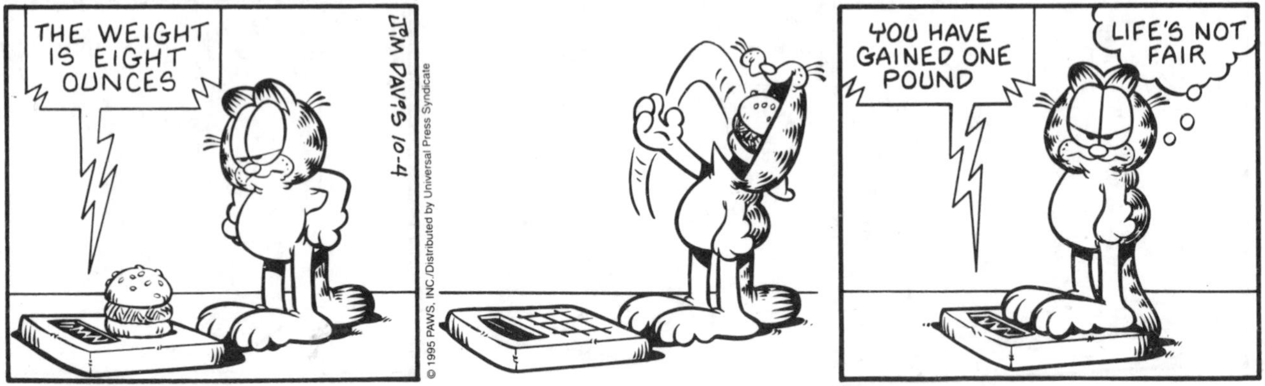
THE WEIGHT IS EIGHT OUNCES
JIM DAVIS 10-4
© 1995 PAWS, INC./Distributed by Universal Press Syndicate
YOU HAVE GAINED ONE POUND
LIFE'S NOT FAIR

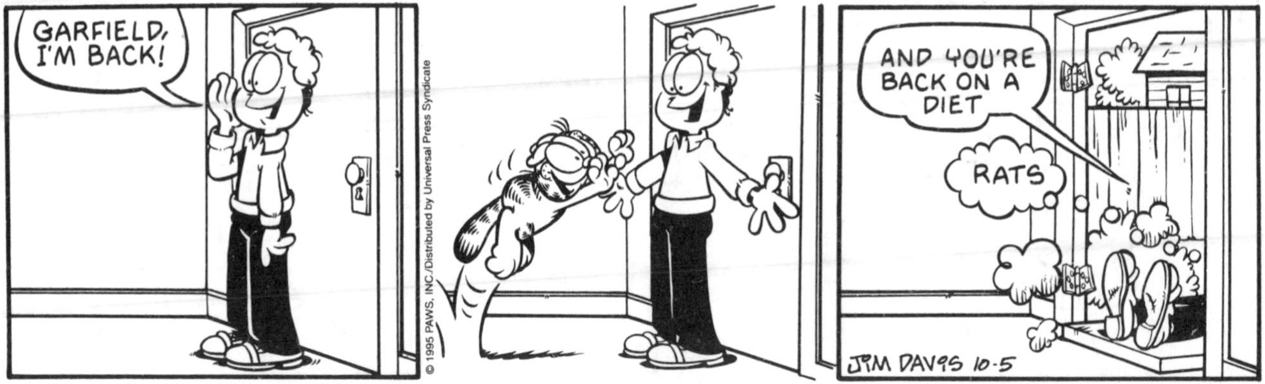
GARFIELD, I'M BACK!
© 1995 PAWS, INC./Distributed by Universal Press Syndicate
AND YOU'RE BACK ON A DIET
RATS
JIM DAVIS 10-5

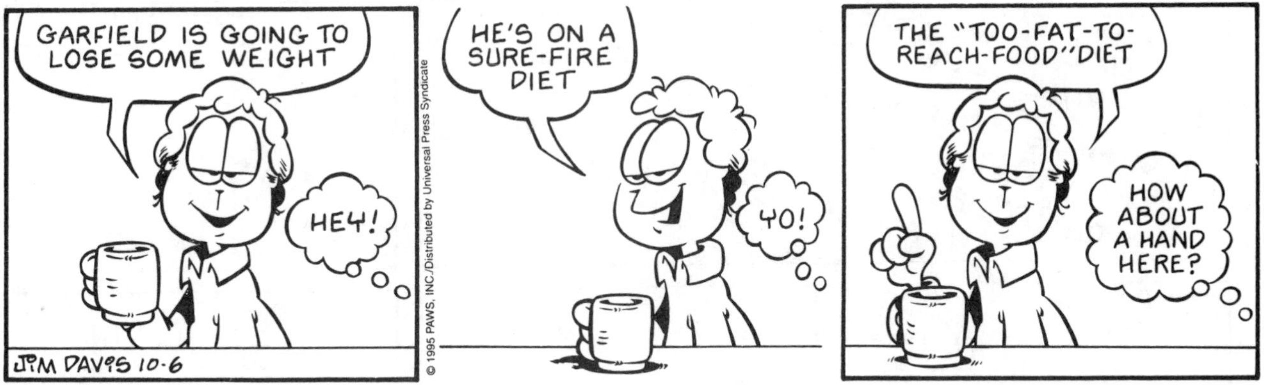
GARFIELD IS GOING TO LOSE SOME WEIGHT
HEY!
HE'S ON A SURE-FIRE DIET
YO!
THE "TOO-FAT-TO-REACH-FOOD" DIET
HOW ABOUT A HAND HERE?
JIM DAVIS 10-6
© 1995 PAWS, INC./Distributed by Universal Press Syndicate

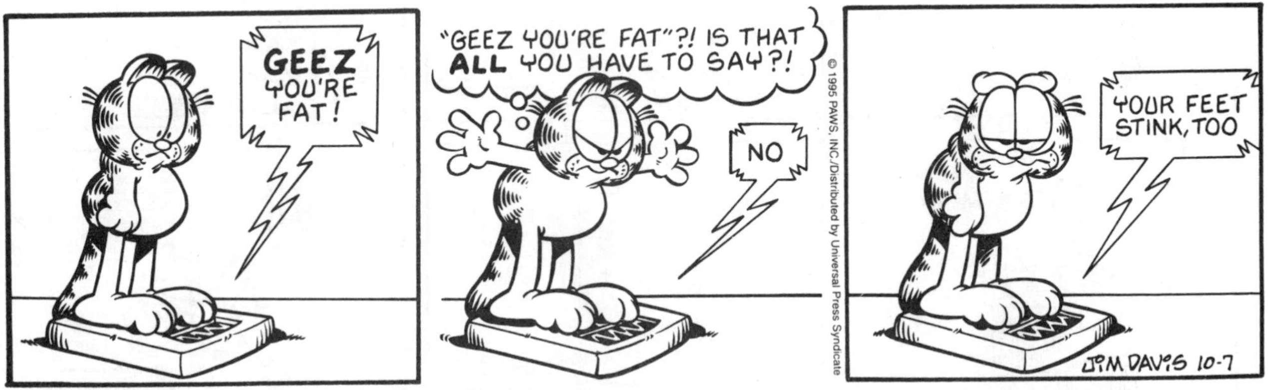
GEEZ YOU'RE FAT!
"GEEZ YOU'RE FAT"?! IS THAT ALL YOU HAVE TO SAY?!
NO
YOUR FEET STINK, TOO
JIM DAVIS 10-7
© 1995 PAWS, INC./Distributed by Universal Press Syndicate

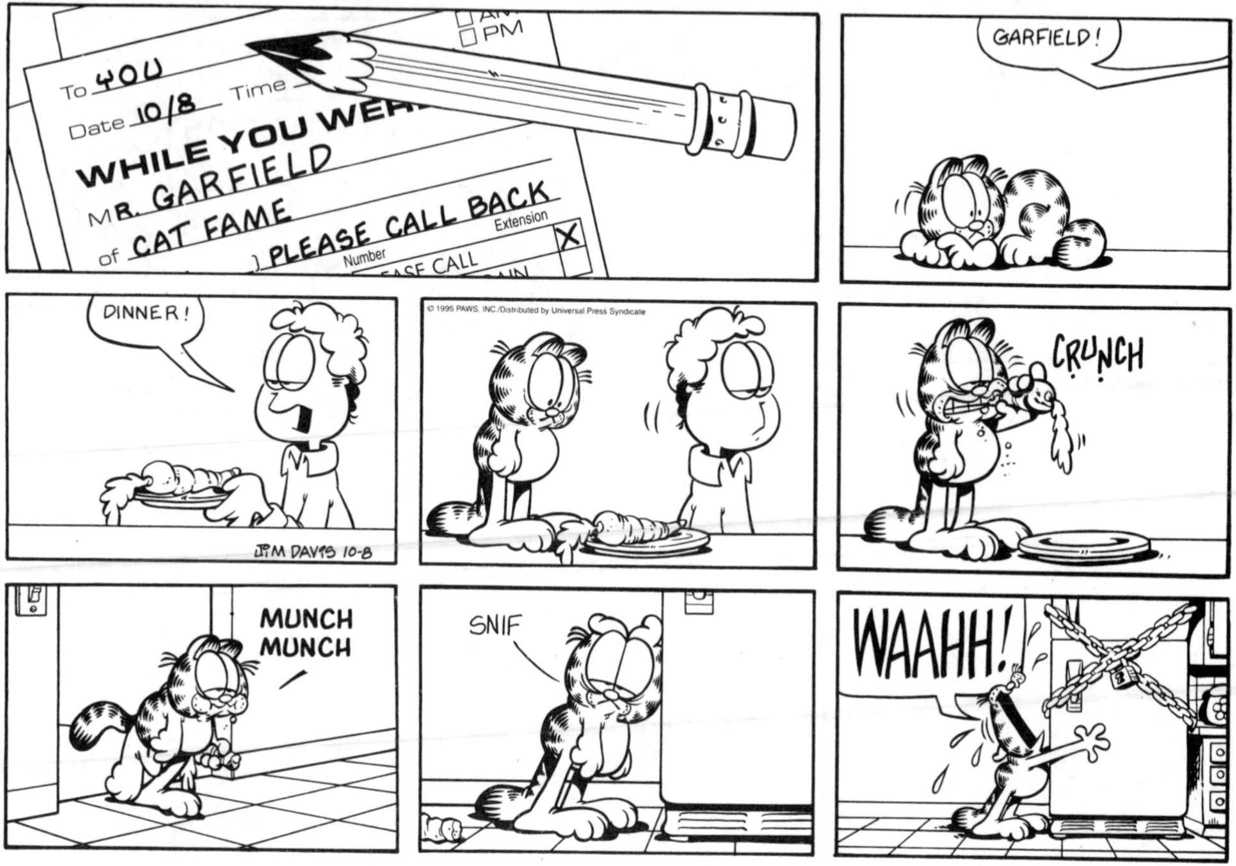
PM
To YOU
Time
Date 10/8
WHILE YOU WER
MR. GARFIELD
of CAT FAME
PLEASE CALL BACK
Extension
Number
EASE CALL
GARFIELD!
DINNER!
JIM DAVIS 10-8
© 1995 PAWS, INC./Distributed by Universal Press Syndicate
CRUNCH
MUNCH
MUNCH
SNIF
WAAHH!

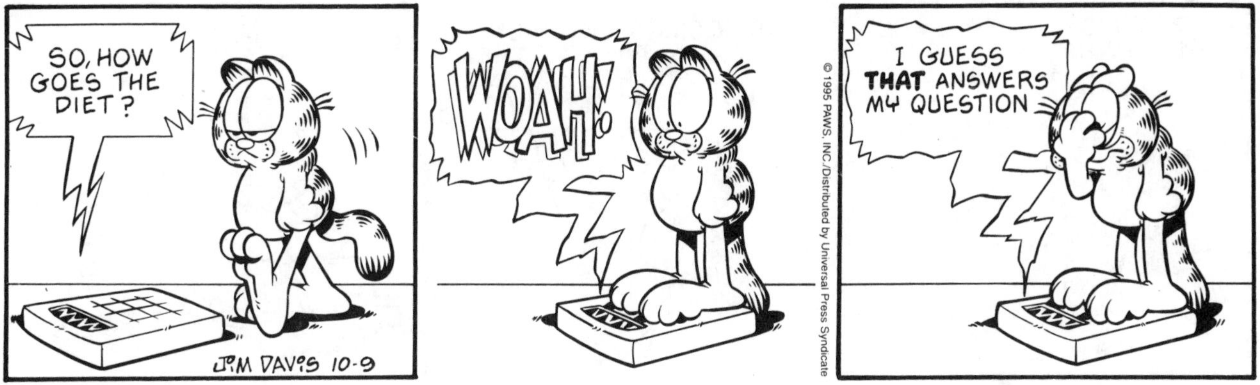
SO, HOW GOES THE DIET?
JIM DAVIS 10-9
WOAH!
I GUESS THAT ANSWERS MY QUESTION

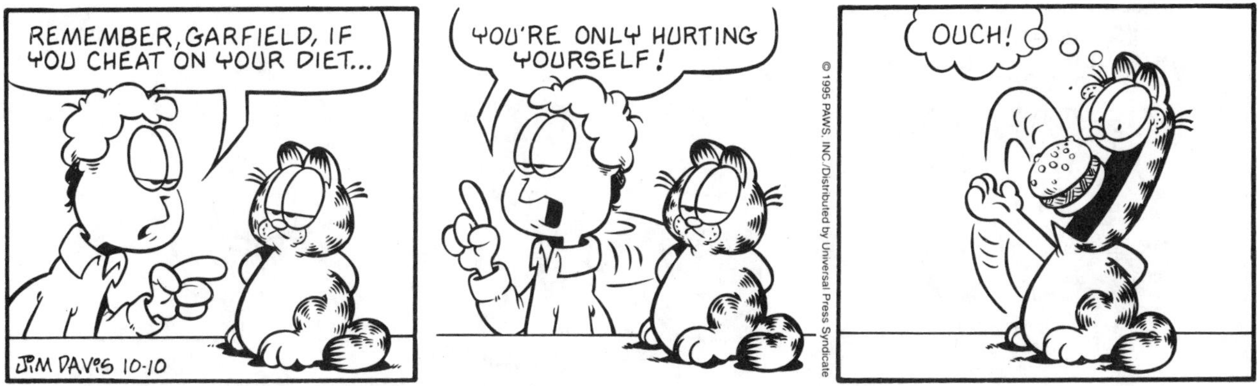
REMEMBER, GARFIELD, IF YOU CHEAT ON YOUR DIET...
JIM DAVIS 10-10
YOU'RE ONLY HURTING YOURSELF!
OUCH!

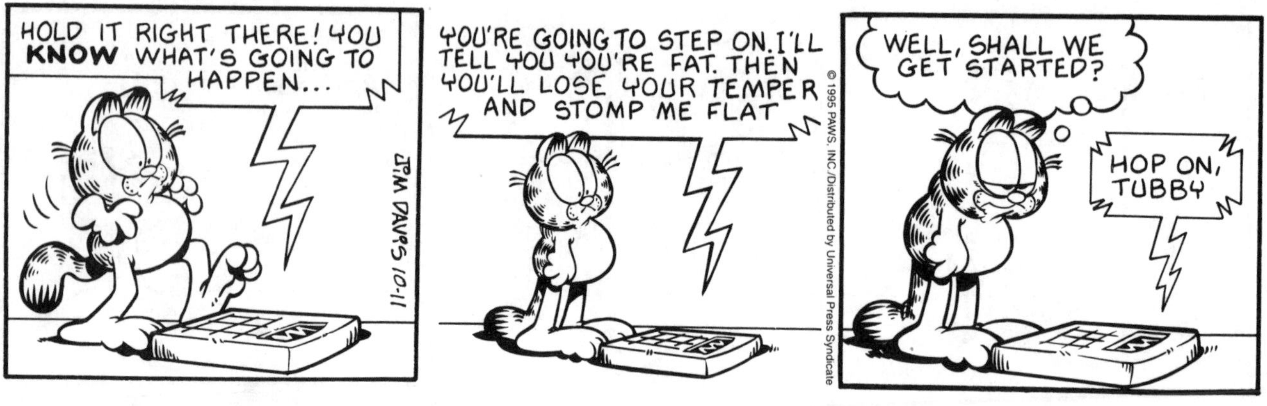
HOLD IT RIGHT THERE! YOU **KNOW** WHAT'S GOING TO HAPPEN...
JIM DAVIS 10-11
YOU'RE GOING TO STEP ON. I'LL TELL YOU YOU'RE FAT. THEN YOU'LL LOSE YOUR TEMPER AND STOMP ME FLAT
© 1995 PAWS, INC./Distributed by Universal Press Syndicate
WELL, SHALL WE GET STARTED?
HOP ON, TUBBY

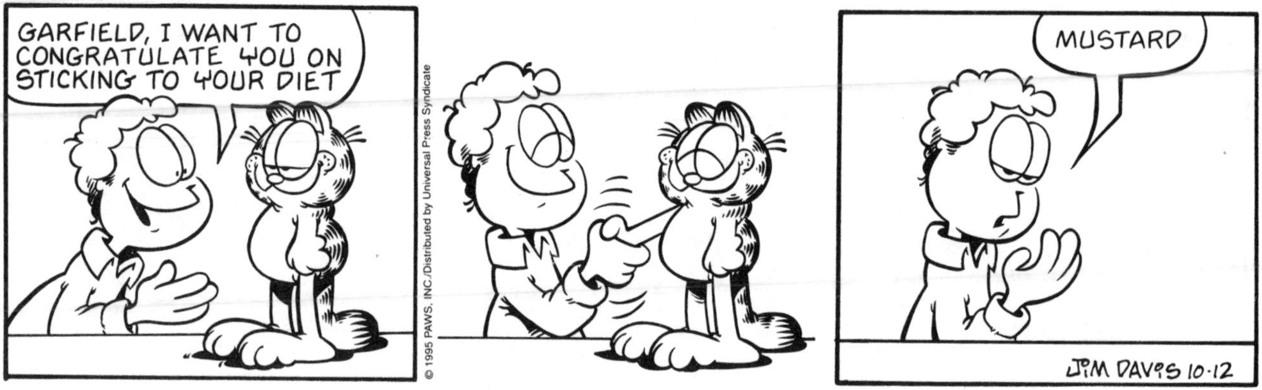
GARFIELD, I WANT TO CONGRATULATE YOU ON STICKING TO YOUR DIET
© 1995 PAWS, INC./Distributed by Universal Press Syndicate
MUSTARD
JIM DAVIS 10-12

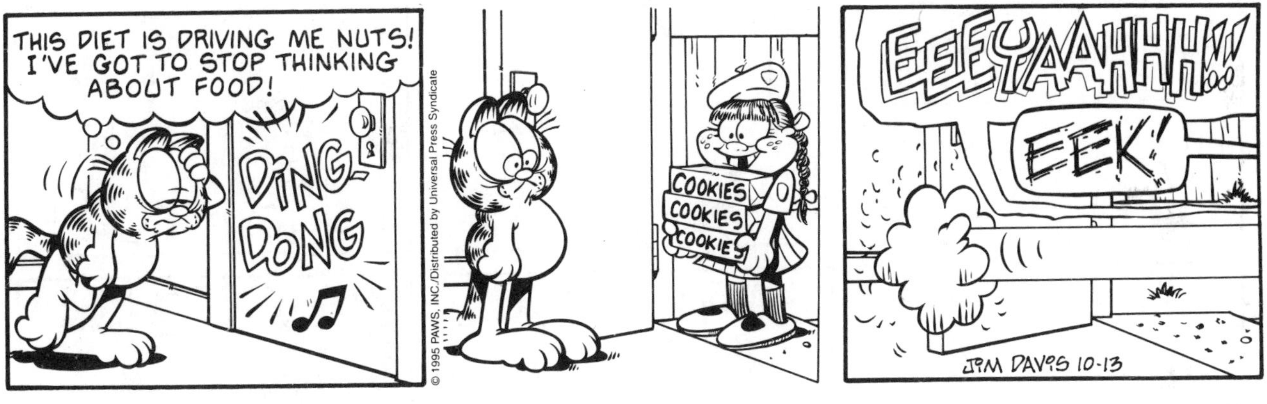
THIS DIET IS DRIVING ME NUTS! I'VE GOT TO STOP THINKING ABOUT FOOD!
DING DONG
© 1995 PAWS, INC./Distributed by Universal Press Syndicate
COOKIES
COOKIES
COOKIES
EEEYAAHHH!!!
EEK!
JIM DAVIS 10-13

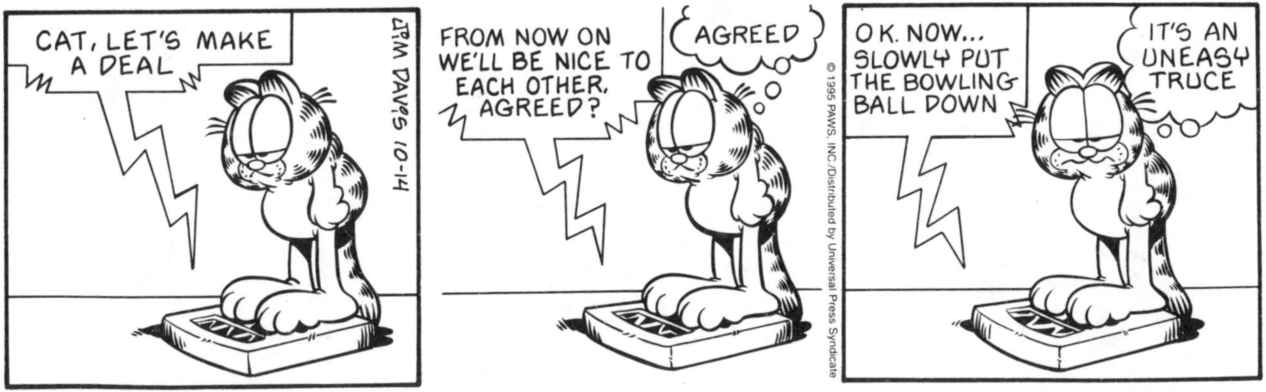
CAT, LET'S MAKE A DEAL
JIM DAVIS 10-14
FROM NOW ON WE'LL BE NICE TO EACH OTHER, AGREED?
AGREED
© 1995 PAWS, INC./Distributed by Universal Press Syndicate
O.K. NOW... SLOWLY PUT THE BOWLING BALL DOWN
IT'S AN UNEASY TRUCE

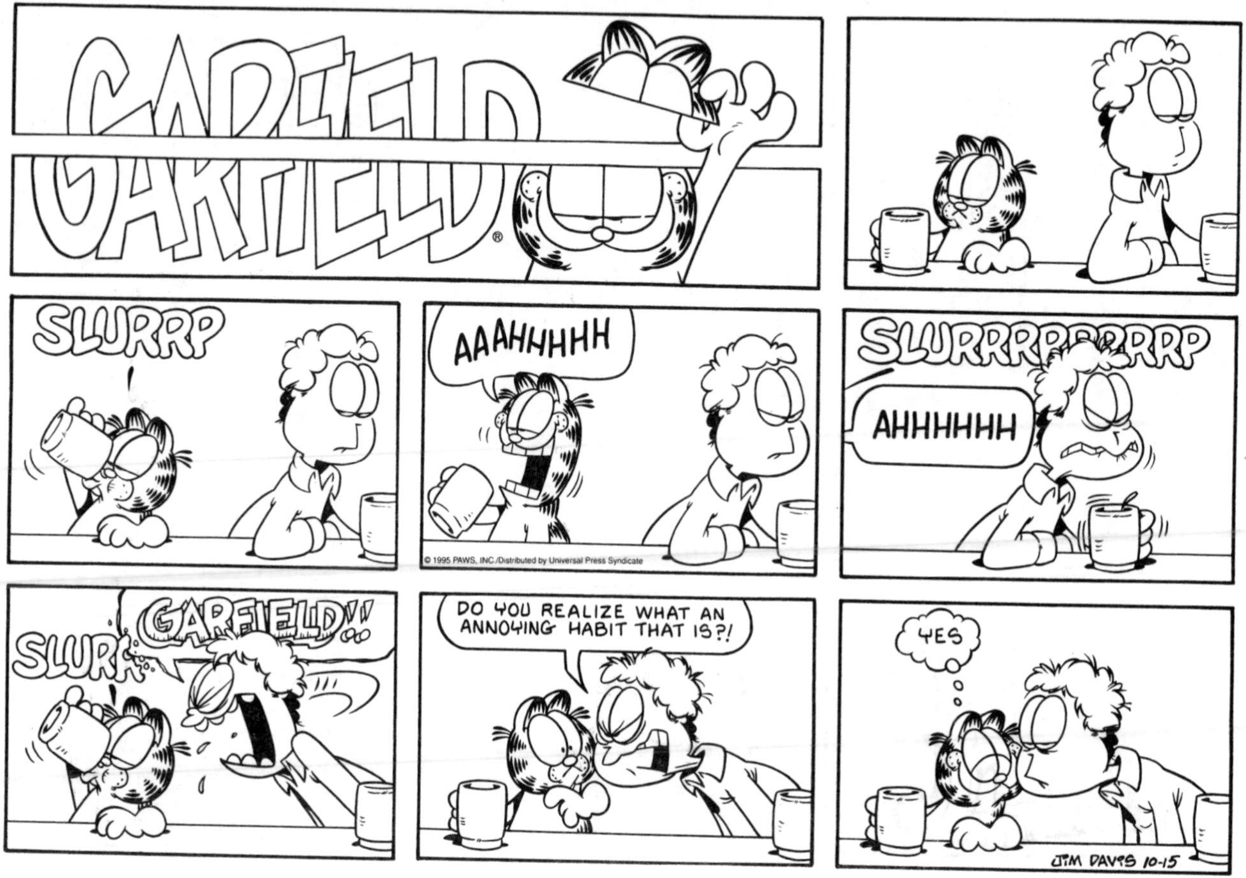
GARFIELD
GARFIELD®
SLURRP
AAAHHHHH
© 1995 PAWS, INC./Distributed by Universal Press Syndicate
SLURRRPPPPRRP
AHHHHHH
SLURP
GARFIELD!!
DO YOU REALIZE WHAT AN ANNOYING HABIT THAT IS?!
YES
JIM DAVIS 10-15

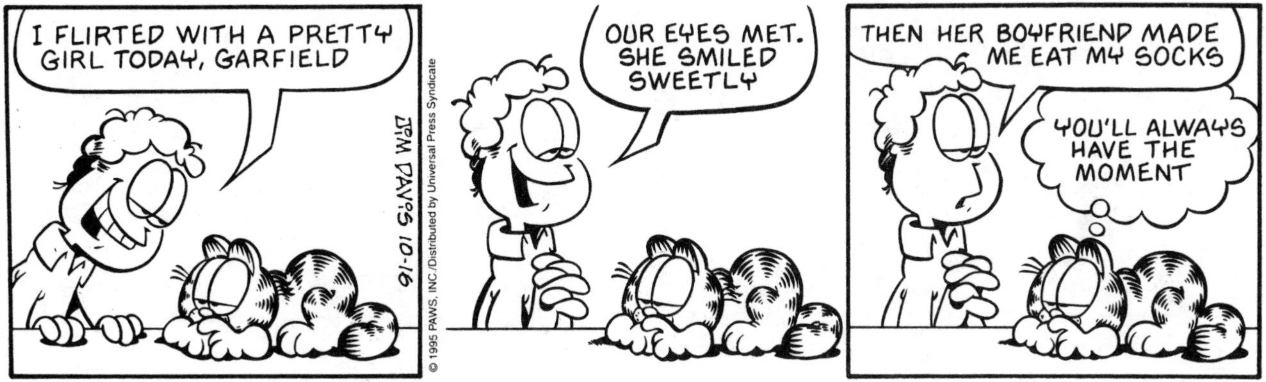
I FLIRTED WITH A PRETTY GIRL TODAY, GARFIELD
JIM DAVIS 10-16
OUR EYES MET. SHE SMILED SWEETLY
THEN HER BOYFRIEND MADE ME EAT MY SOCKS
YOU'LL ALWAYS HAVE THE MOMENT

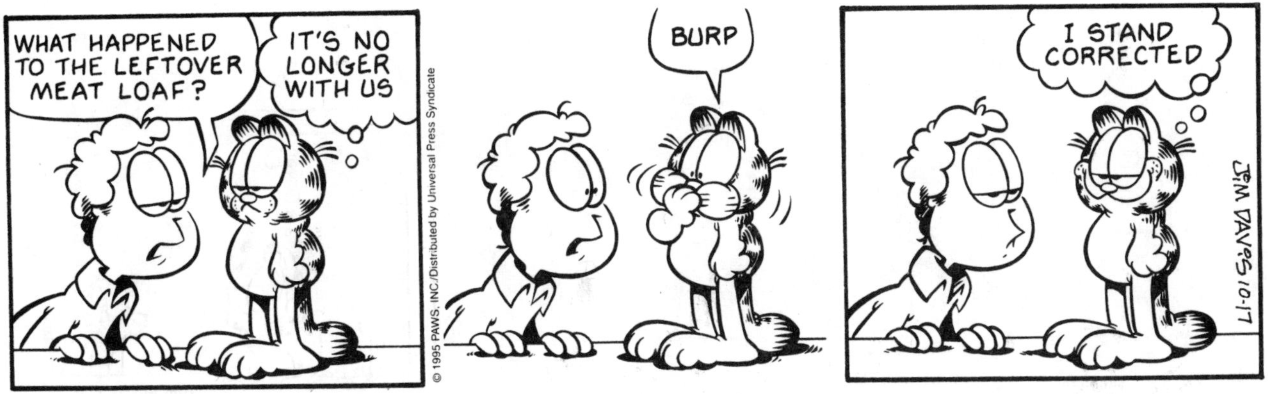
WHAT HAPPENED TO THE LEFTOVER MEAT LOAF?
IT'S NO LONGER WITH US
BURP
I STAND CORRECTED
JIM DAVIS 10-17

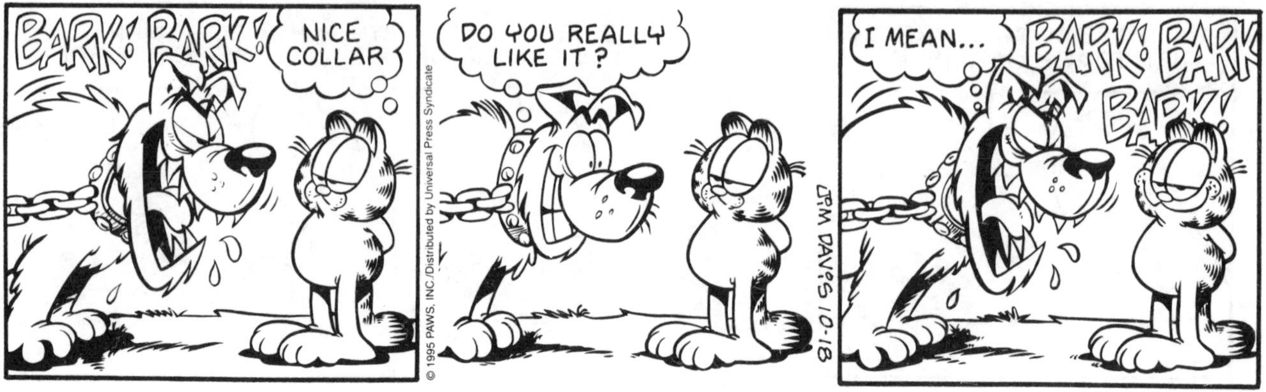
BARK! BARK!
NICE COLLAR
© 1995 PAWS, INC./Distributed by Universal Press Syndicate
DO YOU REALLY LIKE IT?
JIM DAVIS 10-18
I MEAN...
BARK! BARK! BARK!

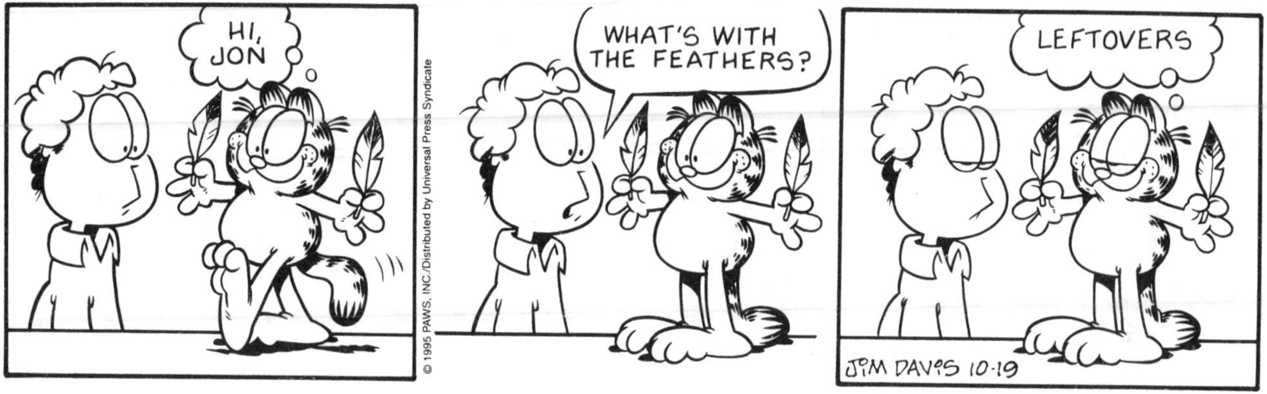
HI, JON
© 1995 PAWS, INC./Distributed by Universal Press Syndicate
WHAT'S WITH THE FEATHERS?
LEFTOVERS
JIM DAVIS 10-19

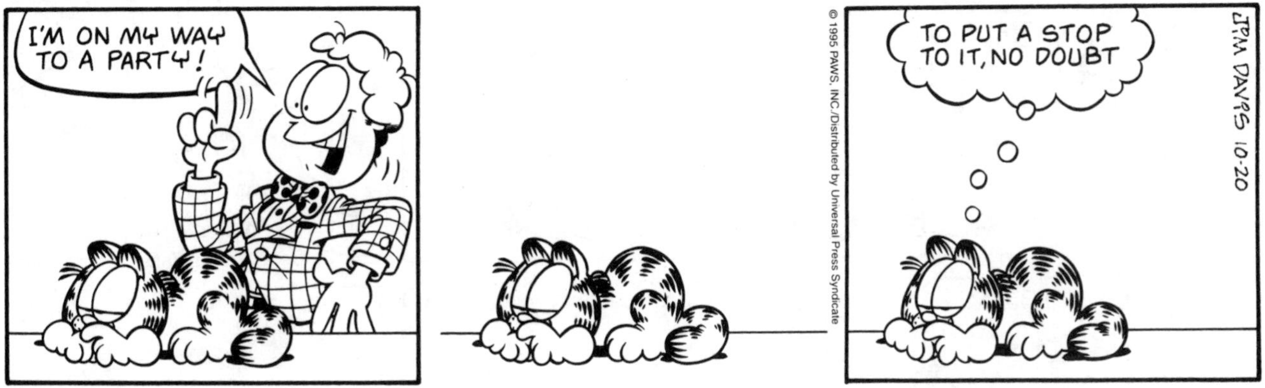
I'M ON MY WAY TO A PARTY!
TO PUT A STOP TO IT, NO DOUBT
JIM DAVIS 10-20
© 1995 PAWS, INC./Distributed by Universal Press Syndicate

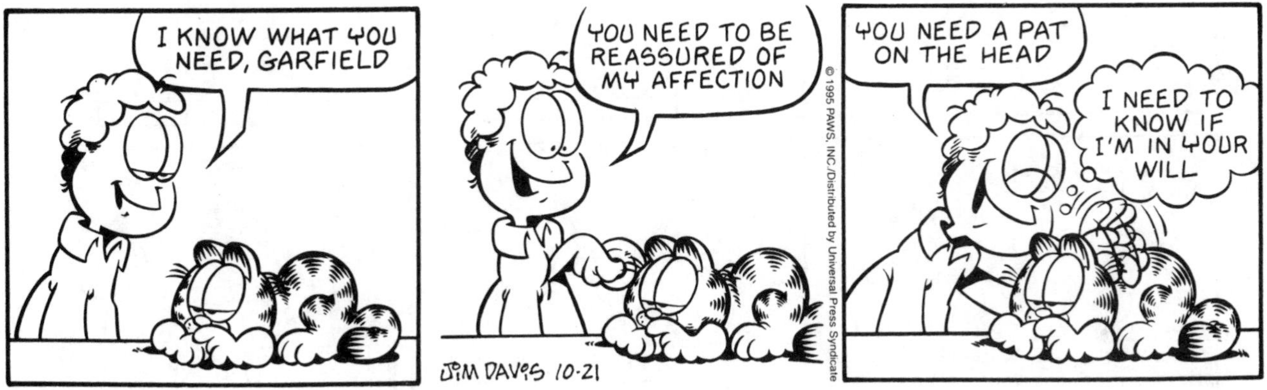
I KNOW WHAT YOU NEED, GARFIELD
YOU NEED TO BE REASSURED OF MY AFFECTION
JIM DAVIS 10-21
YOU NEED A PAT ON THE HEAD
I NEED TO KNOW IF I'M IN YOUR WILL
© 1995 PAWS, INC./Distributed by Universal Press Syndicate

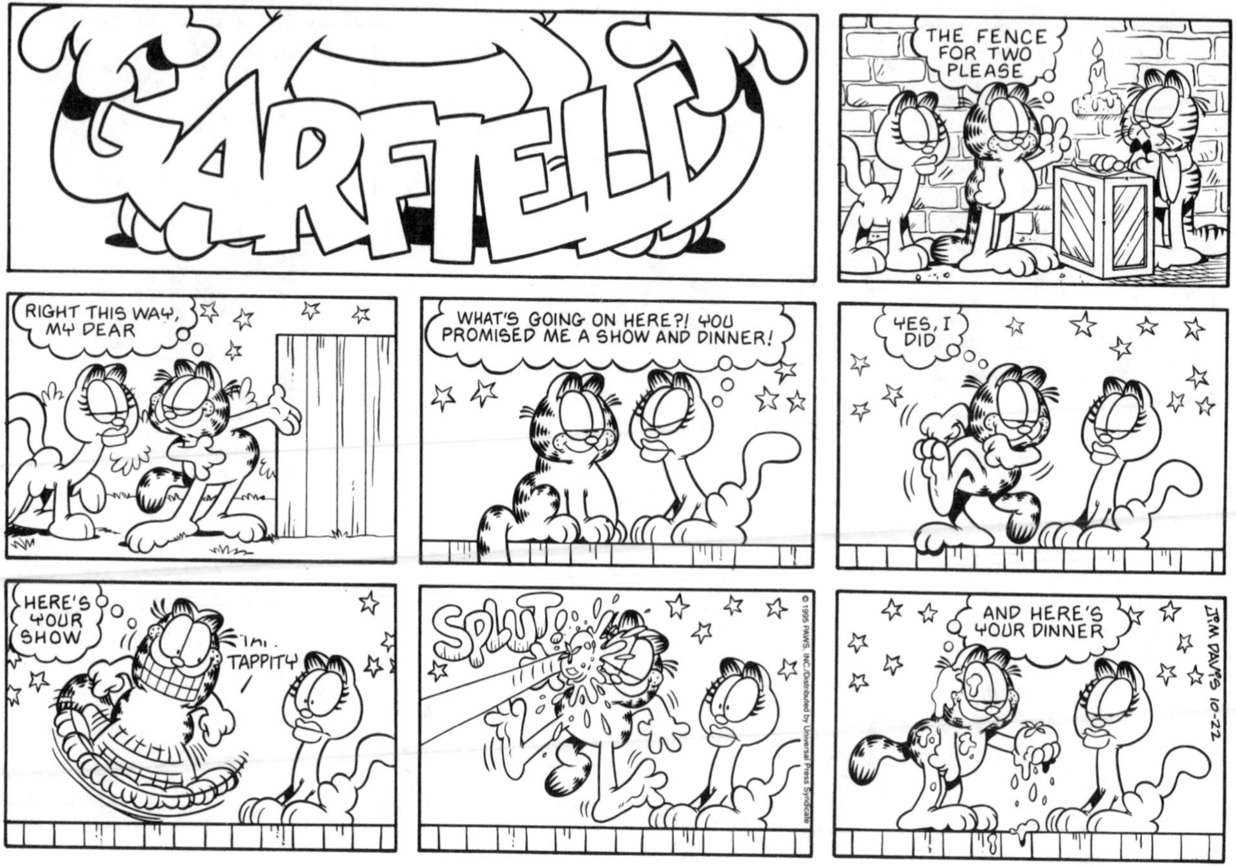
GARFIELD
THE FENCE FOR TWO PLEASE
RIGHT THIS WAY, MY DEAR
WHAT'S GOING ON HERE?! YOU PROMISED ME A SHOW AND DINNER!
YES, I DID
HERE'S YOUR SHOW
TAPPITY
SPLUT!
© 1995 PAWS, INC./Distributed by Universal Press Syndicate
AND HERE'S YOUR DINNER
JIM DAVIS 10-22

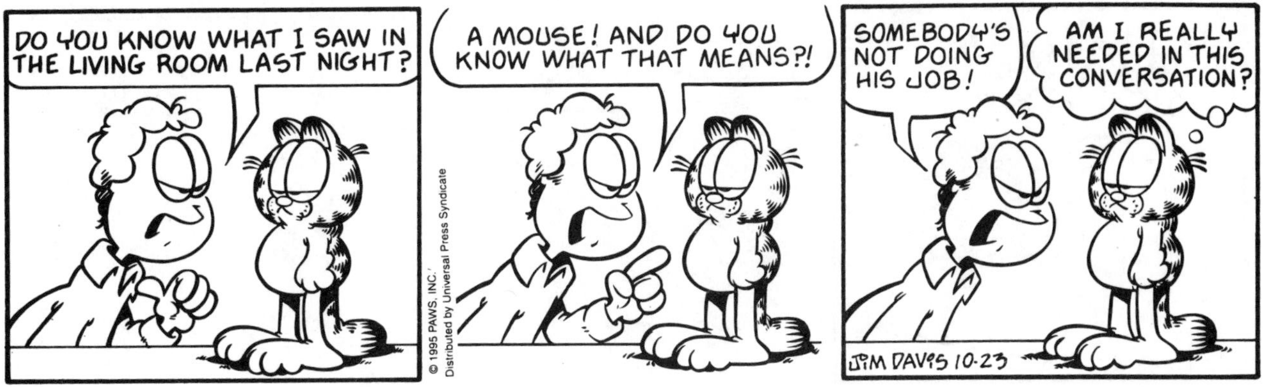
DO YOU KNOW WHAT I SAW IN THE LIVING ROOM LAST NIGHT?
A MOUSE! AND DO YOU KNOW WHAT THAT MEANS?!
SOMEBODY'S NOT DOING HIS JOB!
AM I REALLY NEEDED IN THIS CONVERSATION?
© 1995 PAWS, INC./ Distributed by Universal Press Syndicate
JIM DAVIS 10-23

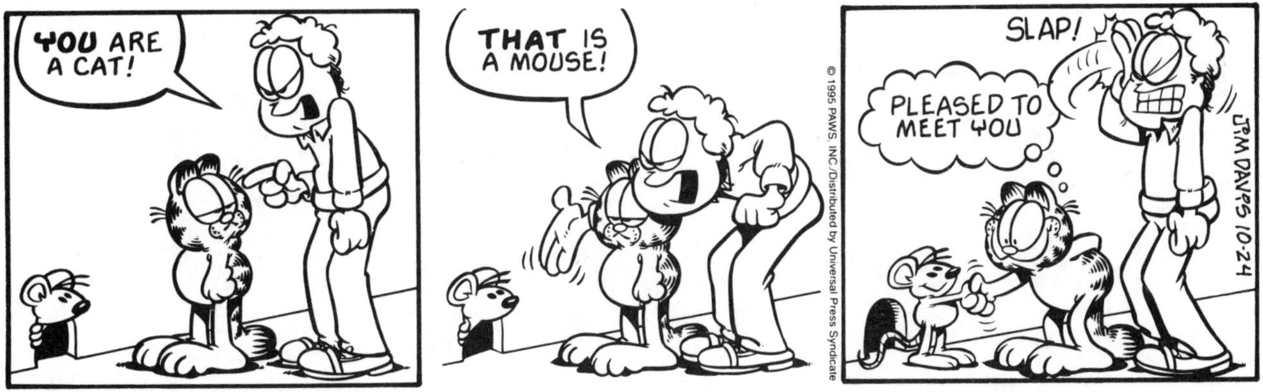
YOU ARE A CAT!
THAT IS A MOUSE!
SLAP!
PLEASED TO MEET YOU
© 1995 PAWS, INC./Distributed by Universal Press Syndicate
JIM DAVIS 10-24

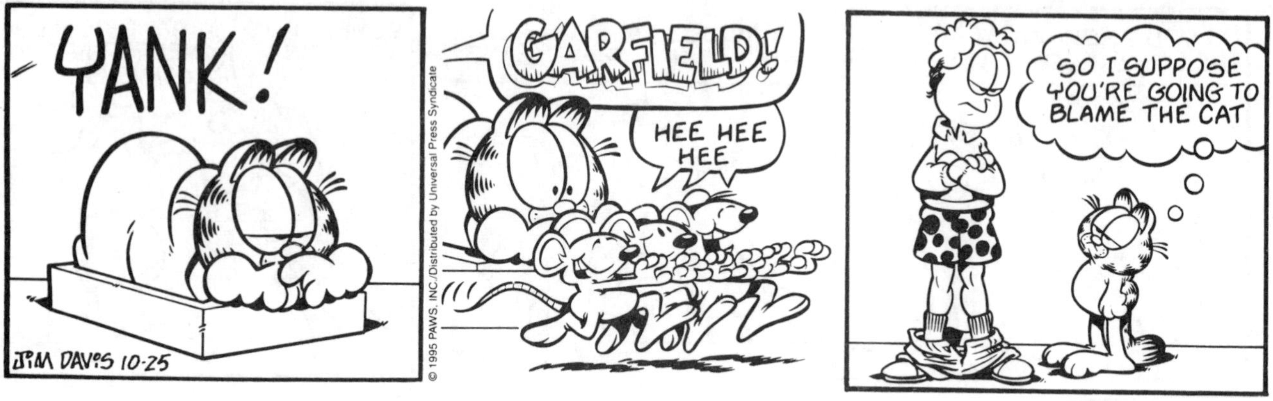
YANK!
JIM DAVIS 10-25
© 1995 PAWS, INC./Distributed by Universal Press Syndicate
GARFIELD!
HEE HEE HEE
SO I SUPPOSE YOU'RE GOING TO BLAME THE CAT

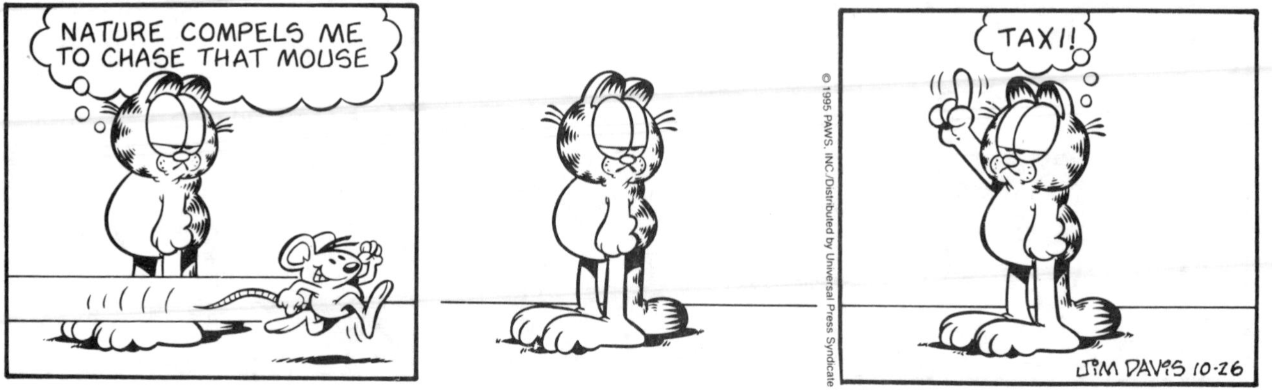
NATURE COMPELS ME TO CHASE THAT MOUSE
© 1995 PAWS, INC./Distributed by Universal Press Syndicate
TAXI!
JIM DAVIS 10-26

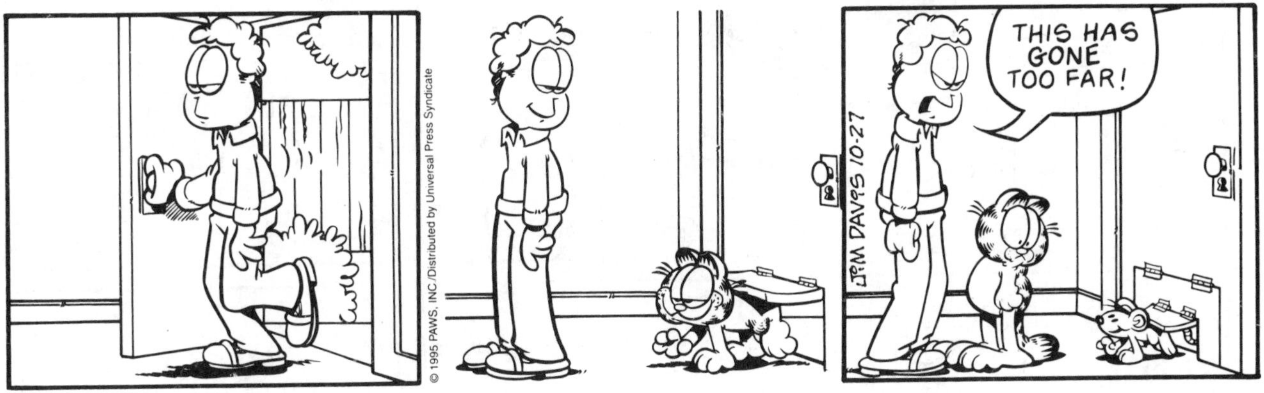
© 1995 PAWS, INC./Distributed by Universal Press Syndicate
JIM DAVIS 10-27
THIS HAS GONE TOO FAR!

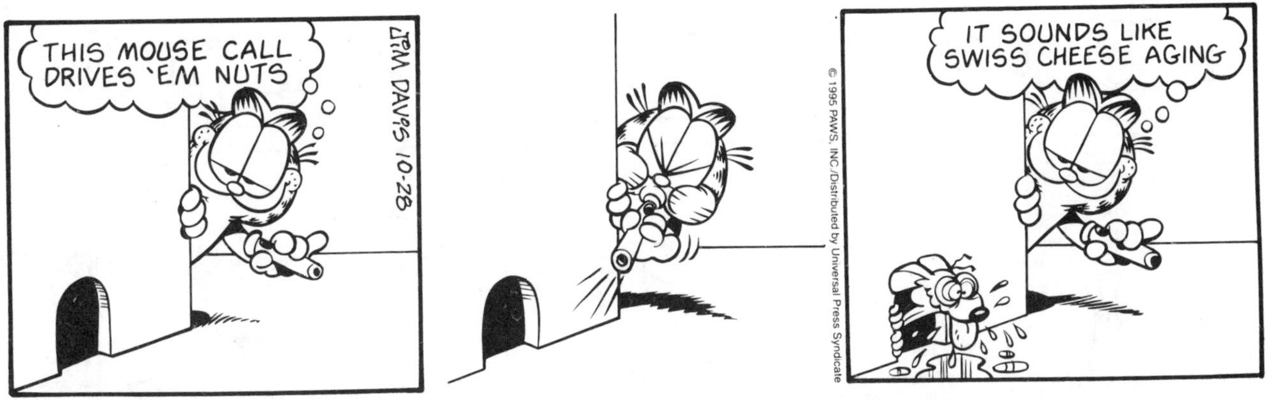
THIS MOUSE CALL DRIVES 'EM NUTS
JIM DAVIS 10-28
© 1995 PAWS, INC./Distributed by Universal Press Syndicate
IT SOUNDS LIKE SWISS CHEESE AGING

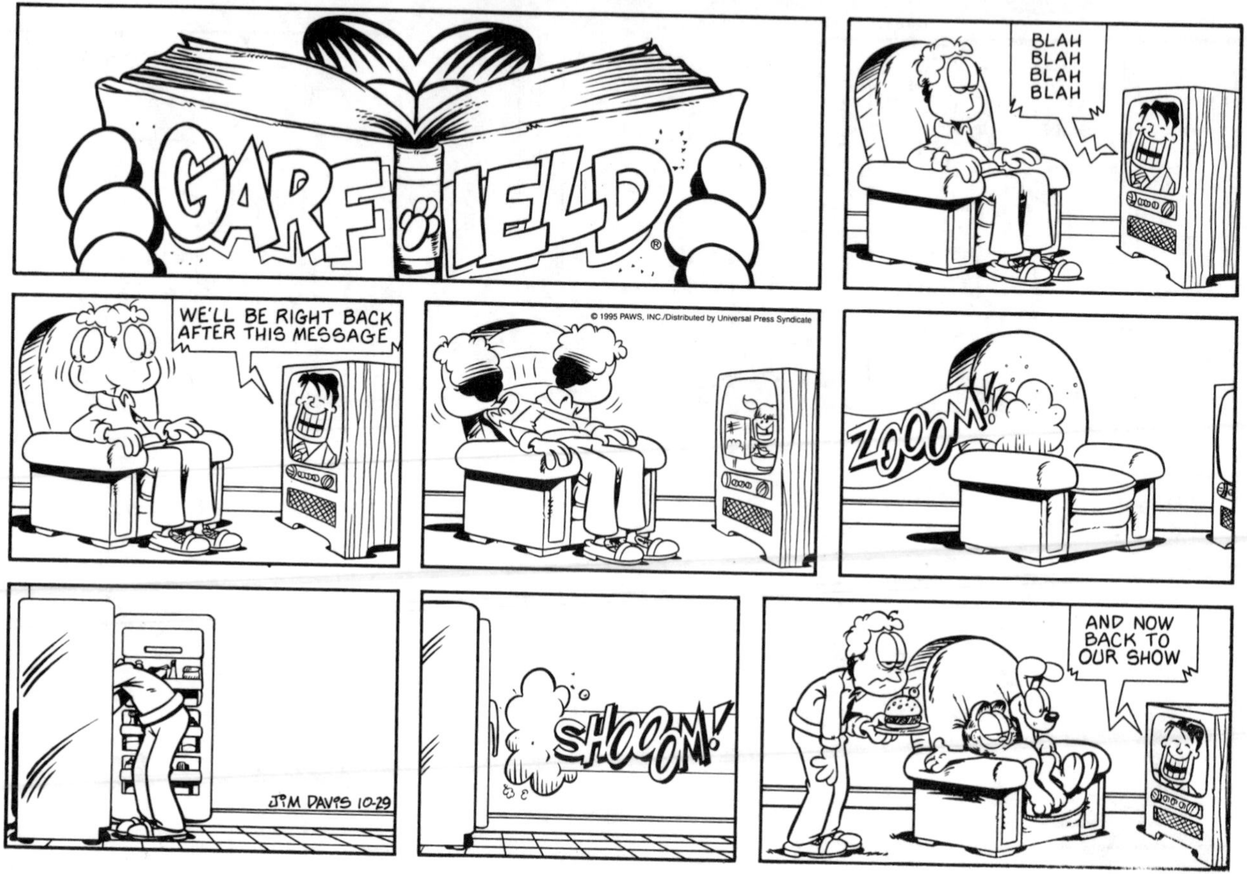

GARFIELD®
BLAH BLAH BLAH BLAH
WE'LL BE RIGHT BACK AFTER THIS MESSAGE
© 1995 PAWS, INC./Distributed by Universal Press Syndicate
ZOOOM!
JIM DAVIS 10-29
SHOOOM!
AND NOW BACK TO OUR SHOW

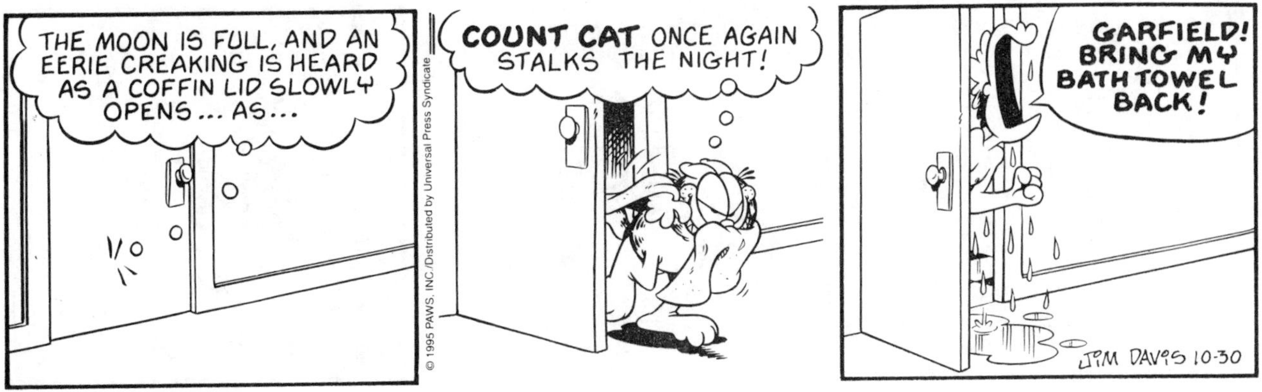
THE MOON IS FULL, AND AN EERIE CREAKING IS HEARD AS A COFFIN LID SLOWLY OPENS ... AS ...
1/0
COUNT CAT ONCE AGAIN STALKS THE NIGHT!
GARFIELD! BRING MY BATH TOWEL BACK!
JIM DAVIS 10-30

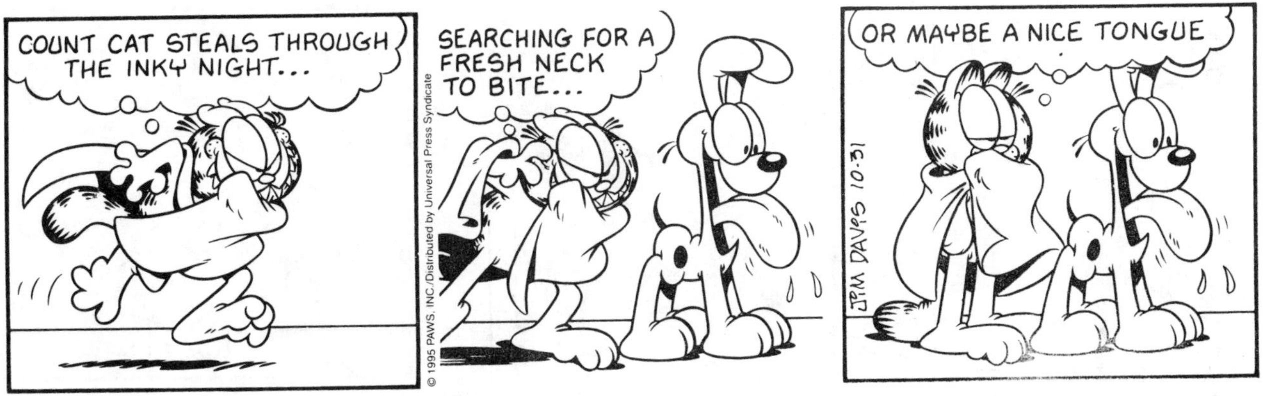
COUNT CAT STEALS THROUGH THE INKY NIGHT...
SEARCHING FOR A FRESH NECK TO BITE...
OR MAYBE A NICE TONGUE
JIM DAVIS 10-31

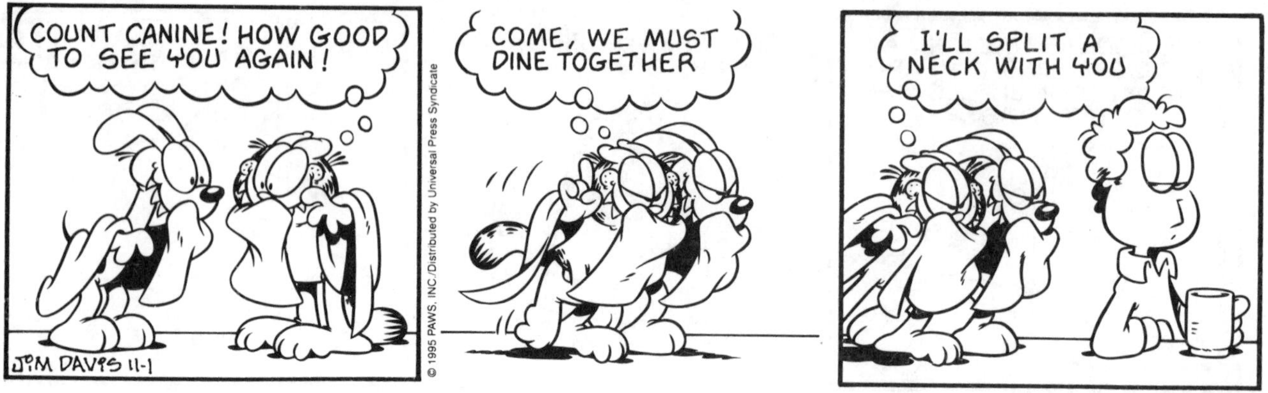
COUNT CANINE! HOW GOOD TO SEE YOU AGAIN!
COME, WE MUST DINE TOGETHER
I'LL SPLIT A NECK WITH YOU
JIM DAVIS 11-1

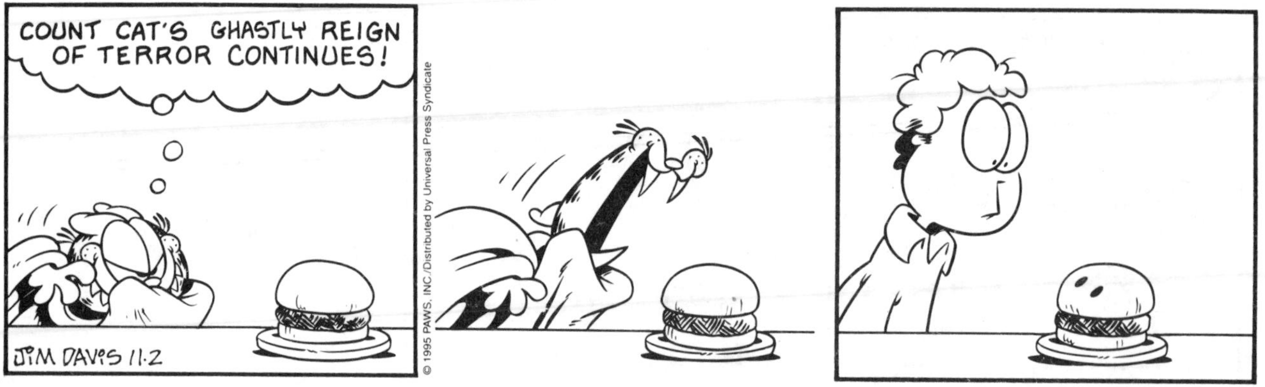
COUNT CAT'S GHASTLY REIGN OF TERROR CONTINUES!
JIM DAVIS 11-2

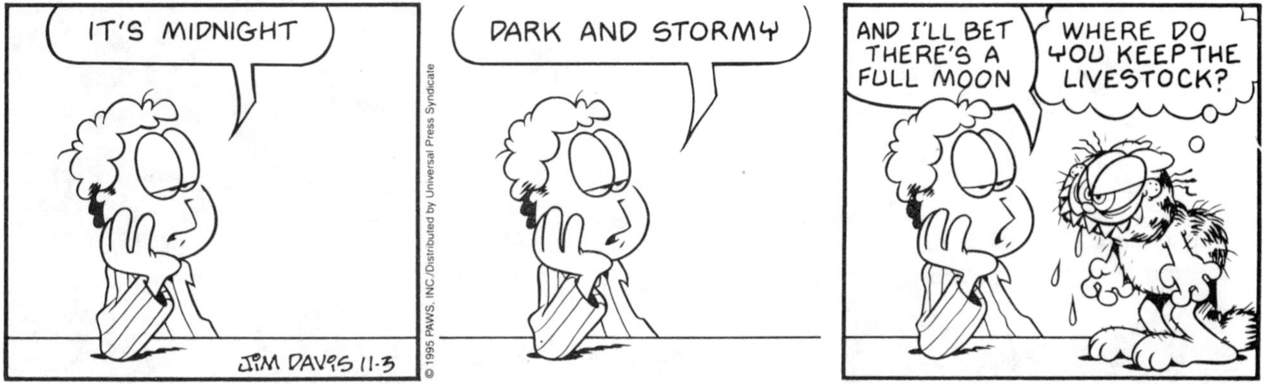
IT'S MIDNIGHT
JIM DAVIS 11-3
DARK AND STORMY
AND I'LL BET THERE'S A FULL MOON
WHERE DO YOU KEEP THE LIVESTOCK?

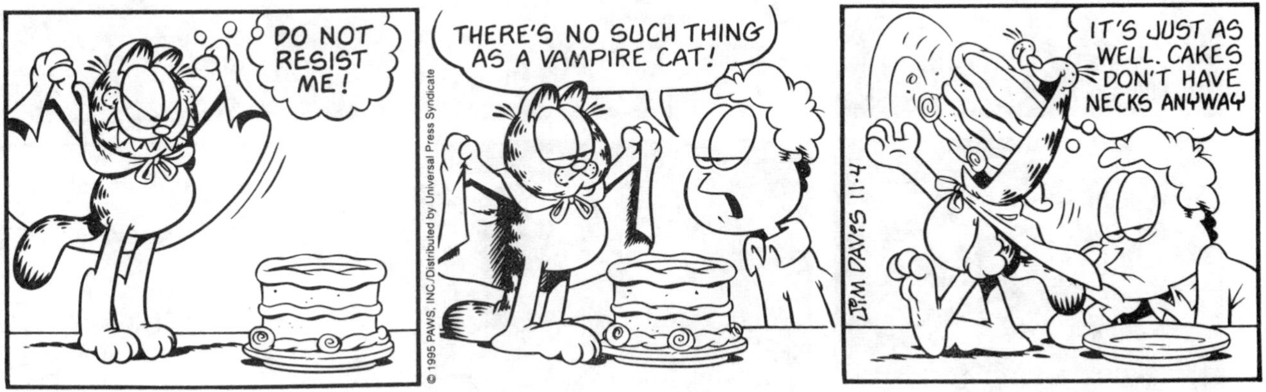
DO NOT RESIST ME!
THERE'S NO SUCH THING AS A VAMPIRE CAT!
JIM DAVIS 11-4
IT'S JUST AS WELL. CAKES DON'T HAVE NECKS ANYWAY

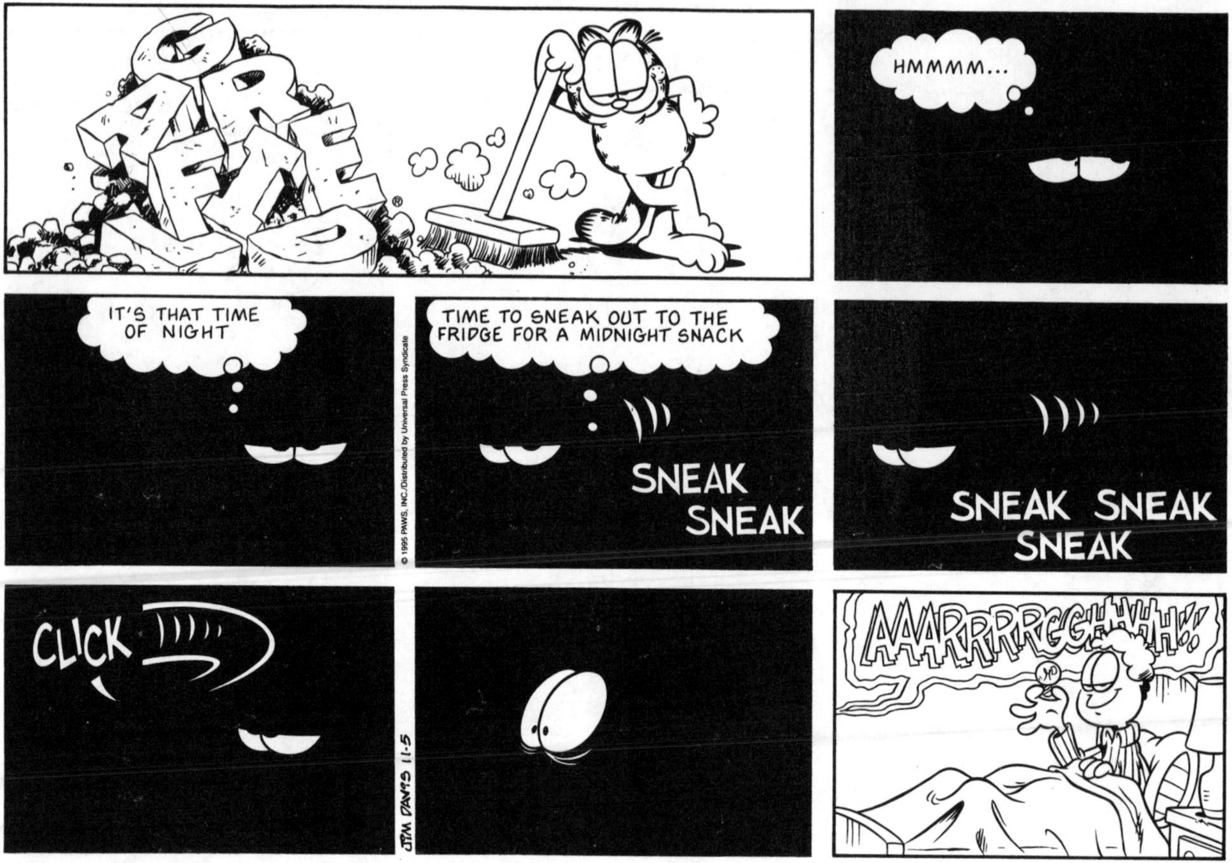
HMMMM...
IT'S THAT TIME OF NIGHT
TIME TO SNEAK OUT TO THE FRIDGE FOR A MIDNIGHT SNACK
SNEAK
SNEAK
SNEAK SNEAK
SNEAK
CLICK
AAARRRRGGHHHH!!
© 1995 PAWS, INC./Distributed by Universal Press Syndicate
JIM DAVIS 11-5

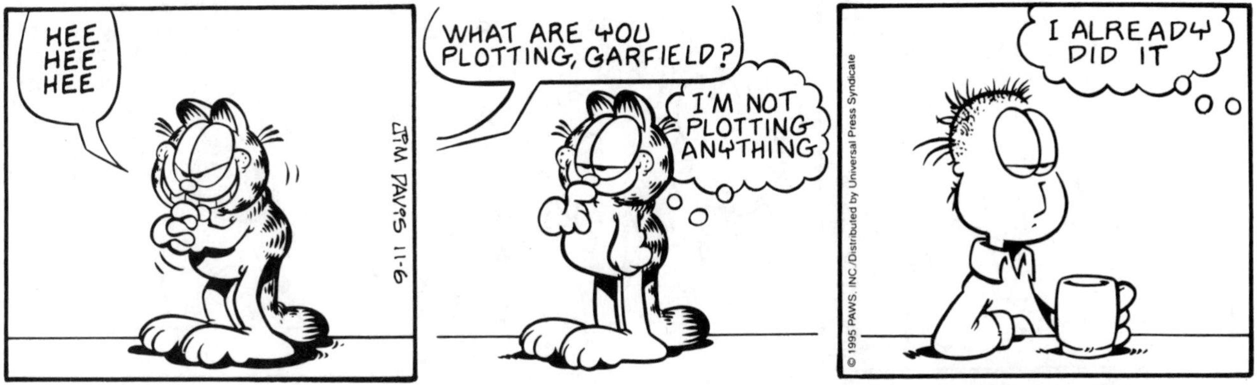
HEE HEE HEE
JPM DAVPS 11-6
WHAT ARE YOU PLOTTING, GARFIELD?
I'M NOT PLOTTING ANYTHING
I ALREADY DID IT
© 1995 PAWS, INC./Distributed by Universal Press Syndicate

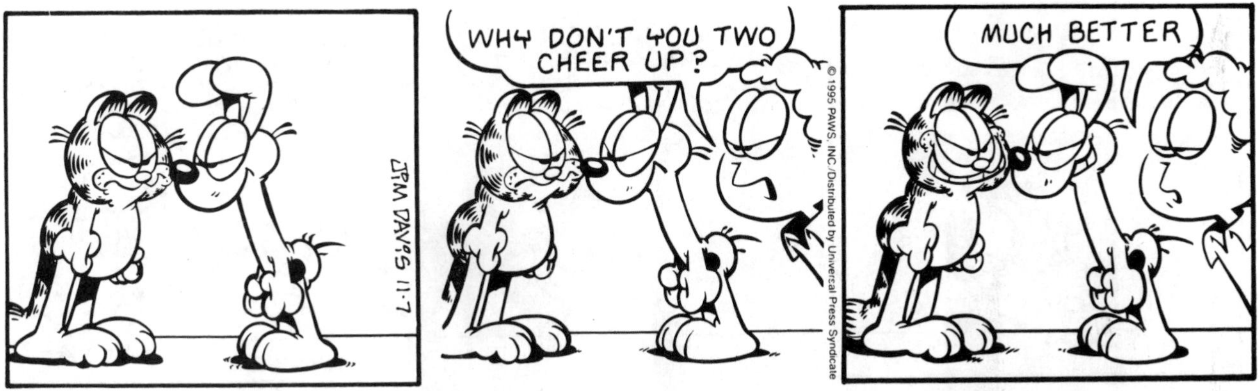
JPM DAVPS 11-7
WHY DON'T YOU TWO CHEER UP?
MUCH BETTER
© 1995 PAWS, INC./Distributed by Universal Press Syndicate

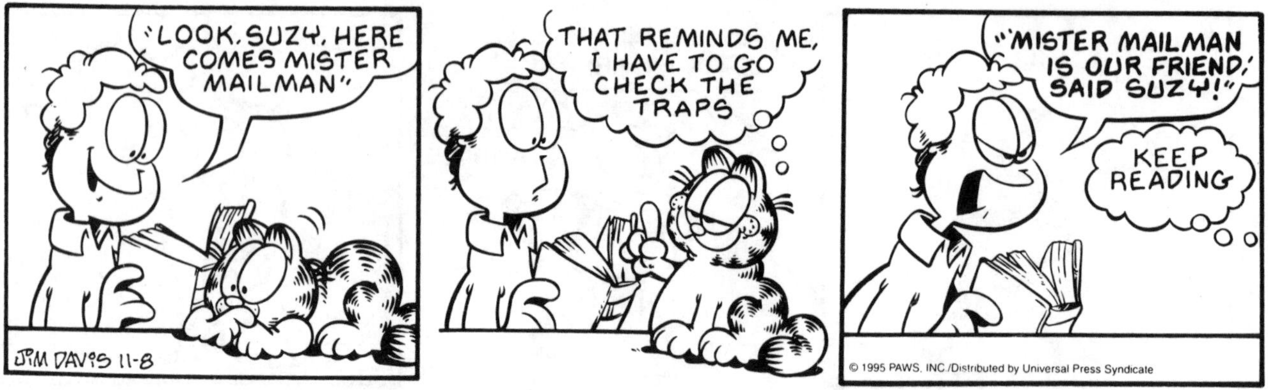
"LOOK, SUZY, HERE COMES MISTER MAILMAN"
THAT REMINDS ME, I HAVE TO GO CHECK THE TRAPS
"'MISTER MAILMAN IS OUR FRIEND,' SAID SUZY!"
KEEP READING
JIM DAVIS 11-8
© 1995 PAWS, INC./Distributed by Universal Press Syndicate

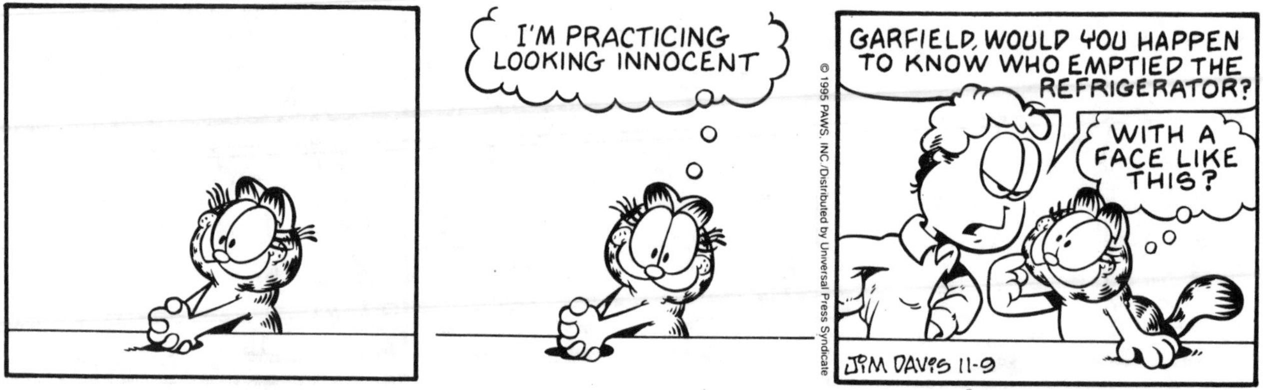
I'M PRACTICING LOOKING INNOCENT
GARFIELD, WOULD YOU HAPPEN TO KNOW WHO EMPTIED THE REFRIGERATOR?
WITH A FACE LIKE THIS?
JIM DAVIS 11-9
© 1995 PAWS, INC./Distributed by Universal Press Syndicate

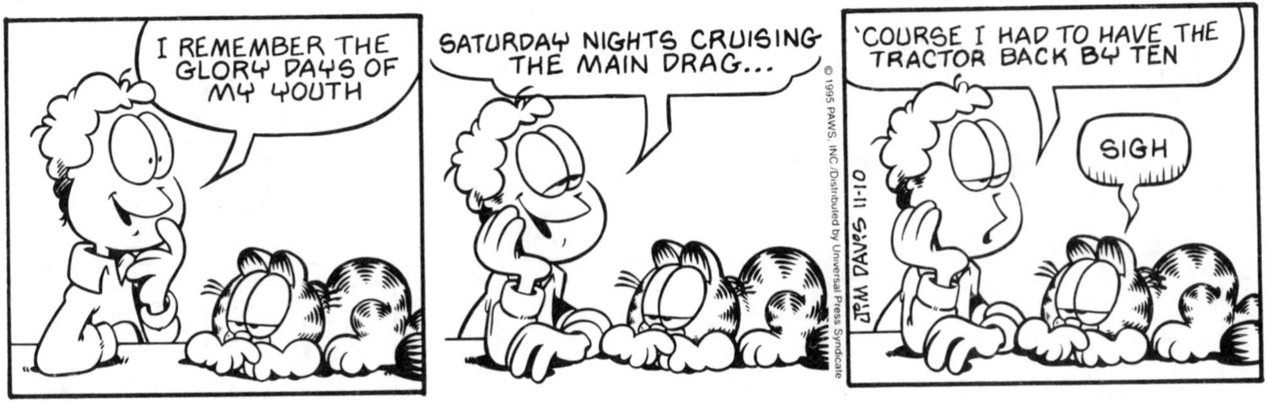
I REMEMBER THE GLORY DAYS OF MY YOUTH
SATURDAY NIGHTS CRUISING THE MAIN DRAG...
'COURSE I HAD TO HAVE THE TRACTOR BACK BY TEN
SIGH
JIM DAVIS 11-10

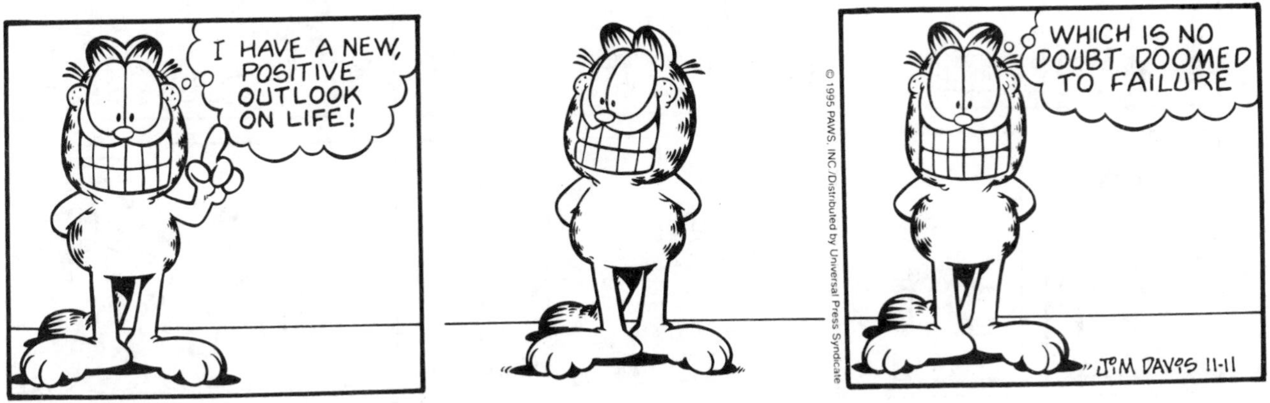
I HAVE A NEW, POSITIVE OUTLOOK ON LIFE!
WHICH IS NO DOUBT DOOMED TO FAILURE
JIM DAVIS 11-11

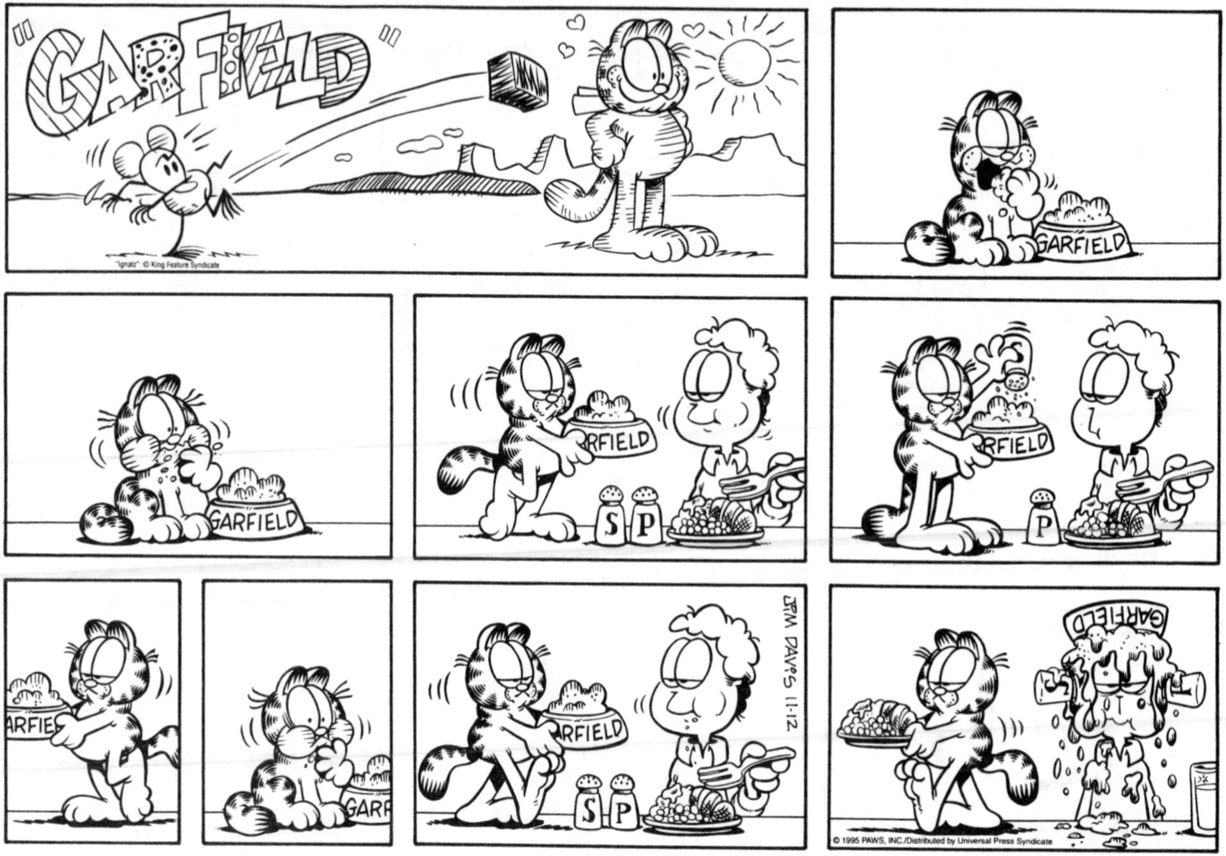
"GARFIELD"
GARFIELD
GARFIELD
RFIELD
S
P
RFIELD
P
ARFIEL
GARF
RFIELD
S
P
JIM DAVIS 11-12
GARFIELD

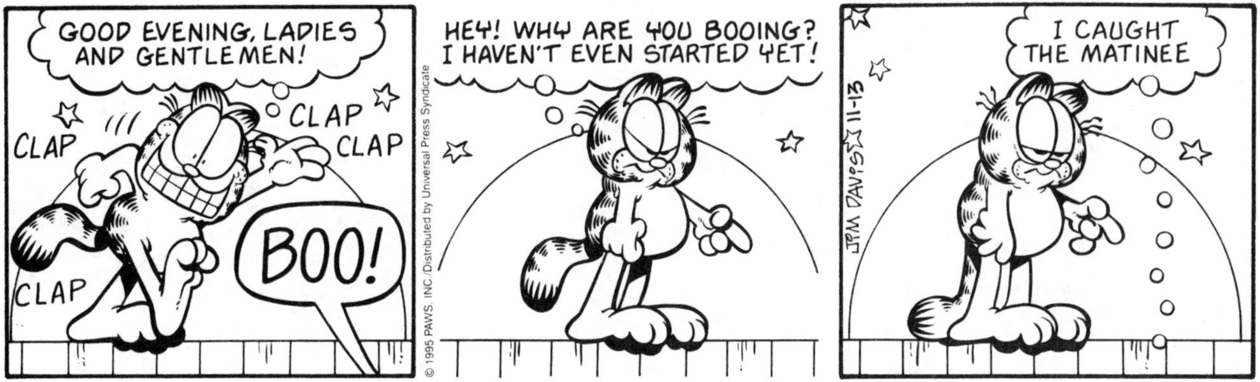
GOOD EVENING, LADIES AND GENTLEMEN!
CLAP
CLAP
CLAP
CLAP
BOO!
HEY! WHY ARE YOU BOOING? I HAVEN'T EVEN STARTED YET!
I CAUGHT THE MATINEE
JIM DAVIS 11-13
© 1995 PAWS, INC./Distributed by Universal Press Syndicate

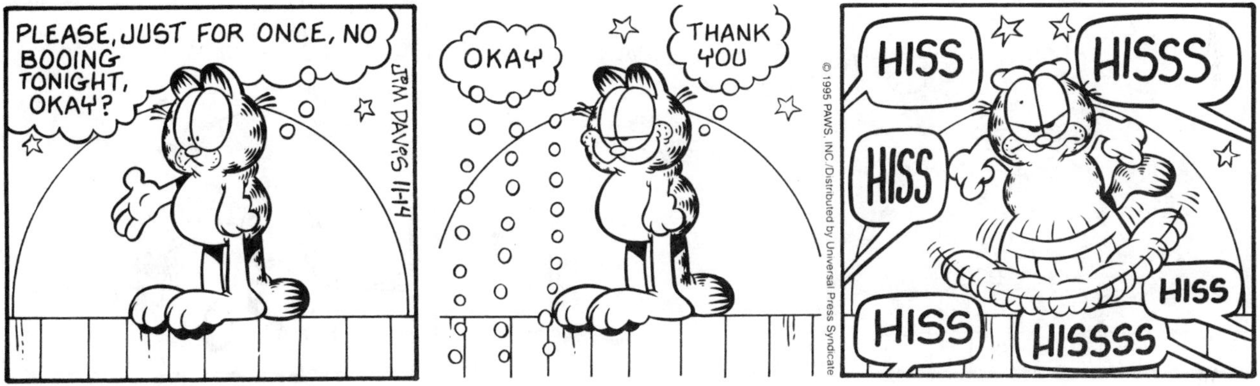
PLEASE, JUST FOR ONCE, NO BOOING TONIGHT, OKAY?
JIM DAVIS 11-14
OKAY
THANK YOU
HISS
HISSS
HISS
HISS
HISSSS
HISS
© 1995 PAWS, INC./Distributed by Universal Press Syndicate

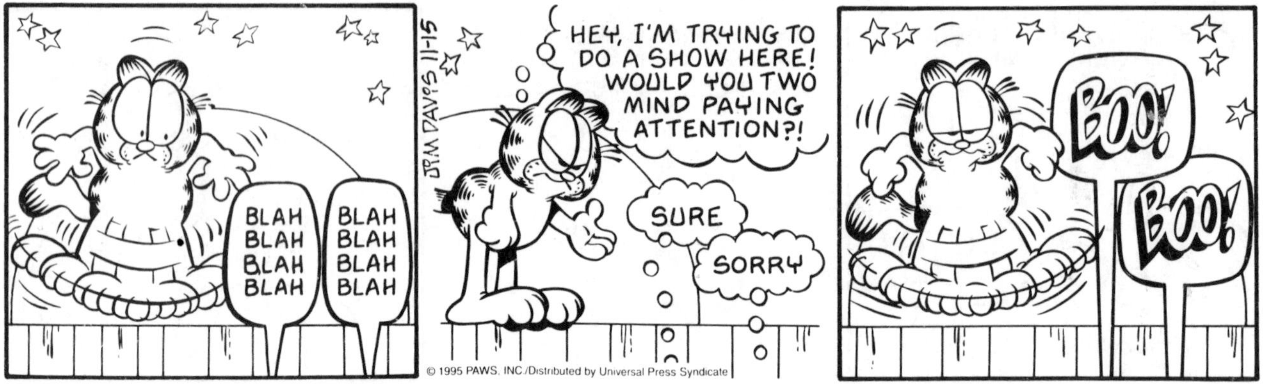
BLAH BLAH BLAH BLAH
BLAH BLAH BLAH BLAH
JIM DAVIS 11-15
HEY, I'M TRYING TO DO A SHOW HERE! WOULD YOU TWO MIND PAYING ATTENTION?!
SURE
SORRY
BOO!
BOO!

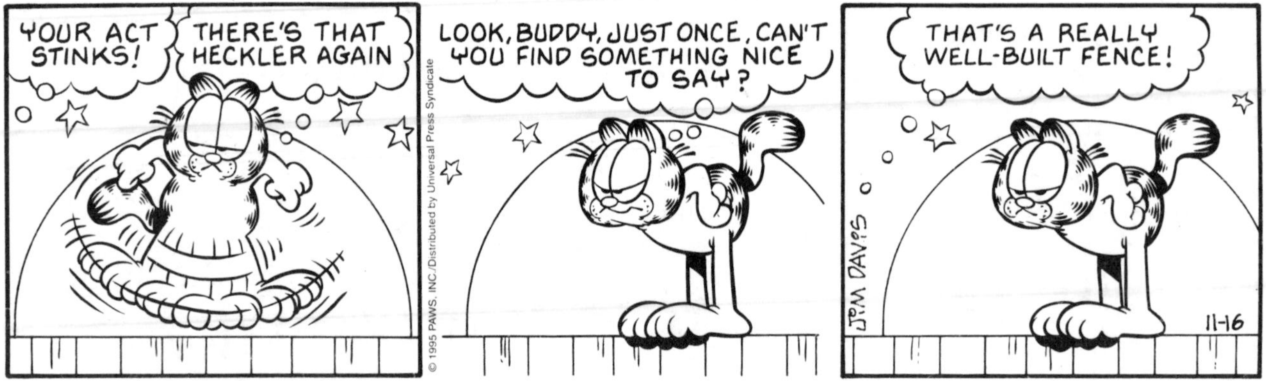
YOUR ACT STINKS!
THERE'S THAT HECKLER AGAIN
LOOK, BUDDY, JUST ONCE, CAN'T YOU FIND SOMETHING NICE TO SAY?
THAT'S A REALLY WELL-BUILT FENCE!
JIM DAVIS
11-16

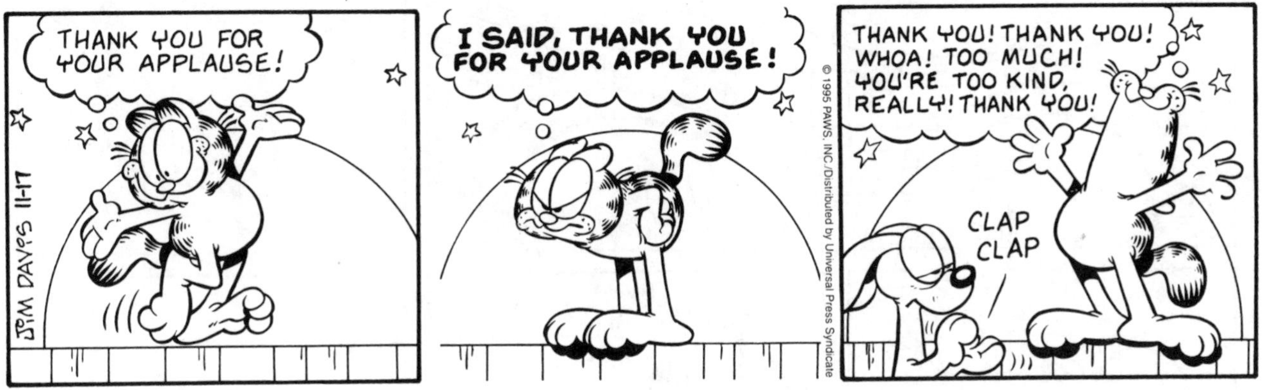
THANK YOU FOR YOUR APPLAUSE!
JIM DAVIS 11-17
I SAID, THANK YOU FOR YOUR APPLAUSE!
© 1995 PAWS, INC./Distributed by Universal Press Syndicate
THANK YOU! THANK YOU! WHOA! TOO MUCH! YOU'RE TOO KIND, REALLY! THANK YOU!
CLAP CLAP

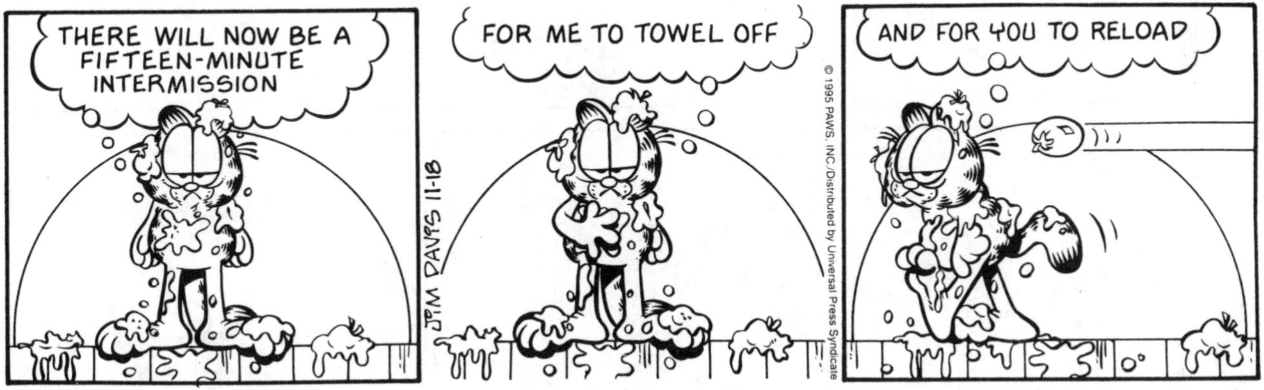
THERE WILL NOW BE A FIFTEEN-MINUTE INTERMISSION
JIM DAVIS 11-18
FOR ME TO TOWEL OFF
© 1995 PAWS, INC./Distributed by Universal Press Syndicate
AND FOR YOU TO RELOAD

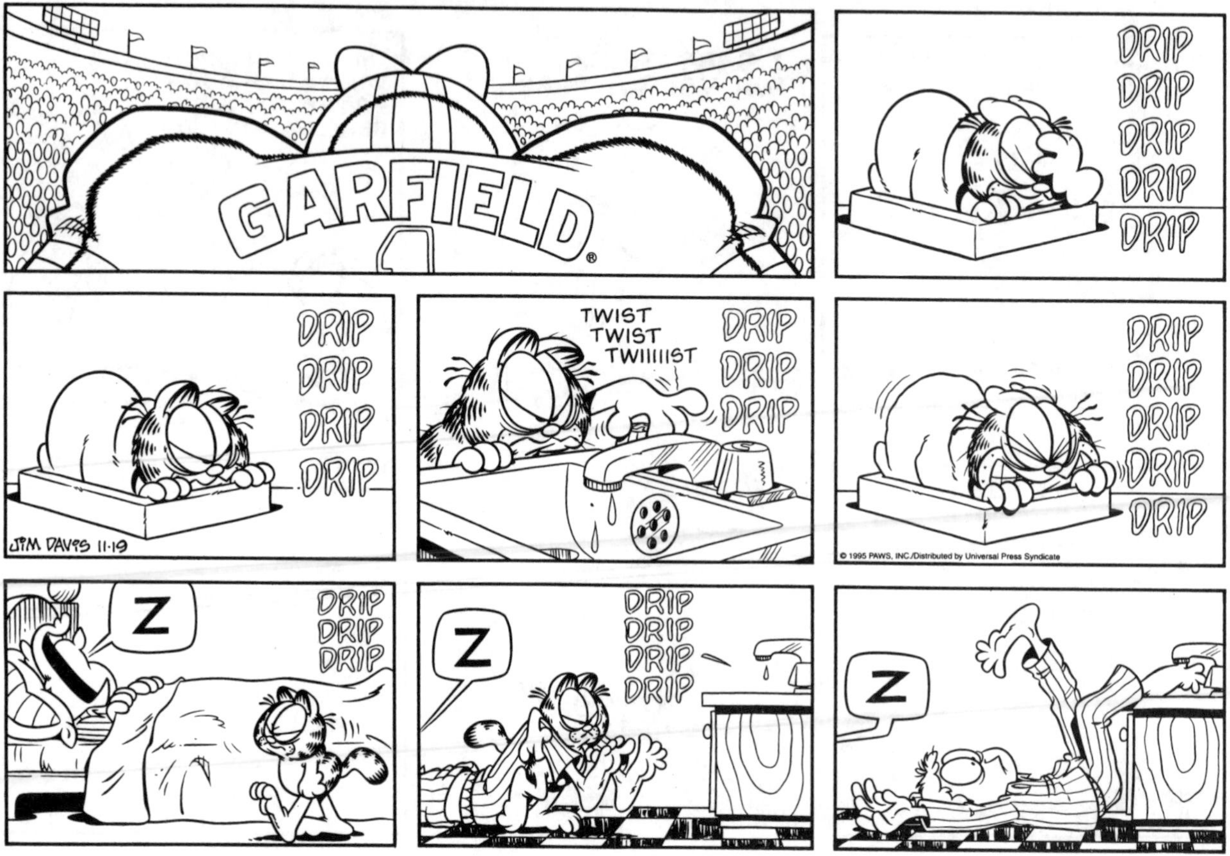
GARFIELD®
DRIP
DRIP
DRIP
DRIP
DRIP
DRIP
DRIP
DRIP
DRIP
JIM DAVIS 11·19
TWIST
TWIST
TWIIIIIST
DRIP
DRIP
DRIP
DRIP
DRIP
DRIP
DRIP
DRIP
© 1995 PAWS, INC./Distributed by Universal Press Syndicate
Z
DRIP
DRIP
DRIP
Z
DRIP
DRIP
DRIP
DRIP
Z

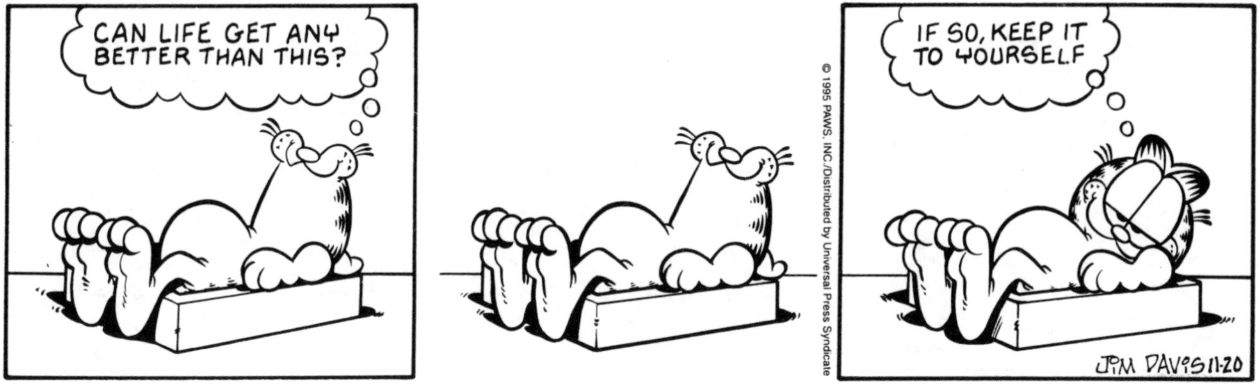
CAN LIFE GET ANY BETTER THAN THIS?
IF SO, KEEP IT TO YOURSELF
© 1995 PAWS, INC./Distributed by Universal Press Syndicate
JIM DAVIS 11-20

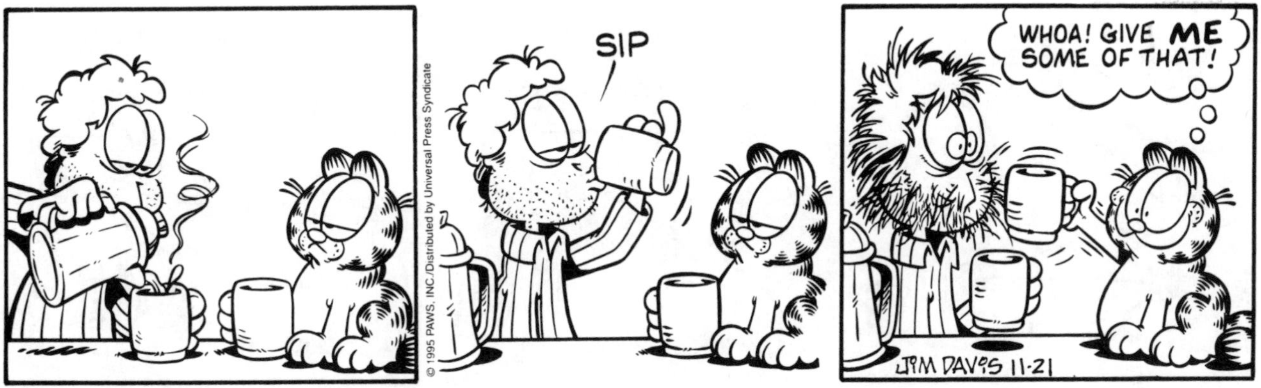
© 1995 PAWS, INC./Distributed by Universal Press Syndicate
SIP
WHOA! GIVE ME SOME OF THAT!
JIM DAVIS 11-21

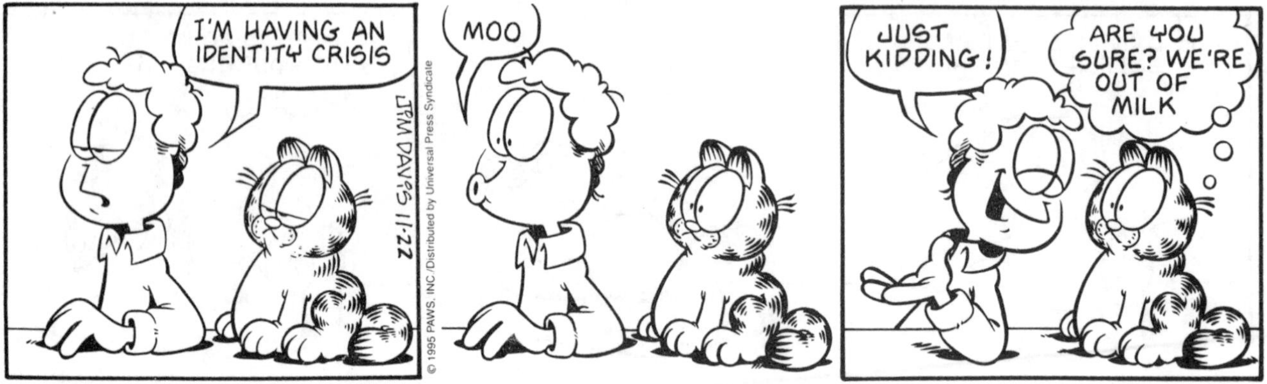
I'M HAVING AN IDENTITY CRISIS
JIM DAVIS 11-22
© 1995 PAWS, INC./Distributed by Universal Press Syndicate
MOO
JUST KIDDING!
ARE YOU SURE? WE'RE OUT OF MILK

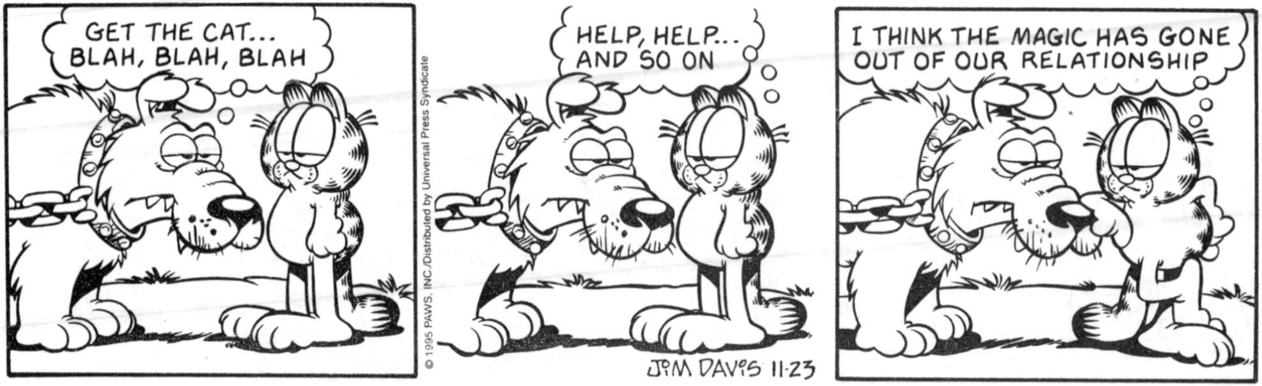
GET THE CAT... BLAH, BLAH, BLAH
© 1995 PAWS, INC./Distributed by Universal Press Syndicate
HELP, HELP... AND SO ON
JIM DAVIS 11-23
I THINK THE MAGIC HAS GONE OUT OF OUR RELATIONSHIP

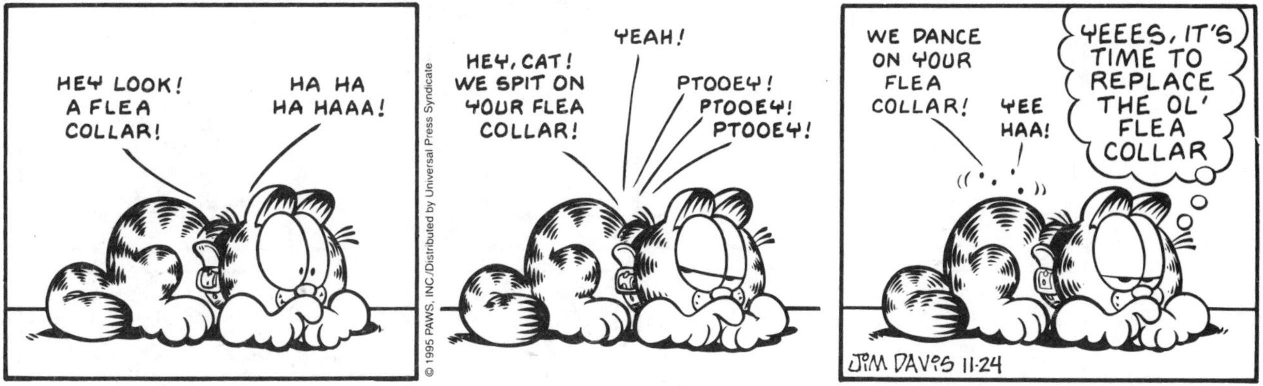
HEY LOOK! A FLEA COLLAR!
HA HA HA HAAA!
HEY, CAT! WE SPIT ON YOUR FLEA COLLAR!
YEAH!
PTOOEY! PTOOEY! PTOOEY!
WE DANCE ON YOUR FLEA COLLAR!
YEE HAA!
YEEES, IT'S TIME TO REPLACE THE OL' FLEA COLLAR
JIM DAVIS 11-24

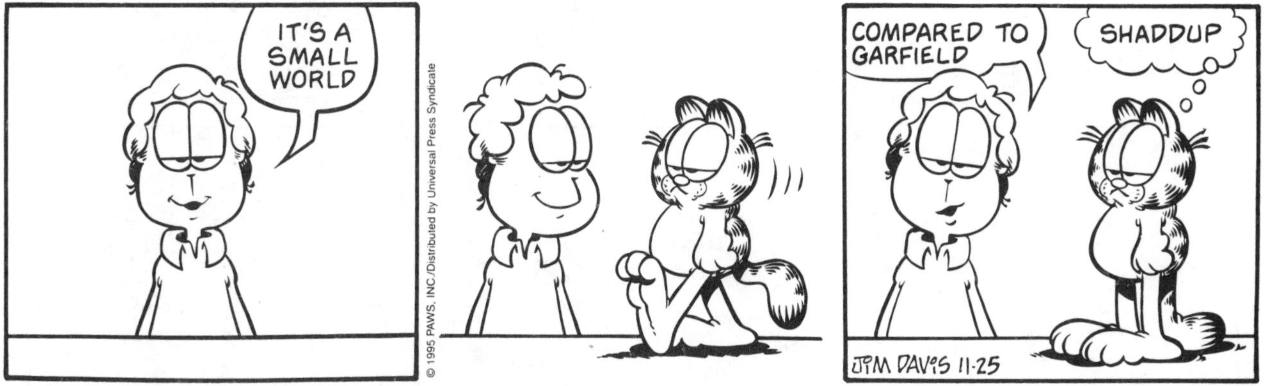
IT'S A SMALL WORLD
COMPARED TO GARFIELD
SHADDUP
JIM DAVIS 11-25

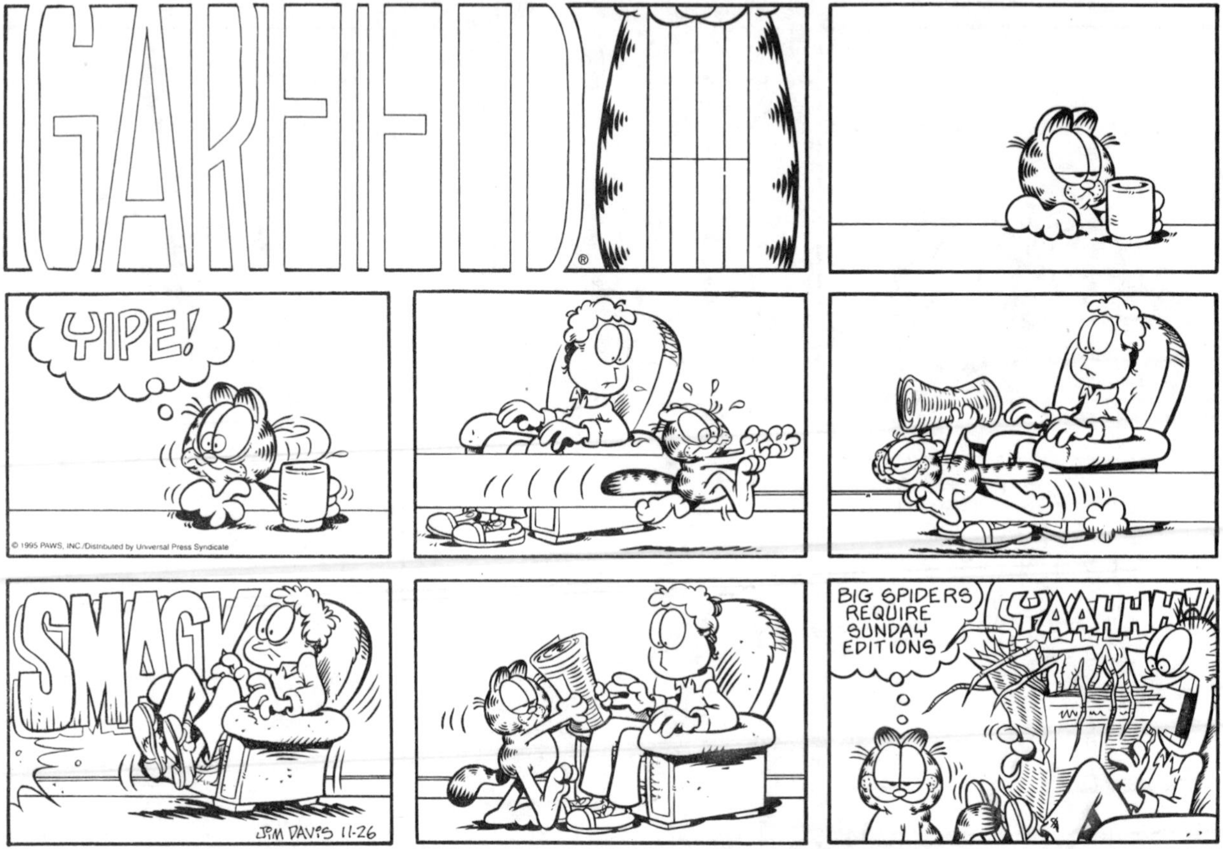
GARFIELD®
YIPE!
© 1995 PAWS, INC./Distributed by Universal Press Syndicate
SMACK
JIM DAVIS 11-26
BIG SPIDERS REQUIRE SUNDAY EDITIONS
YAAHHH!

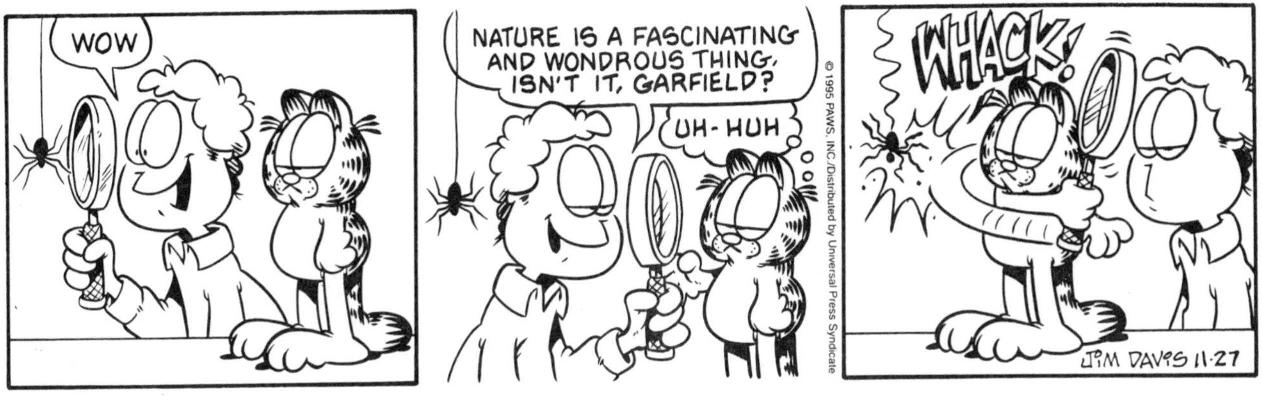
WOW
NATURE IS A FASCINATING AND WONDROUS THING, ISN'T IT, GARFIELD?
UH-HUH
© 1995 PAWS, INC./Distributed by Universal Press Syndicate
WHACK!
JIM DAVIS 11·27

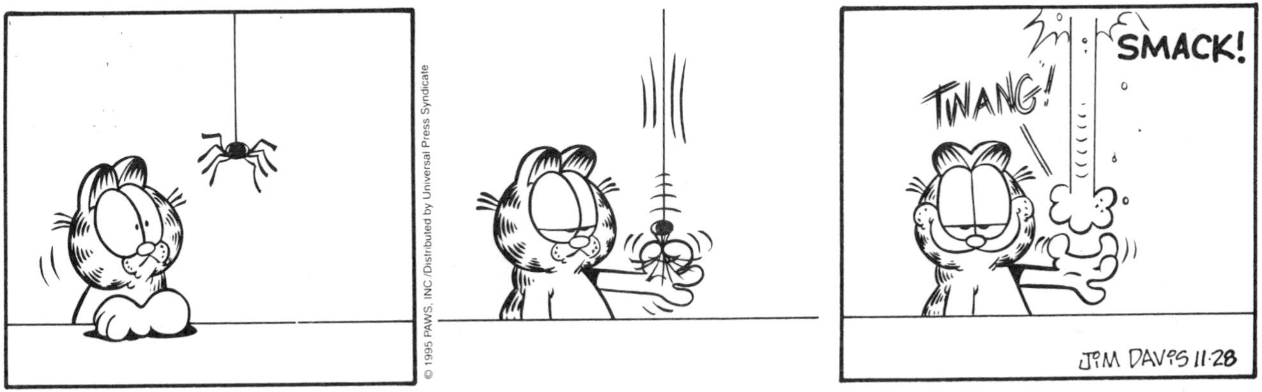
© 1995 PAWS, INC./Distributed by Universal Press Syndicate
TWANG!
SMACK!
JIM DAVIS 11·28

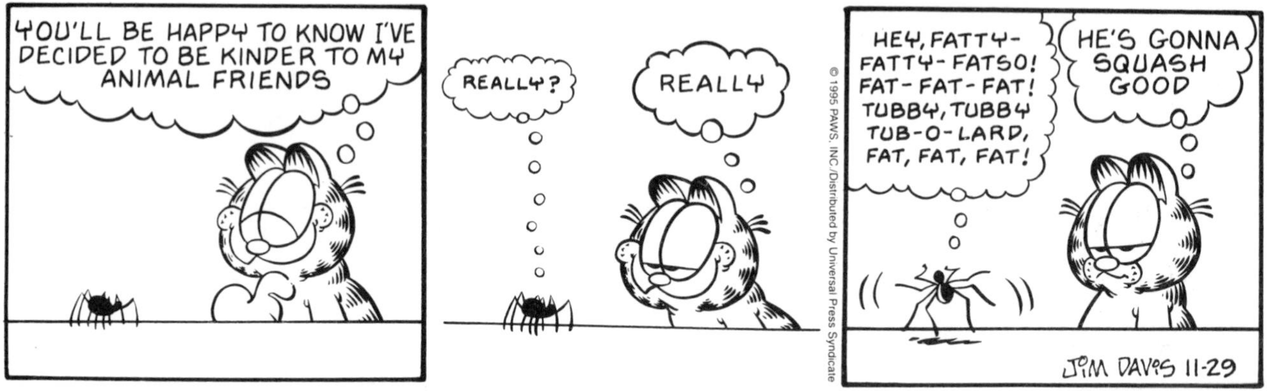
YOU'LL BE HAPPY TO KNOW I'VE DECIDED TO BE KINDER TO MY ANIMAL FRIENDS
REALLY?
REALLY
HEY, FATTY-FATTY-FATSO! FAT-FAT-FAT! TUBBY, TUBBY TUB-O-LARD, FAT, FAT, FAT!
HE'S GONNA SQUASH GOOD
JIM DAVIS 11-29

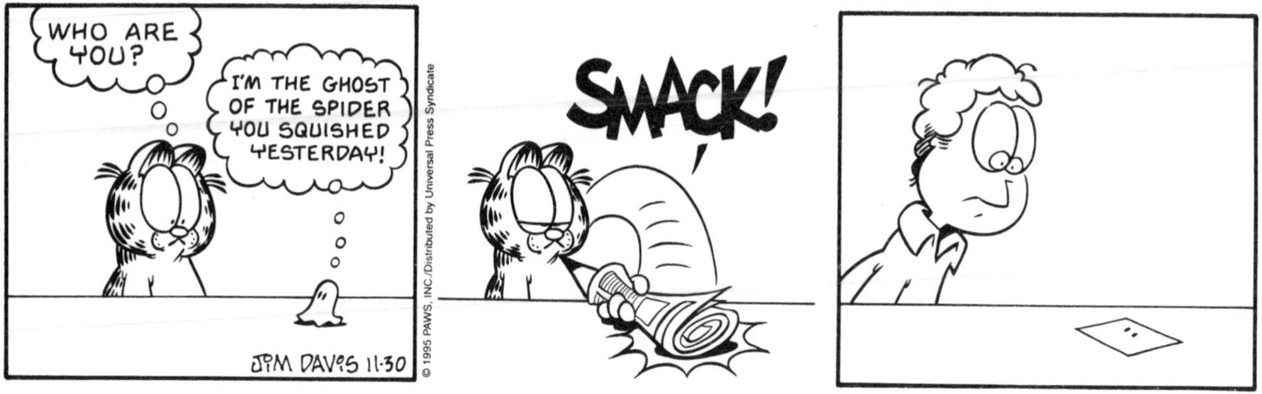
WHO ARE YOU?
I'M THE GHOST OF THE SPIDER YOU SQUISHED YESTERDAY!
JIM DAVIS 11-30
SMACK!

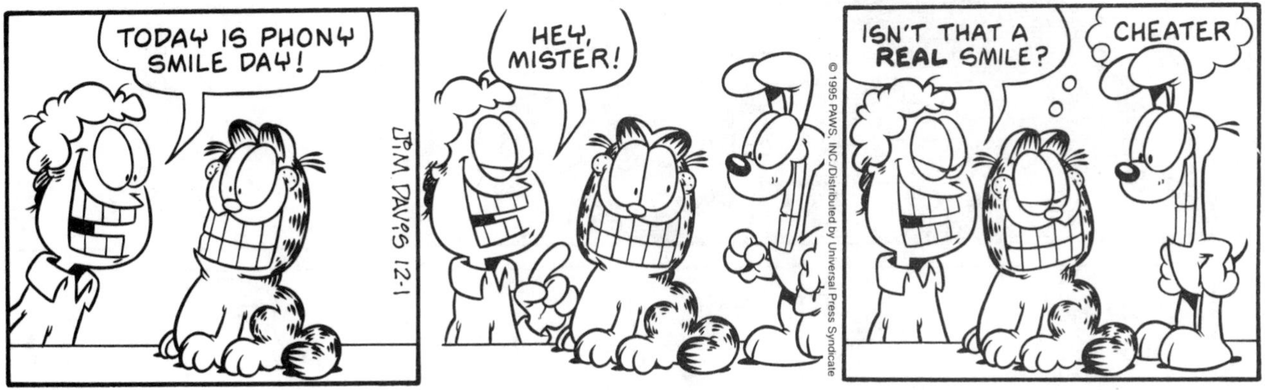
TODAY IS PHONY SMILE DAY!
JIM DAVIS 12-1
HEY, MISTER!
© 1995 PAWS, INC./Distributed by Universal Press Syndicate
ISN'T THAT A **REAL** SMILE?
CHEATER

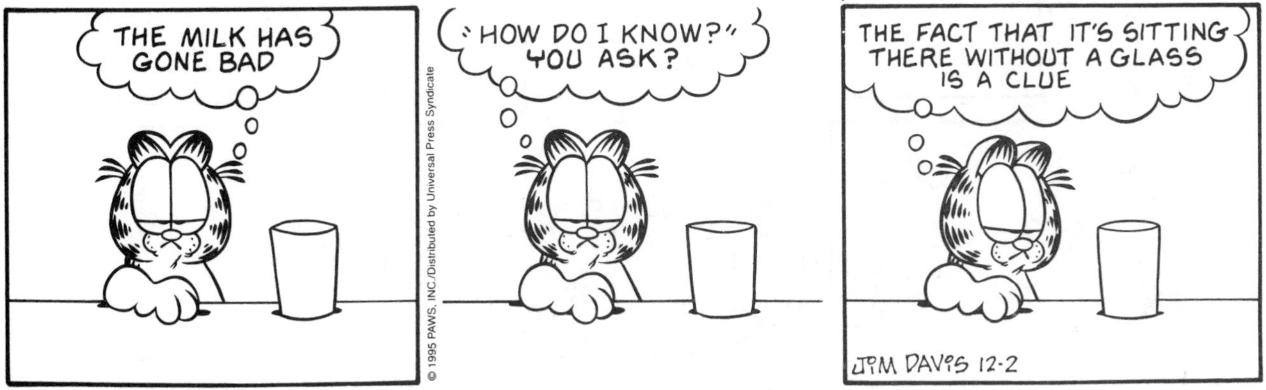
THE MILK HAS GONE BAD
© 1995 PAWS, INC./Distributed by Universal Press Syndicate
"HOW DO I KNOW?" YOU ASK?
THE FACT THAT IT'S SITTING THERE WITHOUT A GLASS IS A CLUE
JIM DAVIS 12-2

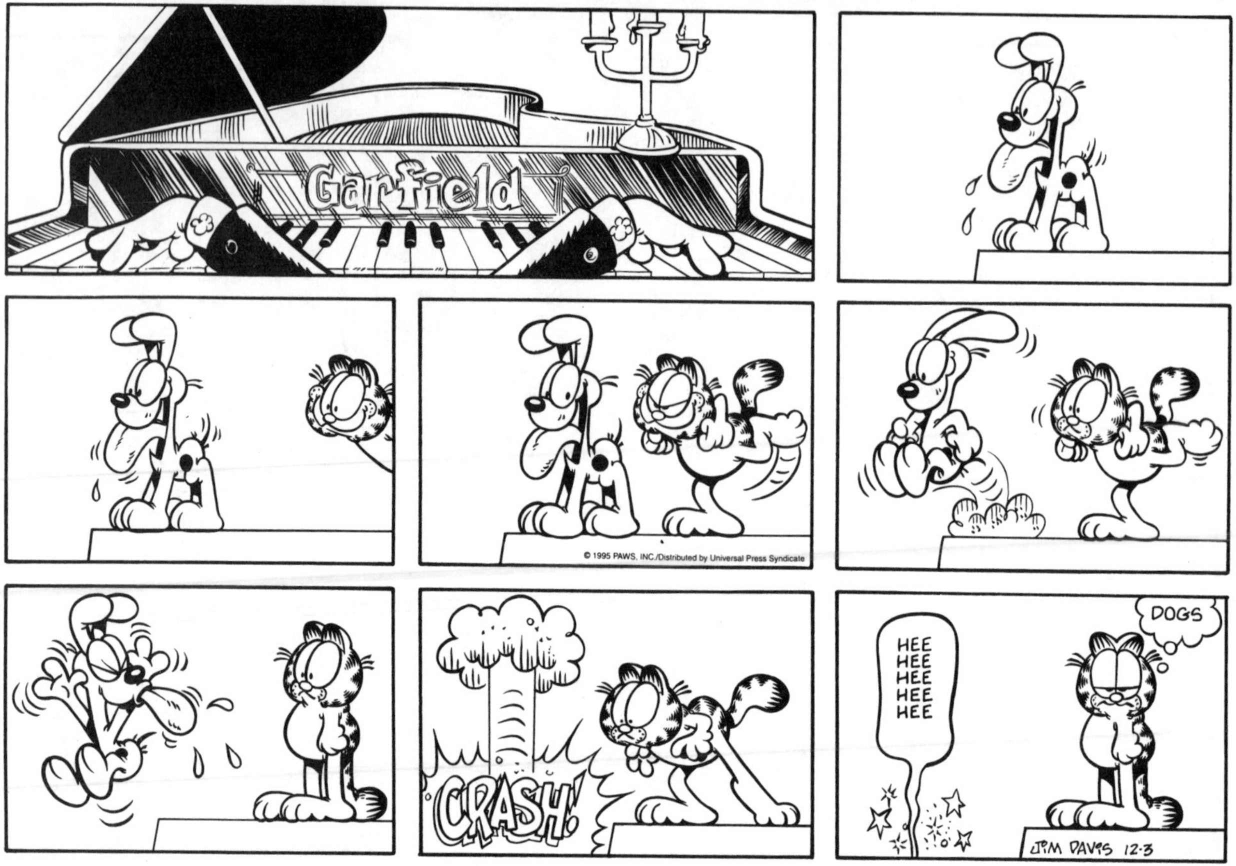
Garfield
© 1995 PAWS, INC./Distributed by Universal Press Syndicate
CRASH!
HEE HEE HEE HEE HEE
DOGS
JIM DAVIS 12-3

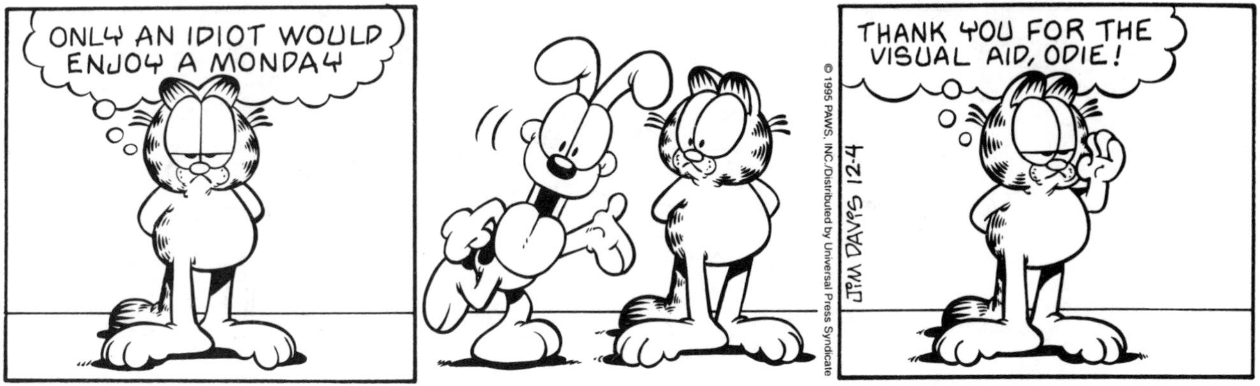
ONLY AN IDIOT WOULD ENJOY A MONDAY
THANK YOU FOR THE VISUAL AID, ODIE!
JIM DAVIS 12-4

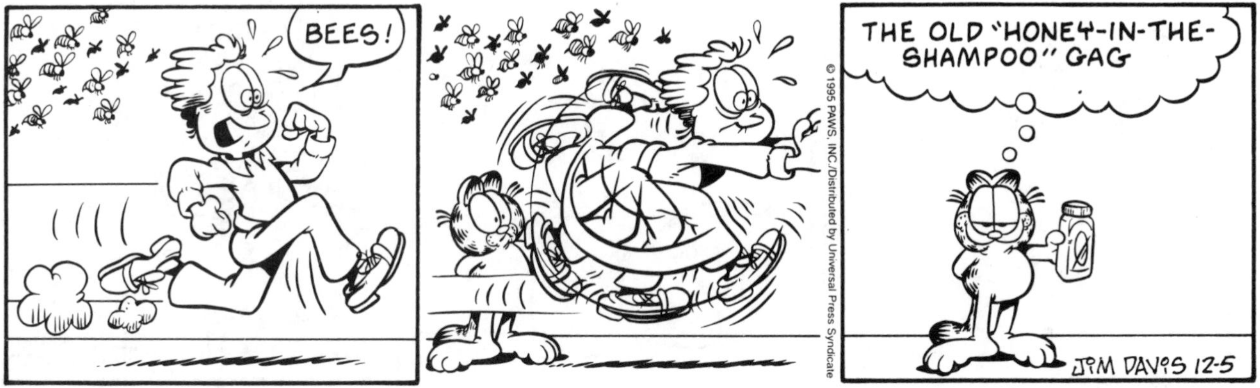
BEES!
THE OLD "HONEY-IN-THE-SHAMPOO" GAG
JIM DAVIS 12-5

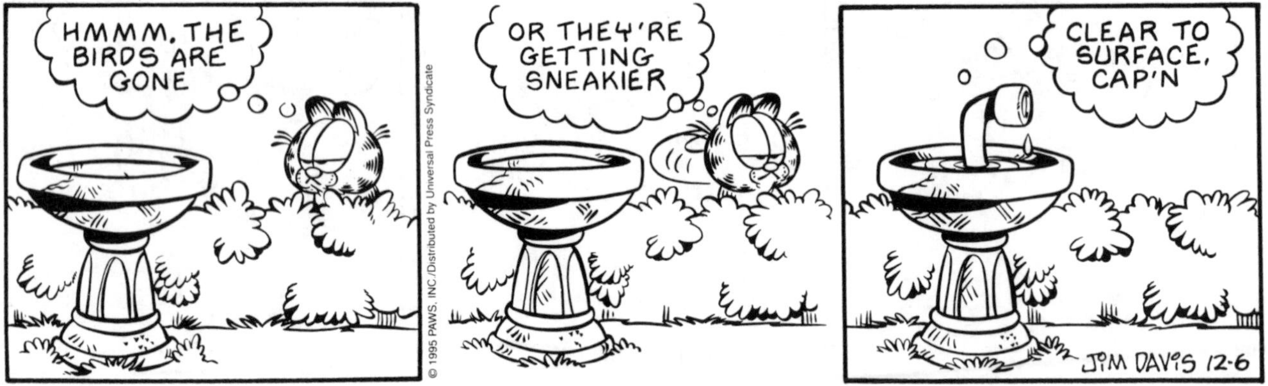
HMMM, THE BIRDS ARE GONE
OR THEY'RE GETTING SNEAKIER
CLEAR TO SURFACE, CAP'N
JIM DAVIS 12-6

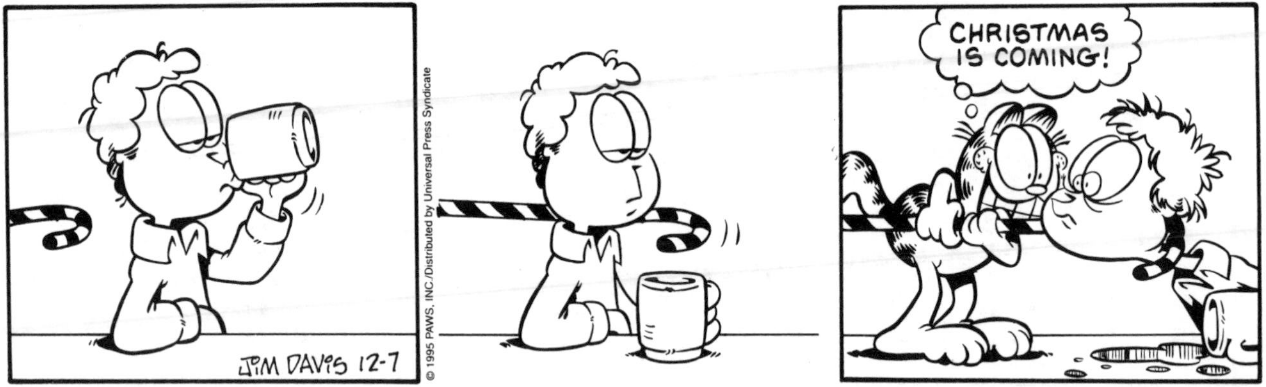
JIM DAVIS 12-7
CHRISTMAS IS COMING!

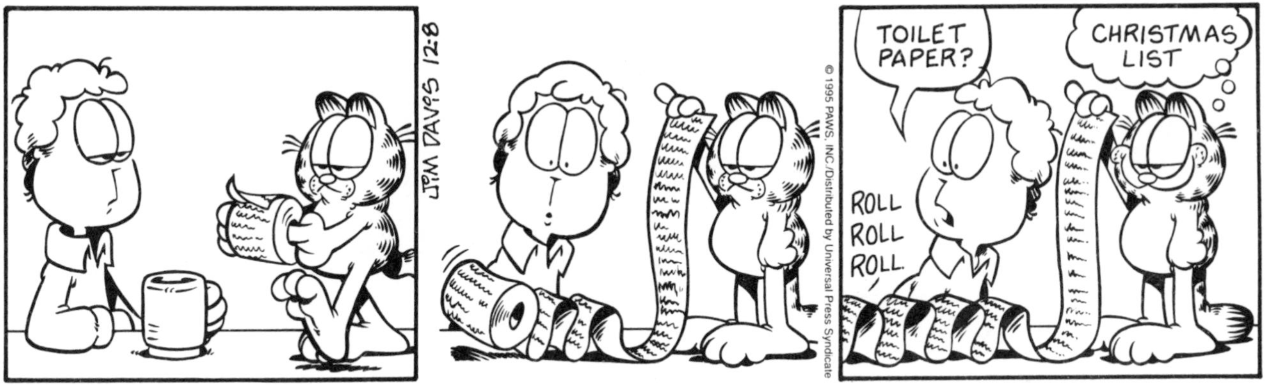
JIM DAVIS 12-8
© 1995 PAWS, INC./Distributed by Universal Press Syndicate
ROLL
ROLL
ROLL.
TOILET PAPER?
CHRISTMAS LIST

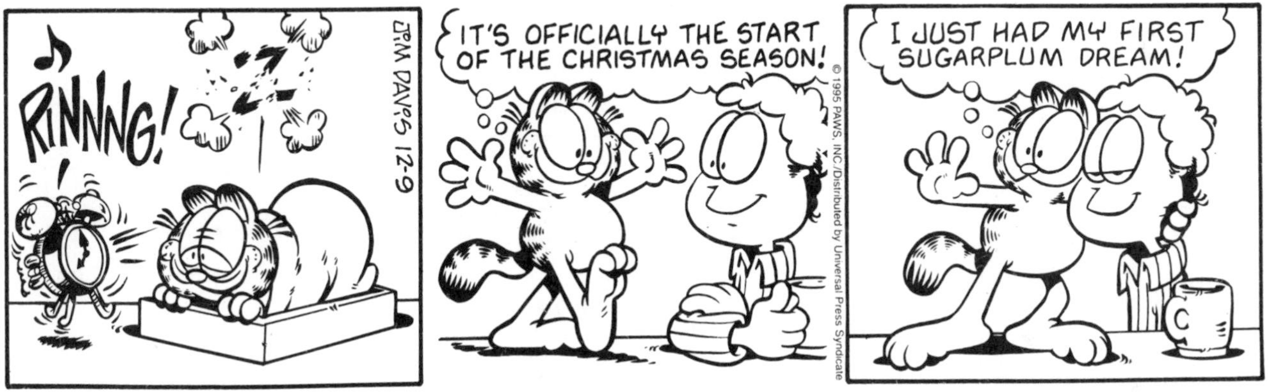
RINNNG!
JIM DAVIS 12-9
IT'S OFFICIALLY THE START OF THE CHRISTMAS SEASON!
© 1995 PAWS, INC./Distributed by Universal Press Syndicate
I JUST HAD MY FIRST SUGARPLUM DREAM!

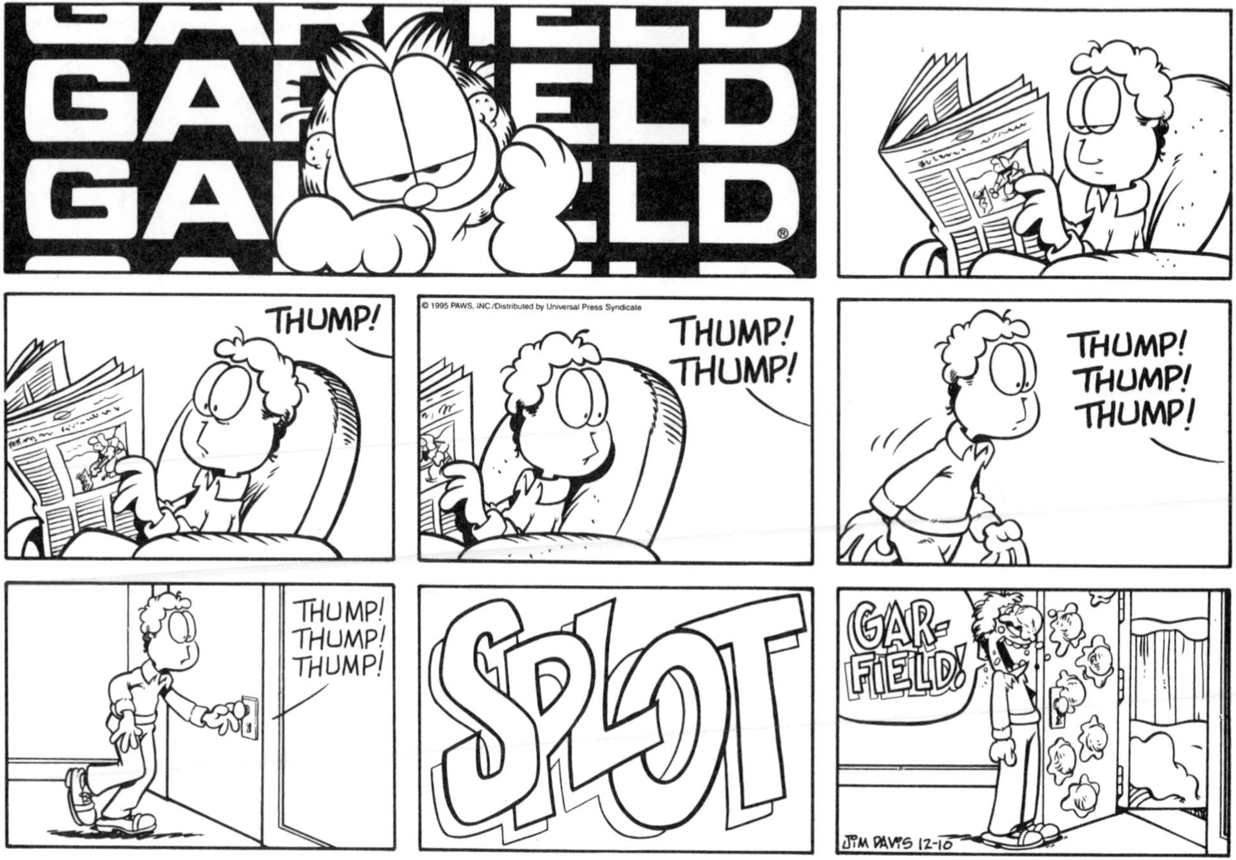
GARFIELD GARFIELD GARFIELD ®
THUMP!
© 1995 PAWS, INC./Distributed by Universal Press Syndicate
THUMP! THUMP!
THUMP! THUMP! THUMP!
THUMP! THUMP! THUMP!
SPLOT
GAR-FIELD!
JIM DAVIS 12-10

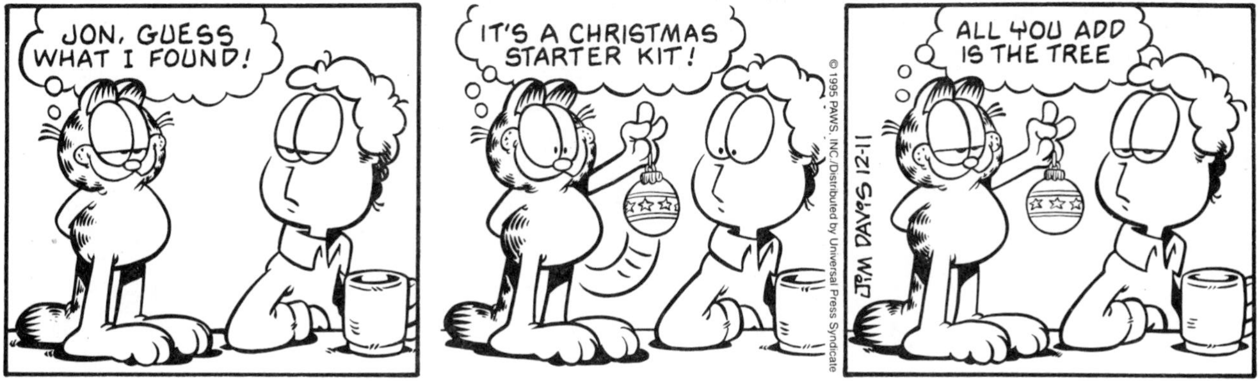
JON, GUESS WHAT I FOUND!
IT'S A CHRISTMAS STARTER KIT!
© 1995 PAWS, INC./Distributed by Universal Press Syndicate
JIM DAVIS 12-11
ALL YOU ADD IS THE TREE

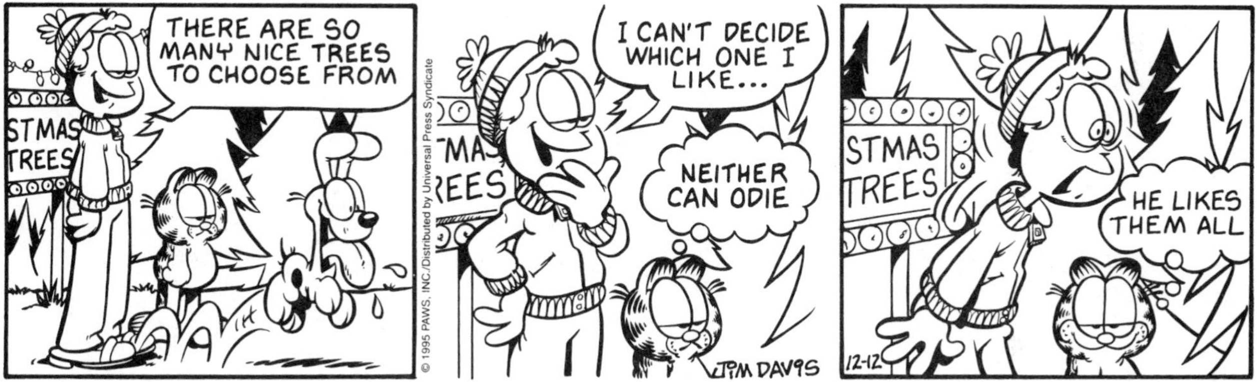
STMAS TREES
THERE ARE SO MANY NICE TREES TO CHOOSE FROM
© 1995 PAWS, INC./Distributed by Universal Press Syndicate
I CAN'T DECIDE WHICH ONE I LIKE...
NEITHER CAN ODIE
JIM DAVIS
STMAS TREES
12-12
HE LIKES THEM ALL

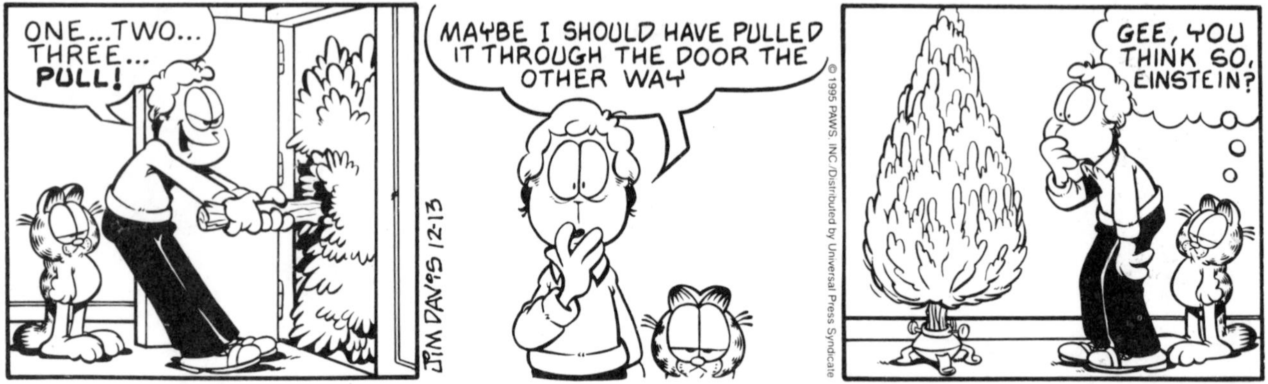
ONE...TWO... THREE... PULL!
JIM DAVIS 12-13
MAYBE I SHOULD HAVE PULLED IT THROUGH THE DOOR THE OTHER WAY
© 1995 PAWS, INC./Distributed by Universal Press Syndicate
GEE, YOU THINK SO, EINSTEIN?

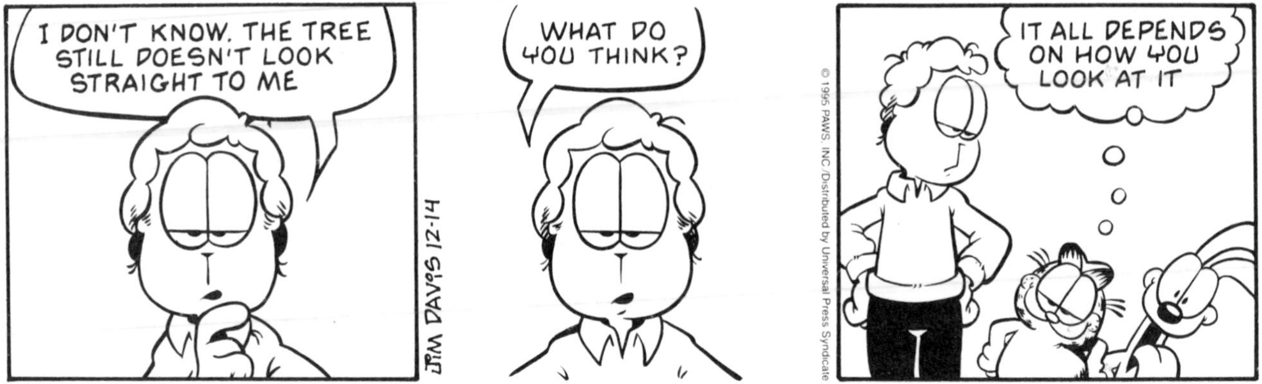
I DON'T KNOW. THE TREE STILL DOESN'T LOOK STRAIGHT TO ME
JIM DAVIS 12-14
WHAT DO YOU THINK?
© 1995 PAWS, INC./Distributed by Universal Press Syndicate
IT ALL DEPENDS ON HOW YOU LOOK AT IT

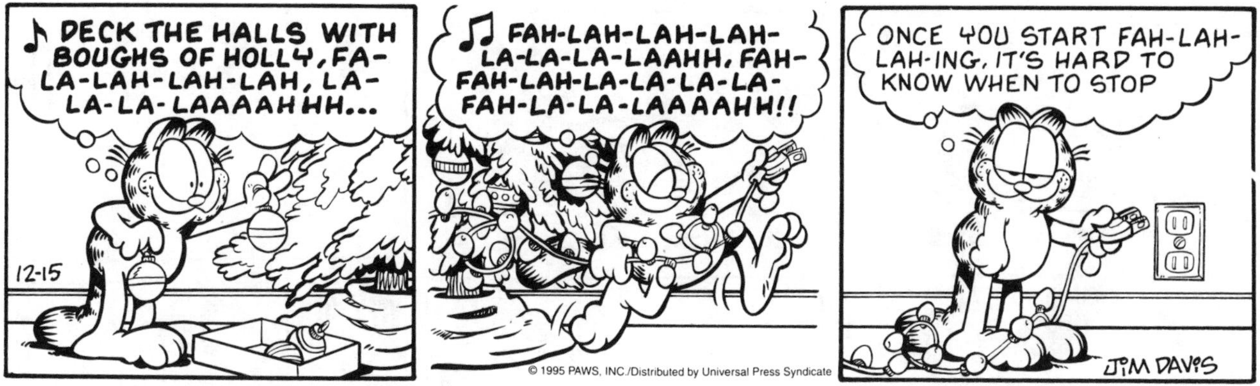
DECK THE HALLS WITH BOUGHS OF HOLLY, FA-LA-LAH-LAH-LAH, LA-LA-LA-LAAAAHHH...
12-15
FAH-LAH-LAH-LAH-LA-LA-LA-LAAHH, FAH-FAH-LAH-LA-LA-LA-LA-FAH-LA-LA-LAAAAHH!!
© 1995 PAWS, INC./Distributed by Universal Press Syndicate
ONCE YOU START FAH-LAH-LAH-ING, IT'S HARD TO KNOW WHEN TO STOP
JIM DAVIS

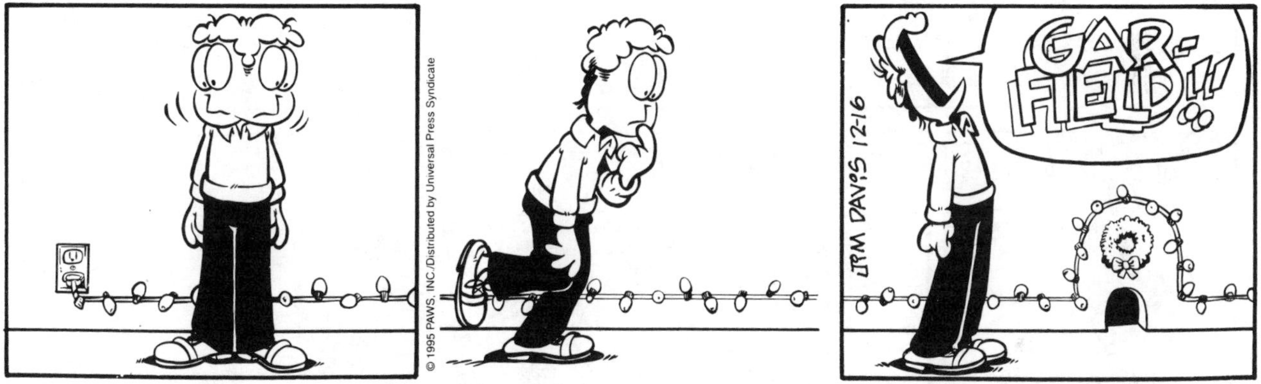
© 1995 PAWS, INC./Distributed by Universal Press Syndicate
JIM DAVIS 12-16
GAR-FIELD!!!

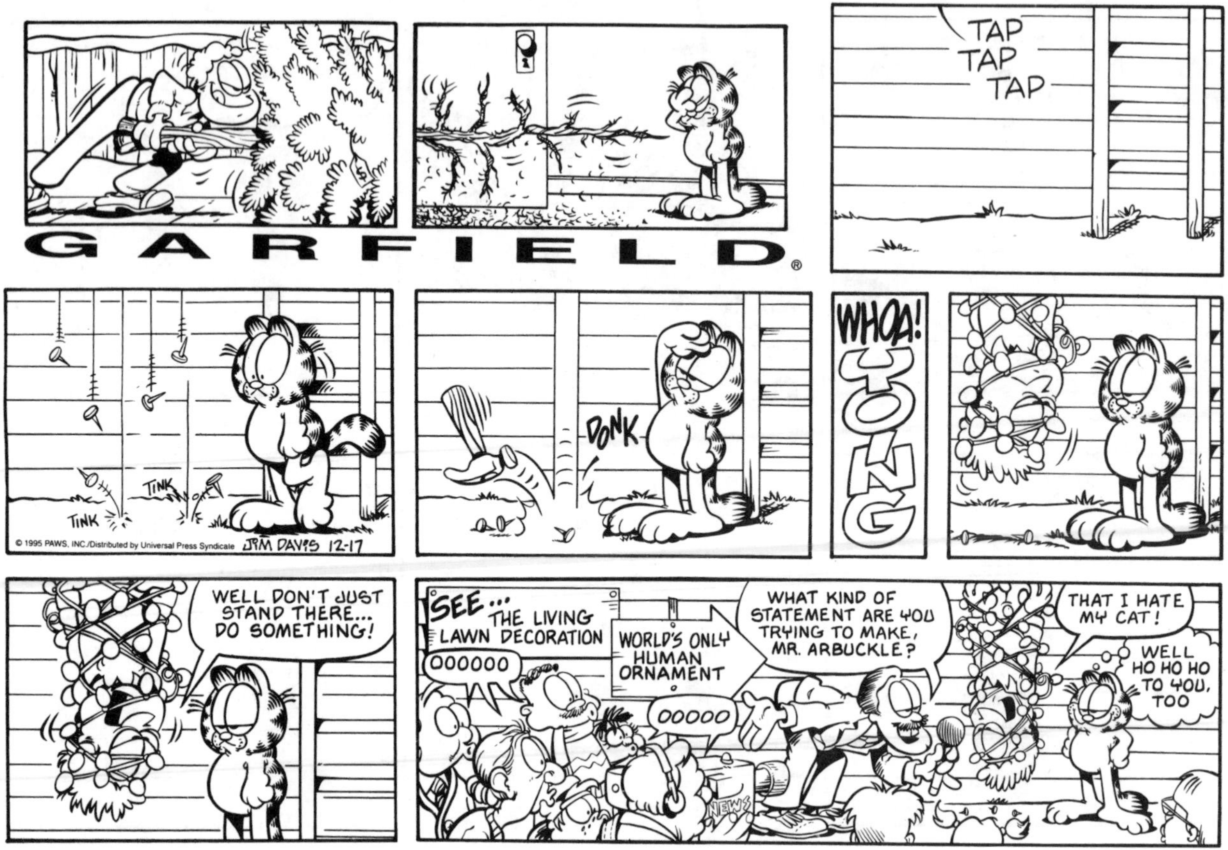
GARFIELD®
TAP
TAP
TAP
© 1995 PAWS, INC./Distributed by Universal Press Syndicate
JIM DAVIS 12-17
TINK
TINK
DONK
WHOA!
YOING
WELL DON'T JUST STAND THERE... DO SOMETHING!
SEE... THE LIVING LAWN DECORATION
WORLD'S ONLY HUMAN ORNAMENT
OOOOOO
OOOOO
NEWS
WHAT KIND OF STATEMENT ARE YOU TRYING TO MAKE, MR. ARBUCKLE?
THAT I HATE MY CAT!
WELL HO HO HO TO YOU, TOO

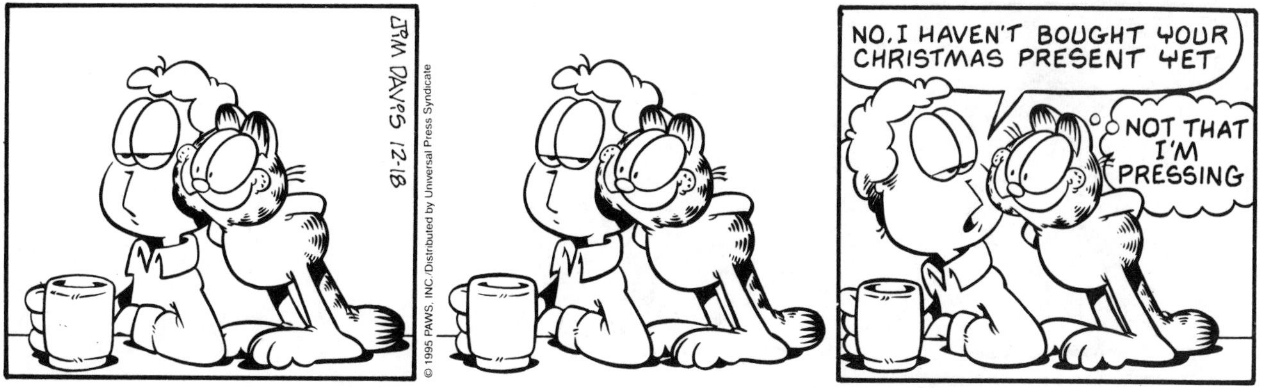
JIM DAVIS 12-18
© 1995 PAWS, INC./Distributed by Universal Press Syndicate
NO, I HAVEN'T BOUGHT YOUR CHRISTMAS PRESENT YET
NOT THAT I'M PRESSING

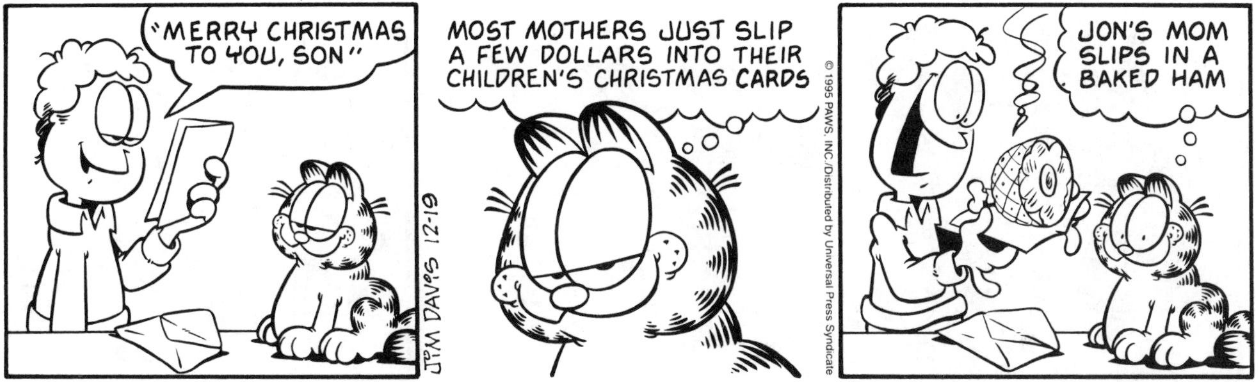
"MERRY CHRISTMAS TO YOU, SON"
JIM DAVIS 12-19
MOST MOTHERS JUST SLIP A FEW DOLLARS INTO THEIR CHILDREN'S CHRISTMAS CARDS
© 1995 PAWS, INC./Distributed by Universal Press Syndicate
JON'S MOM SLIPS IN A BAKED HAM

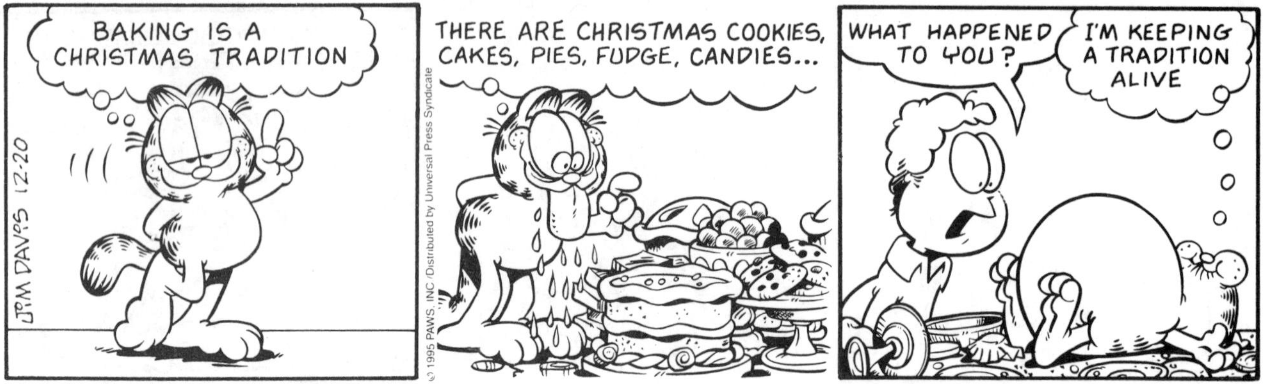
BAKING IS A CHRISTMAS TRADITION
JIM DAVIS 12-20
© 1995 PAWS, INC./Distributed by Universal Press Syndicate
THERE ARE CHRISTMAS COOKIES, CAKES, PIES, FUDGE, CANDIES...
WHAT HAPPENED TO YOU?
I'M KEEPING A TRADITION ALIVE

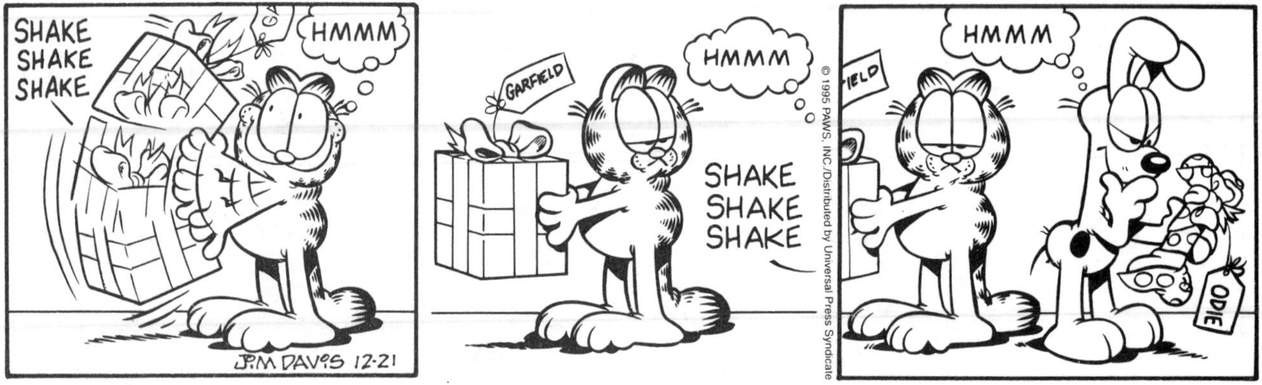
SHAKE SHAKE SHAKE
HMMM
JIM DAVIS 12-21
GARFIELD
HMMM
SHAKE SHAKE SHAKE
© 1995 PAWS, INC./Distributed by Universal Press Syndicate
FIELD
HMMM
ODIE

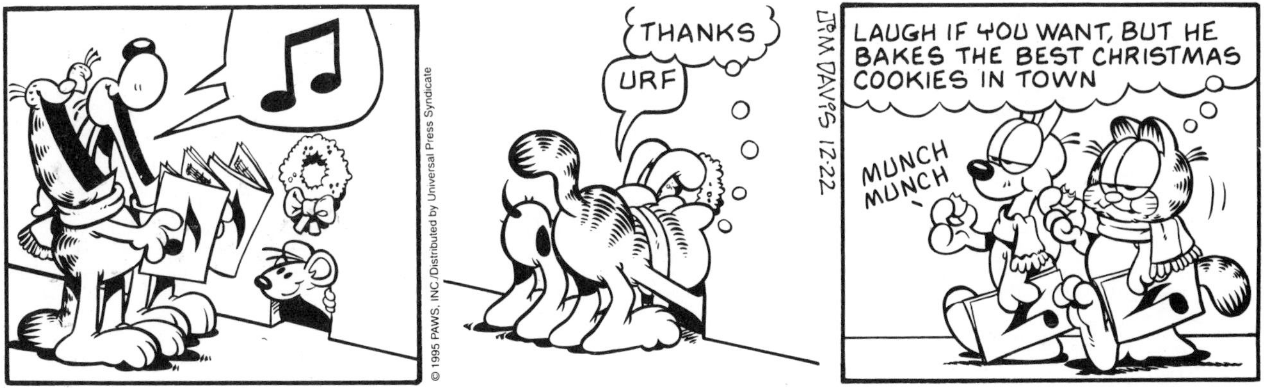
URF
THANKS
LAUGH IF YOU WANT, BUT HE BAKES THE BEST CHRISTMAS COOKIES IN TOWN
MUNCH MUNCH
JIM DAVIS 12-22

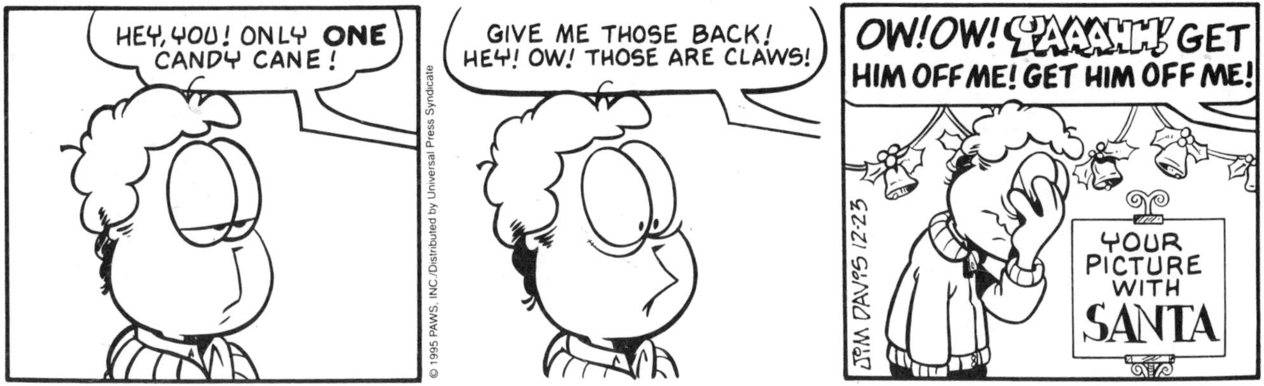
HEY, YOU! ONLY **ONE** CANDY CANE!
GIVE ME THOSE BACK! HEY! OW! THOSE ARE CLAWS!
OW! OW! YAAAHH! GET HIM OFF ME! GET HIM OFF ME!
YOUR PICTURE WITH SANTA
JIM DAVIS 12-23

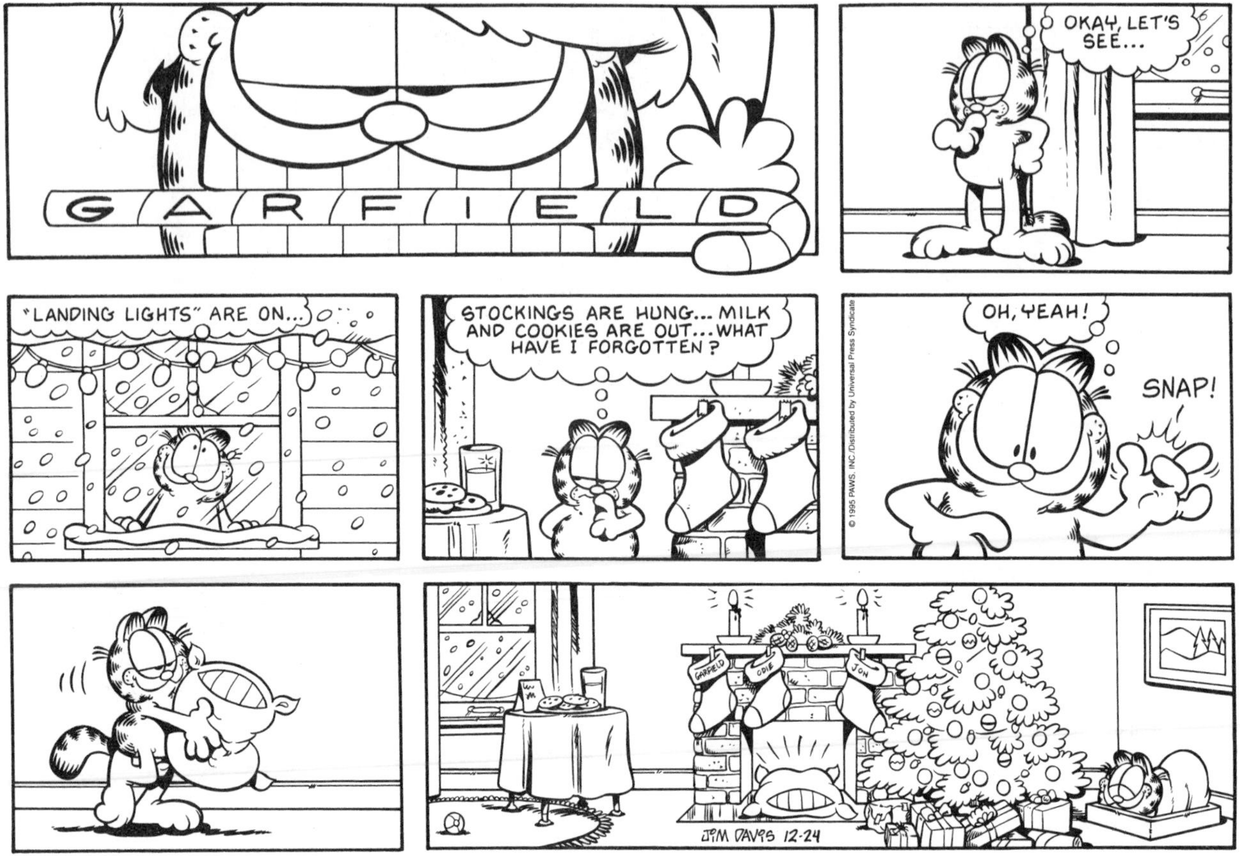
GARFIELD
OKAY, LET'S SEE...
"LANDING LIGHTS" ARE ON...
STOCKINGS ARE HUNG... MILK AND COOKIES ARE OUT... WHAT HAVE I FORGOTTEN?
OH, YEAH!
SNAP!
GARFIELD
ODIE
JON
JIM DAVIS 12-24

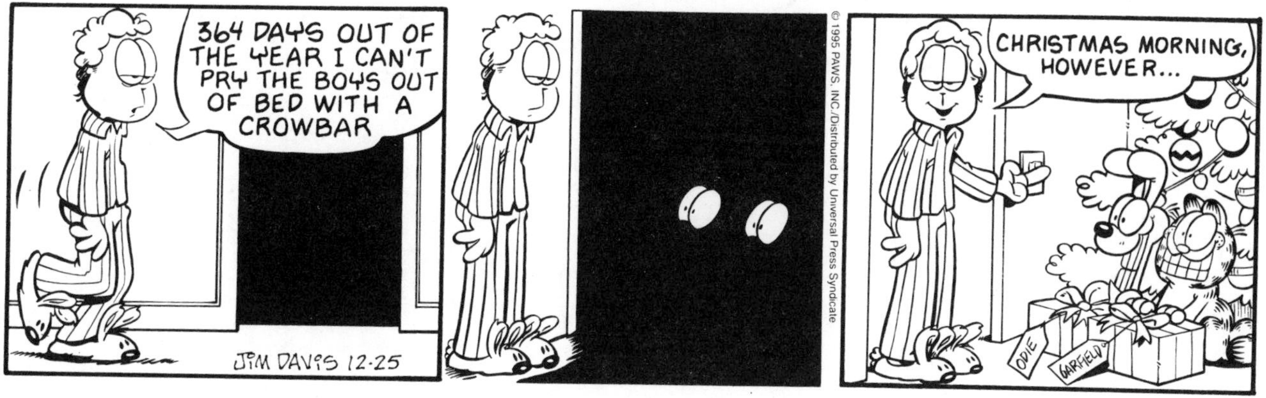
364 DAYS OUT OF THE YEAR I CAN'T PRY THE BOYS OUT OF BED WITH A CROWBAR
JIM DAVIS 12-25
© 1995 PAWS, INC./Distributed by Universal Press Syndicate
CHRISTMAS MORNING, HOWEVER...
ODIE
GARFIELD

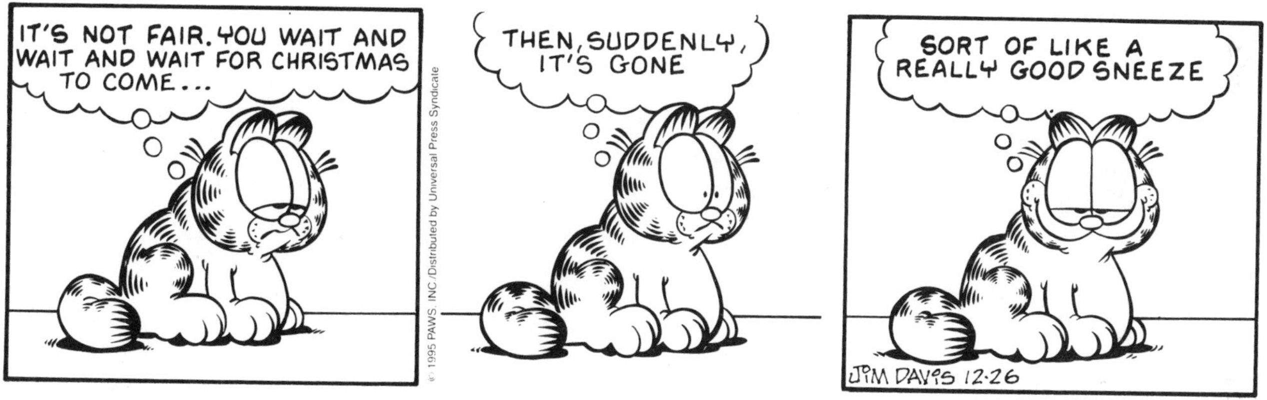
IT'S NOT FAIR. YOU WAIT AND WAIT AND WAIT FOR CHRISTMAS TO COME...
© 1995 PAWS, INC./Distributed by Universal Press Syndicate
THEN, SUDDENLY, IT'S GONE
SORT OF LIKE A REALLY GOOD SNEEZE
JIM DAVIS 12-26

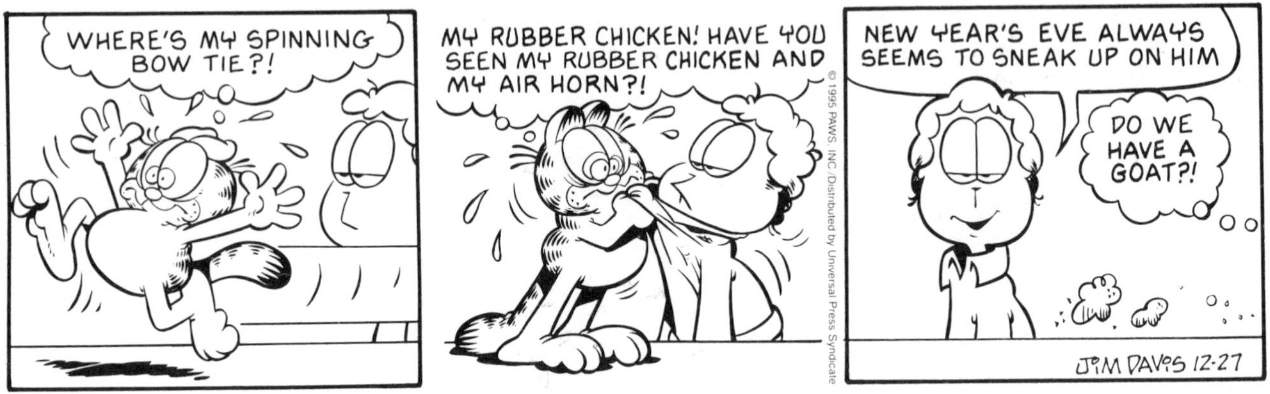
WHERE'S MY SPINNING BOW TIE?!
MY RUBBER CHICKEN! HAVE YOU SEEN MY RUBBER CHICKEN AND MY AIR HORN?!
© 1995 PAWS, INC./Distributed by Universal Press Syndicate
NEW YEAR'S EVE ALWAYS SEEMS TO SNEAK UP ON HIM
DO WE HAVE A GOAT?!
JIM DAVIS 12-27

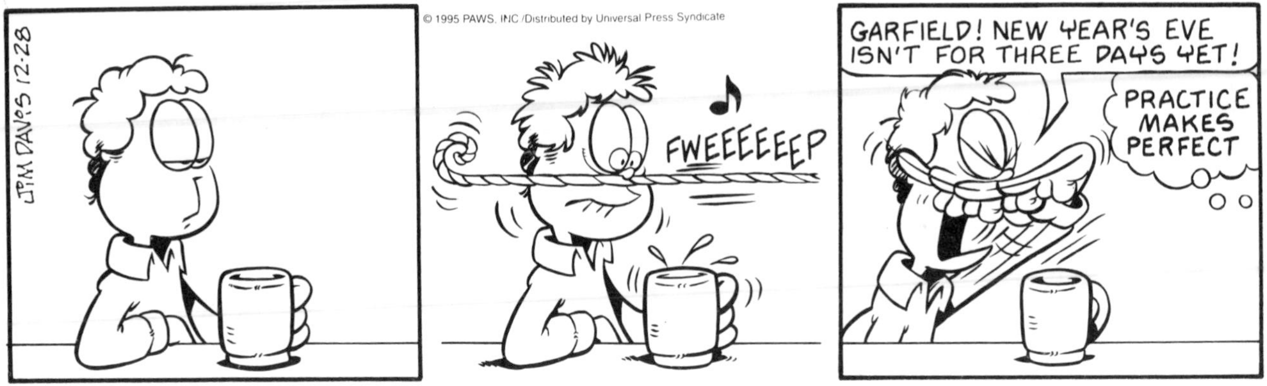
JIM DAVIS 12-28
© 1995 PAWS, INC /Distributed by Universal Press Syndicate
FWEEEEEEEP
GARFIELD! NEW YEAR'S EVE ISN'T FOR THREE DAYS YET!
PRACTICE MAKES PERFECT

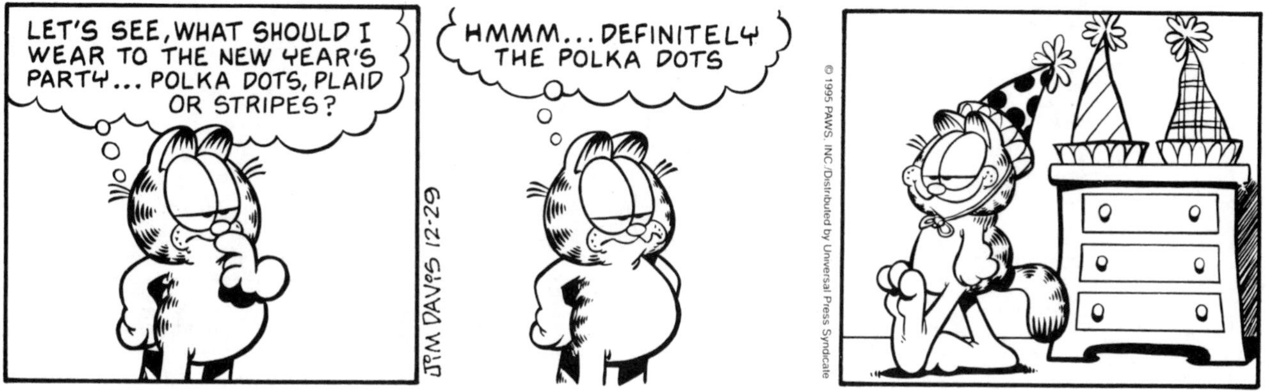
LET'S SEE, WHAT SHOULD I WEAR TO THE NEW YEAR'S PARTY... POLKA DOTS, PLAID OR STRIPES?
JIM DAVIS 12-29
HMMM... DEFINITELY THE POLKA DOTS
© 1995 PAWS, INC./Distributed by Universal Press Syndicate

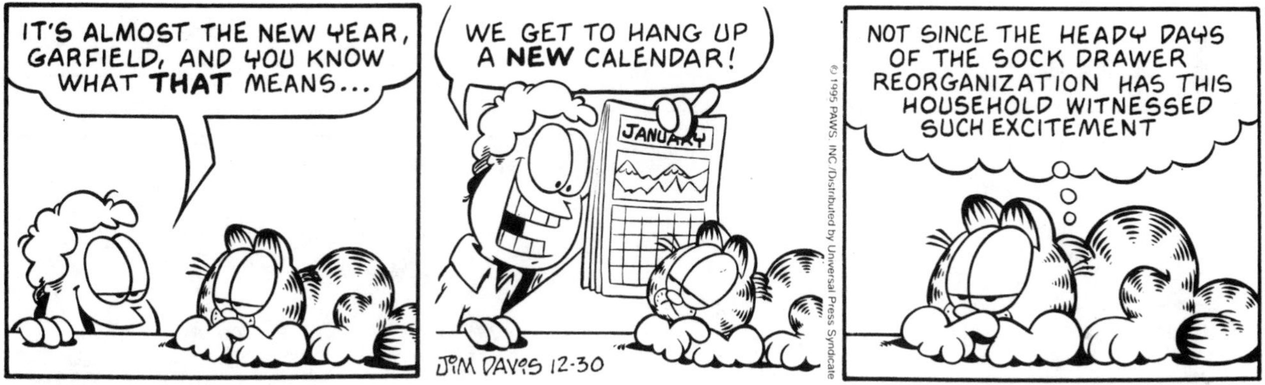
IT'S ALMOST THE NEW YEAR, GARFIELD, AND YOU KNOW WHAT **THAT** MEANS...
WE GET TO HANG UP A **NEW** CALENDAR!
JANUARY
JIM DAVIS 12-30
© 1995 PAWS, INC./Distributed by Universal Press Syndicate
NOT SINCE THE HEADY DAYS OF THE SOCK DRAWER REORGANIZATION HAS THIS HOUSEHOLD WITNESSED SUCH EXCITEMENT

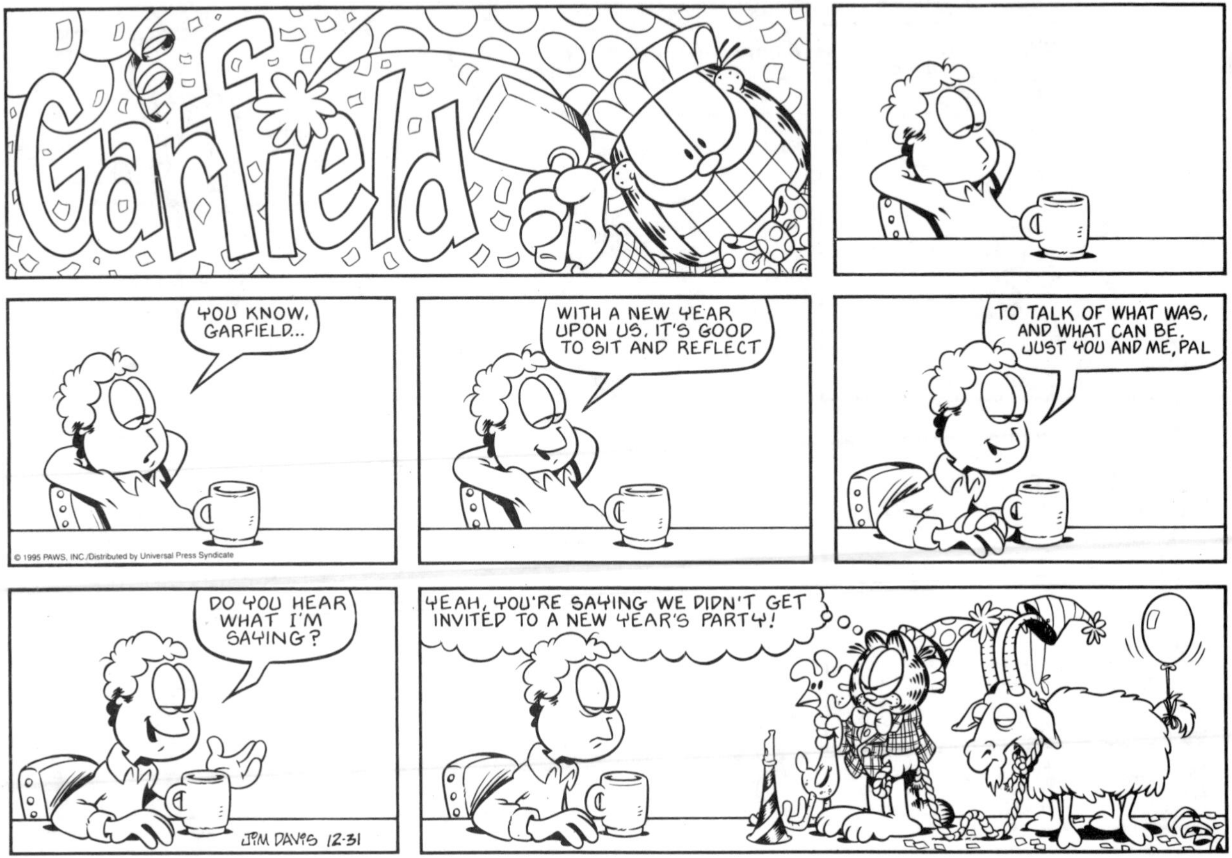
Garfield
YOU KNOW, GARFIELD...
WITH A NEW YEAR UPON US, IT'S GOOD TO SIT AND REFLECT
TO TALK OF WHAT WAS, AND WHAT CAN BE, JUST YOU AND ME, PAL
© 1995 PAWS, INC./Distributed by Universal Press Syndicate
DO YOU HEAR WHAT I'M SAYING?
JIM DAVIS 12-31
YEAH, YOU'RE SAYING WE DIDN'T GET INVITED TO A NEW YEAR'S PARTY!

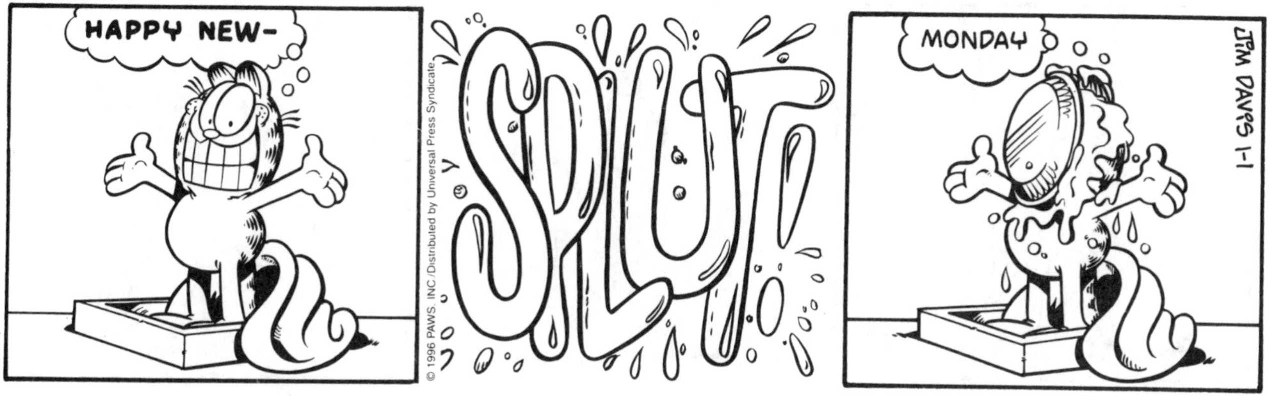
HAPPY NEW-
SPLUT!
MONDAY
JIM DAVIS 1-1

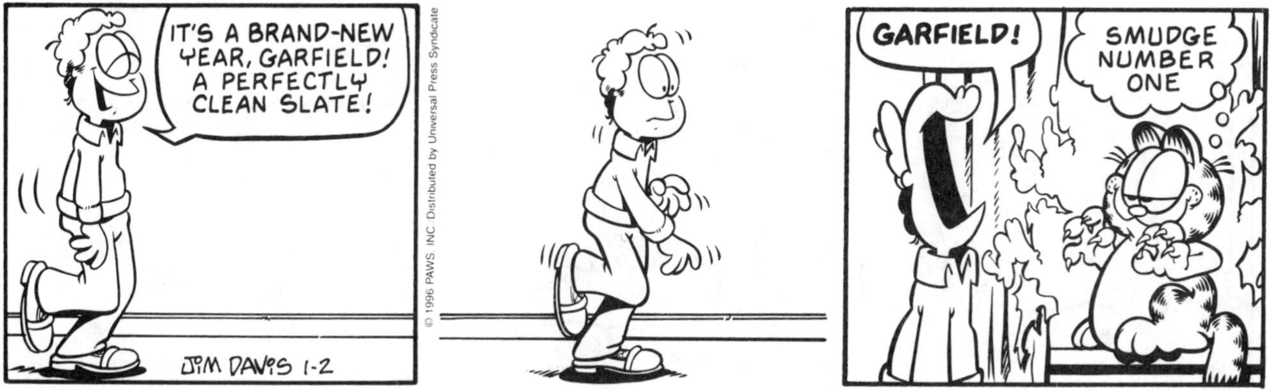
IT'S A BRAND-NEW YEAR, GARFIELD! A PERFECTLY CLEAN SLATE!
JIM DAVIS 1-2
GARFIELD!
SMUDGE NUMBER ONE

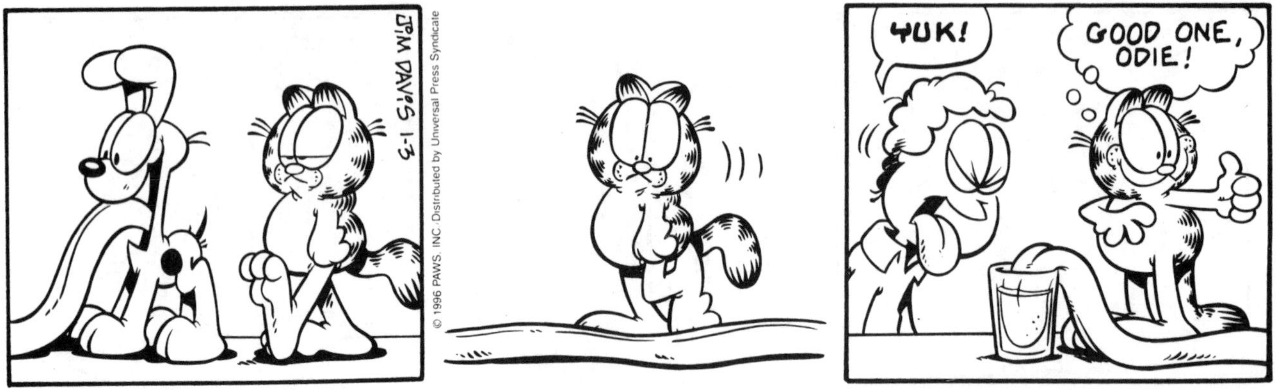
JIM DAVIS 1-3
© 1996 PAWS, INC./Distributed by Universal Press Syndicate
YUK!
GOOD ONE, ODIE!

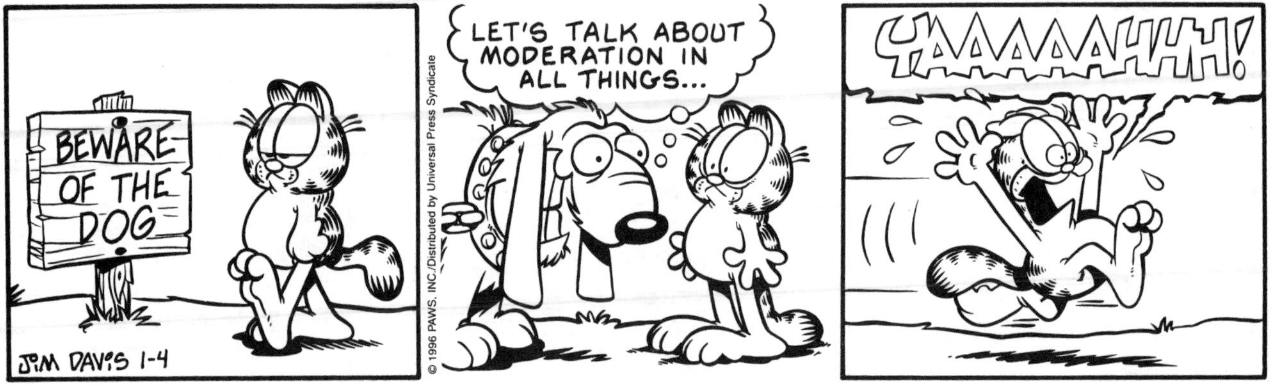
BEWARE OF THE DOG
JIM DAVIS 1-4
© 1996 PAWS, INC./Distributed by Universal Press Syndicate
LET'S TALK ABOUT MODERATION IN ALL THINGS...
YAAAAAHHH!

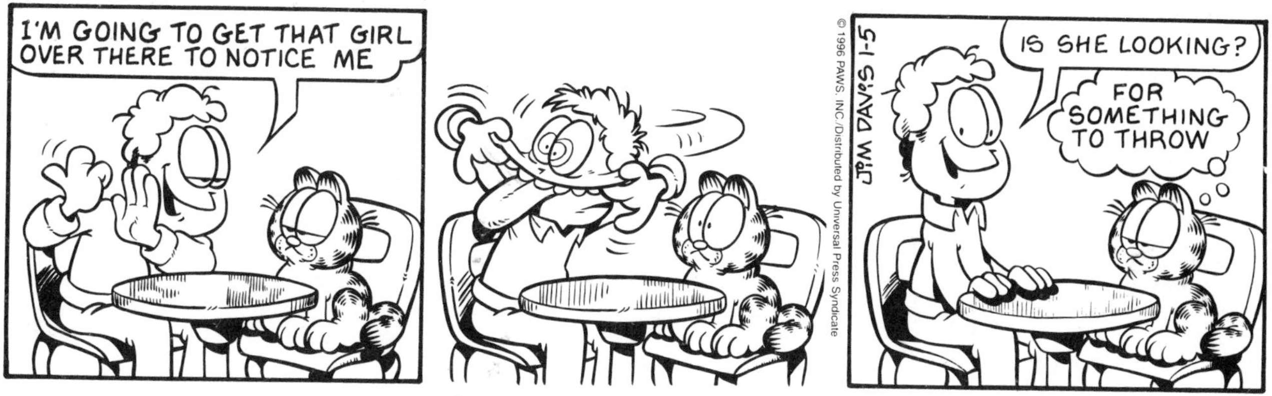
I'M GOING TO GET THAT GIRL OVER THERE TO NOTICE ME
IS SHE LOOKING?
FOR SOMETHING TO THROW
JIM DAVIS 1-5
© 1996 PAWS, INC./Distributed by Universal Press Syndicate

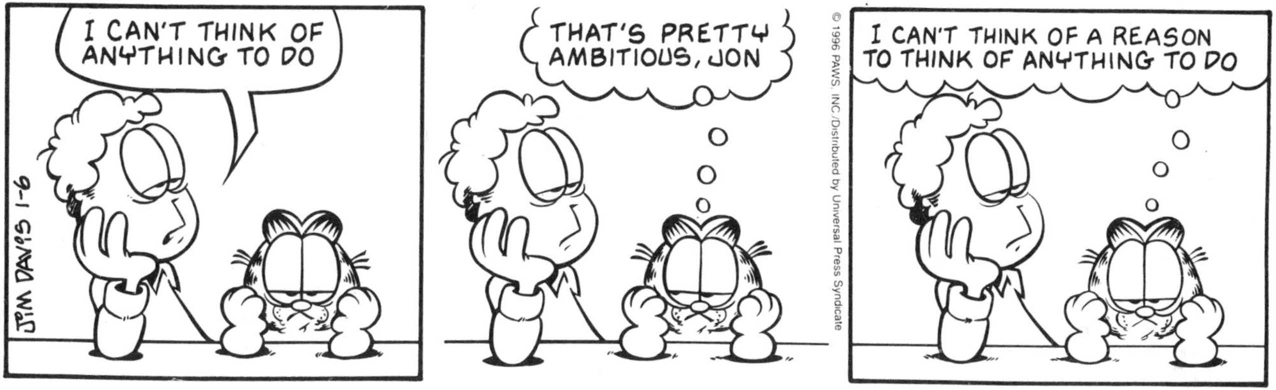
I CAN'T THINK OF ANYTHING TO DO
THAT'S PRETTY AMBITIOUS, JON
I CAN'T THINK OF A REASON TO THINK OF ANYTHING TO DO
JIM DAVIS 1-6
© 1996 PAWS, INC./Distributed by Universal Press Syndicate

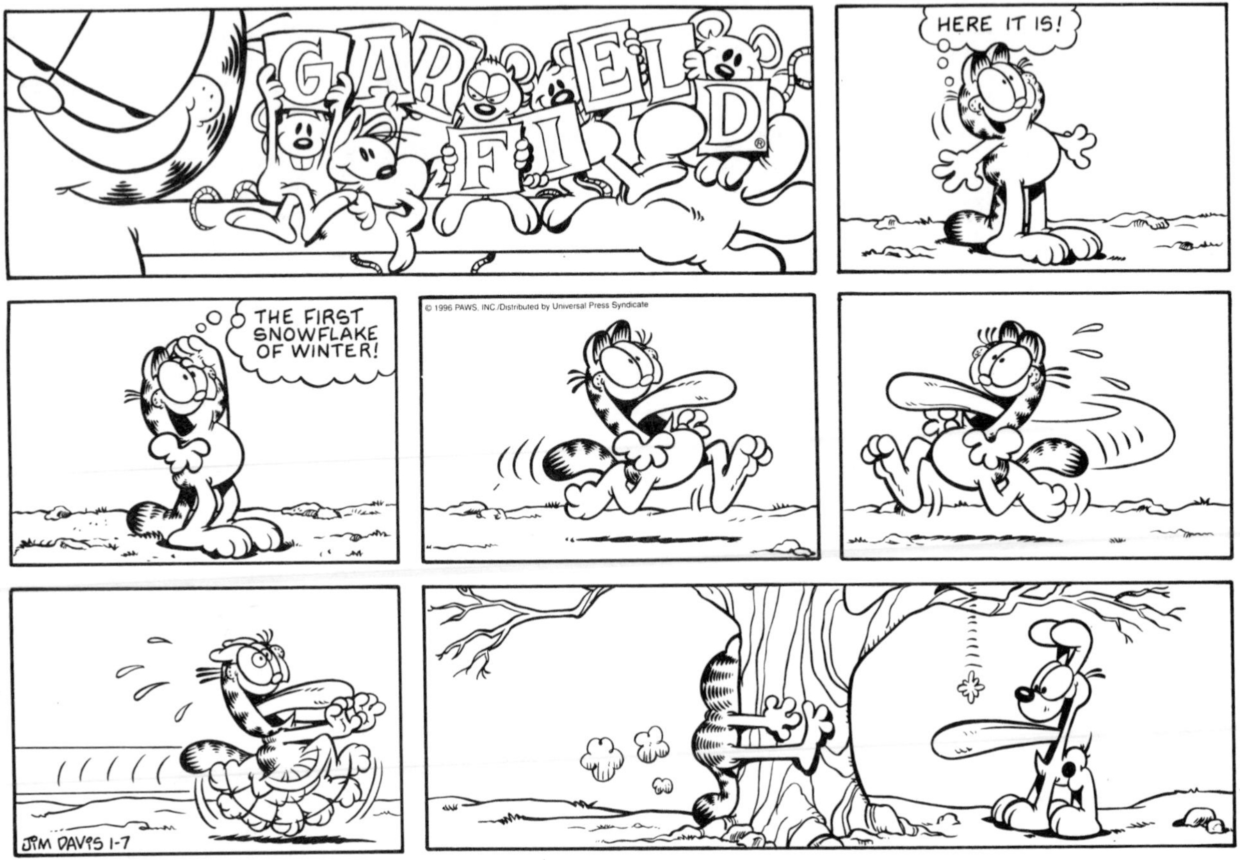
GARFIELD®
HERE IT IS!
THE FIRST SNOWFLAKE OF WINTER!
© 1996 PAWS, INC./Distributed by Universal Press Syndicate
JIM DAVIS 1-7

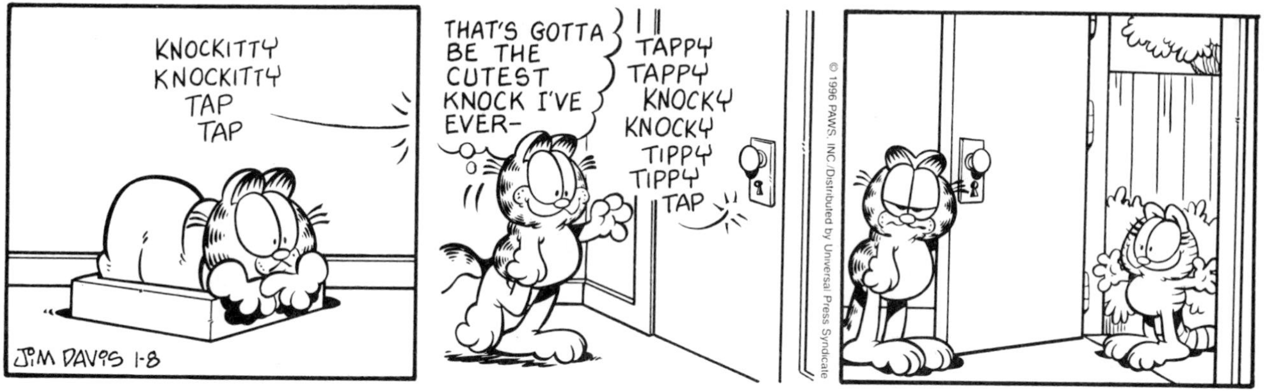
KNOCKITTY KNOCKITTY TAP TAP
JIM DAVIS 1-8
THAT'S GOTTA BE THE CUTEST KNOCK I'VE EVER-
TAPPY TAPPY KNOCKY KNOCKY TIPPY TIPPY TAP
© 1996 PAWS, INC/Distributed by Universal Press Syndicate

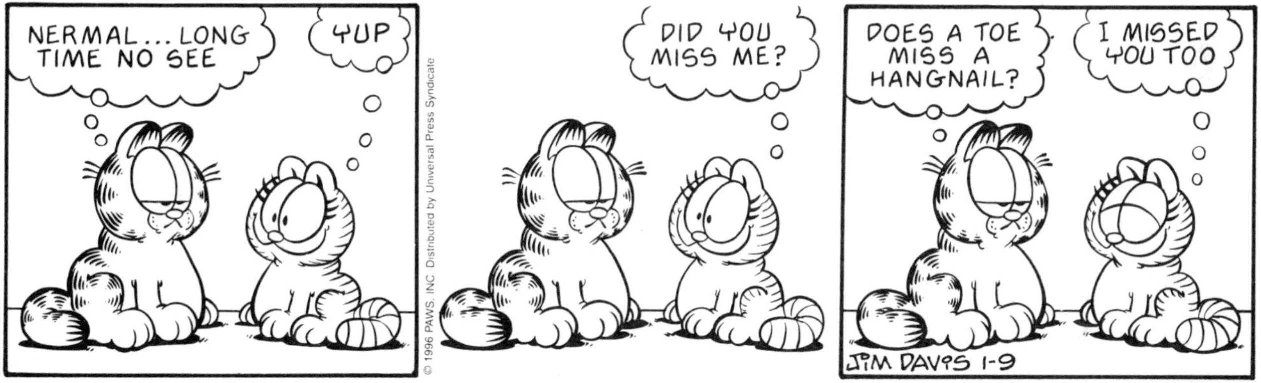
NERMAL... LONG TIME NO SEE
YUP
© 1996 PAWS, INC Distributed by Universal Press Syndicate
DID YOU MISS ME?
DOES A TOE MISS A HANGNAIL?
I MISSED YOU TOO
JIM DAVIS 1-9

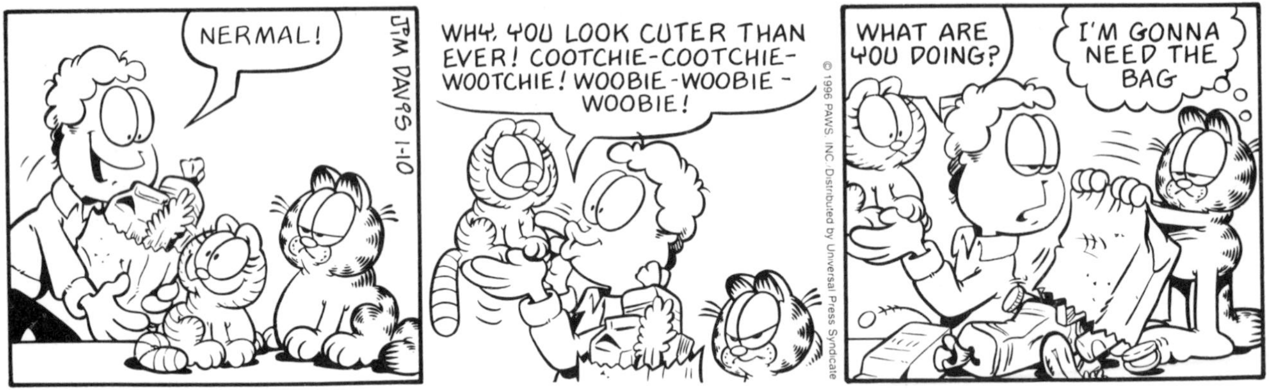
NERMAL!
JPM DAVPS 1-10
WHY, YOU LOOK CUTER THAN EVER! COOTCHIE-COOTCHIE-WOOTCHIE! WOOBIE-WOOBIE-WOOBIE!
© 1996 PAWS, INC./Distributed by Universal Press Syndicate
WHAT ARE YOU DOING?
I'M GONNA NEED THE BAG

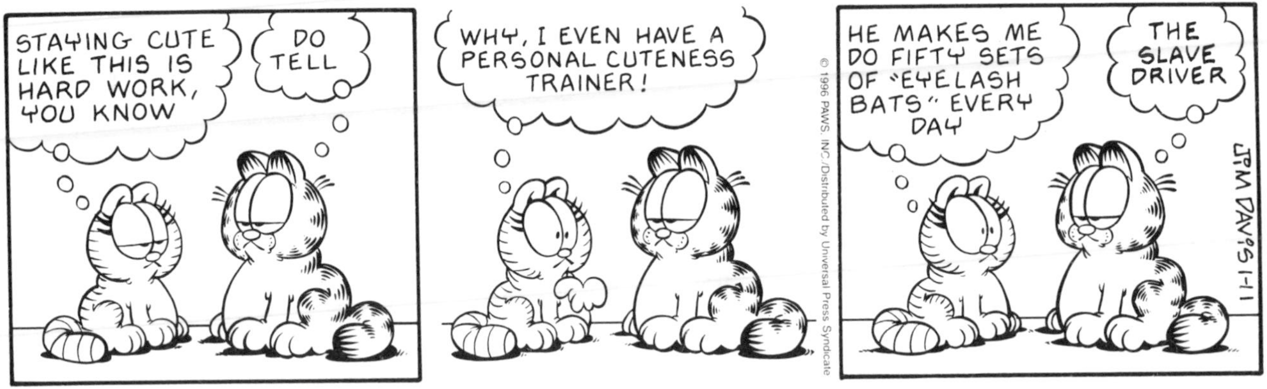
STAYING CUTE LIKE THIS IS HARD WORK, YOU KNOW
DO TELL
WHY, I EVEN HAVE A PERSONAL CUTENESS TRAINER!
© 1996 PAWS, INC./Distributed by Universal Press Syndicate
HE MAKES ME DO FIFTY SETS OF "EYELASH BATS" EVERY DAY
THE SLAVE DRIVER
JPM DAVPS 1-11

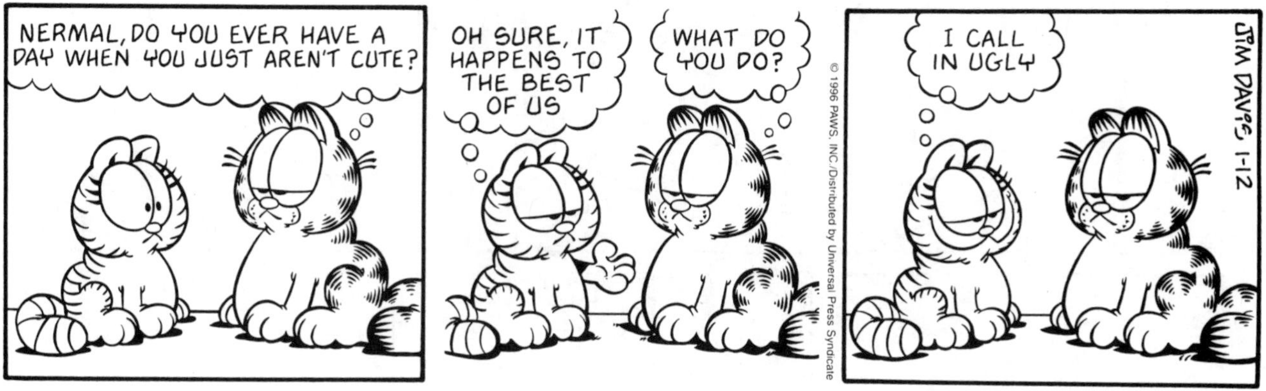
NERMAL, DO YOU EVER HAVE A DAY WHEN YOU JUST AREN'T CUTE?
OH SURE, IT HAPPENS TO THE BEST OF US
WHAT DO YOU DO?
© 1996 PAWS, INC./Distributed by Universal Press Syndicate
I CALL IN UGLY
JIM DAVIS 1-12

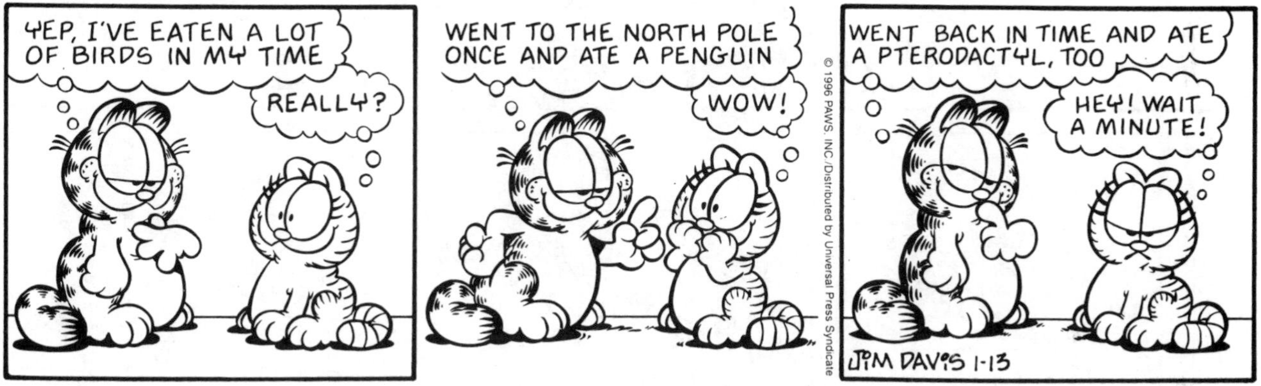
YEP, I'VE EATEN A LOT OF BIRDS IN MY TIME
REALLY?
WENT TO THE NORTH POLE ONCE AND ATE A PENGUIN
WOW!
© 1996 PAWS, INC./Distributed by Universal Press Syndicate
WENT BACK IN TIME AND ATE A PTERODACTYL, TOO
HEY! WAIT A MINUTE!
JIM DAVIS 1-13

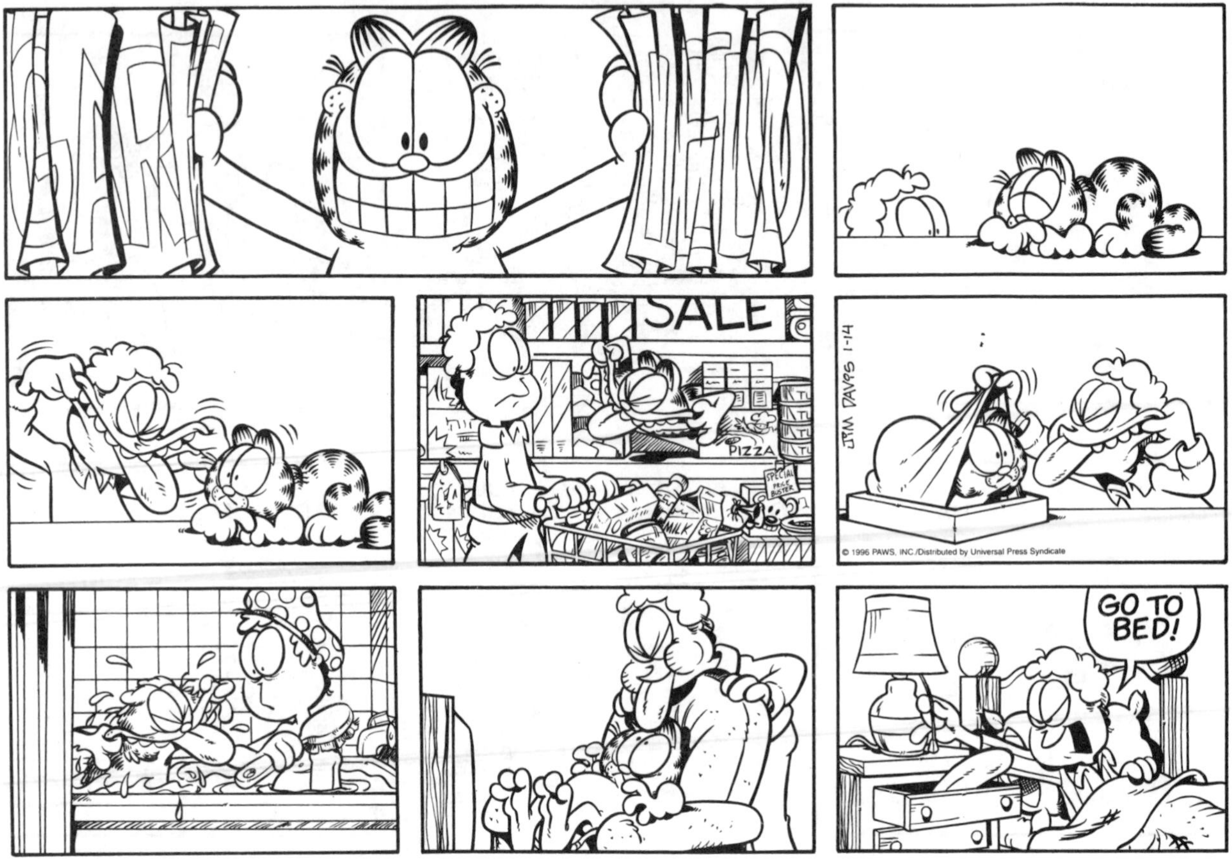
SALE
PIZZA
MILK
SPECIAL PRICE BUSTER
JIM DAVIS 1-14
© 1996 PAWS, INC./Distributed by Universal Press Syndicate
GO TO BED!

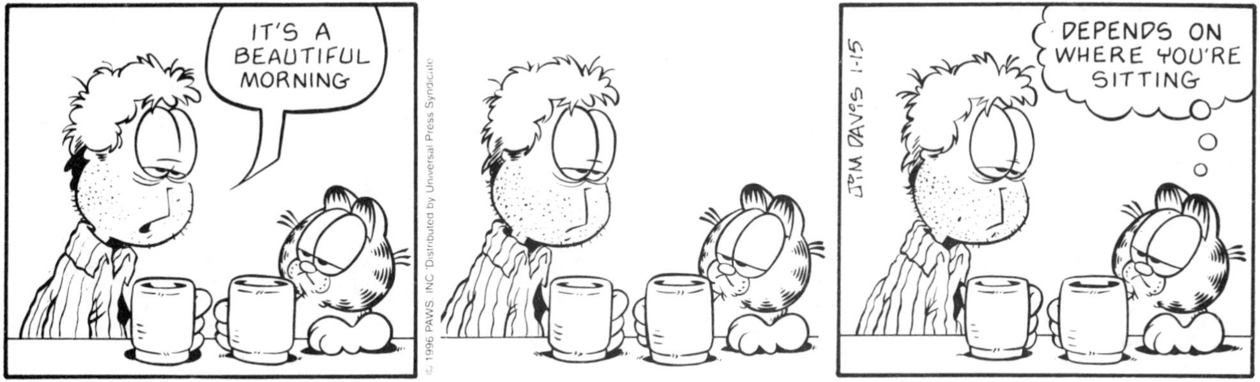
IT'S A BEAUTIFUL MORNING
DEPENDS ON WHERE YOU'RE SITTING
JIM DAVIS 1-15

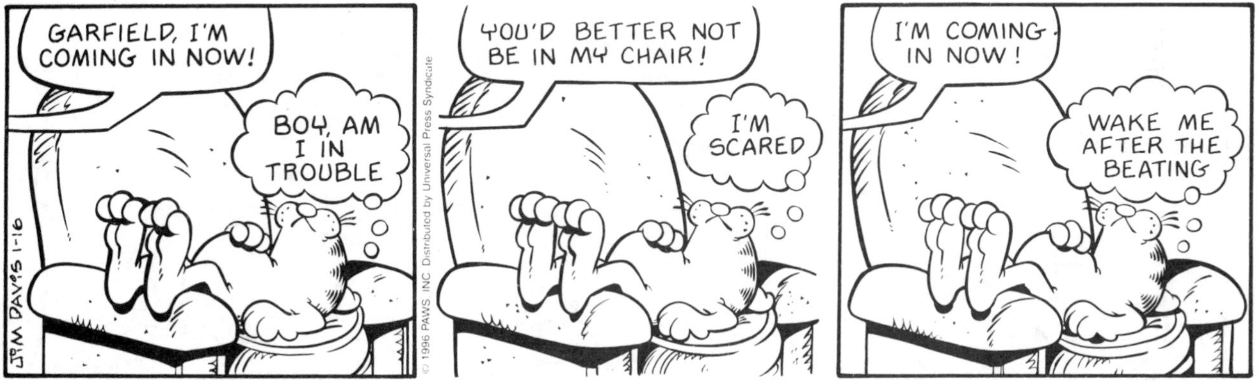
GARFIELD, I'M COMING IN NOW!
BOY, AM I IN TROUBLE
JIM DAVIS 1-16
YOU'D BETTER NOT BE IN MY CHAIR!
I'M SCARED
I'M COMING IN NOW!
WAKE ME AFTER THE BEATING

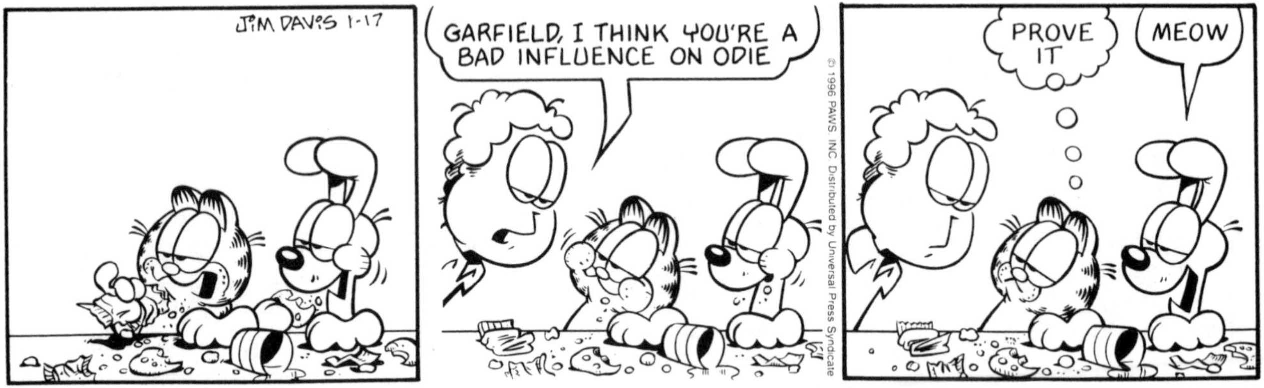
JIM DAVIS 1-17
GARFIELD, I THINK YOU'RE A BAD INFLUENCE ON ODIE
© 1996 PAWS, INC. Distributed by Universal Press Syndicate
PROVE IT
MEOW

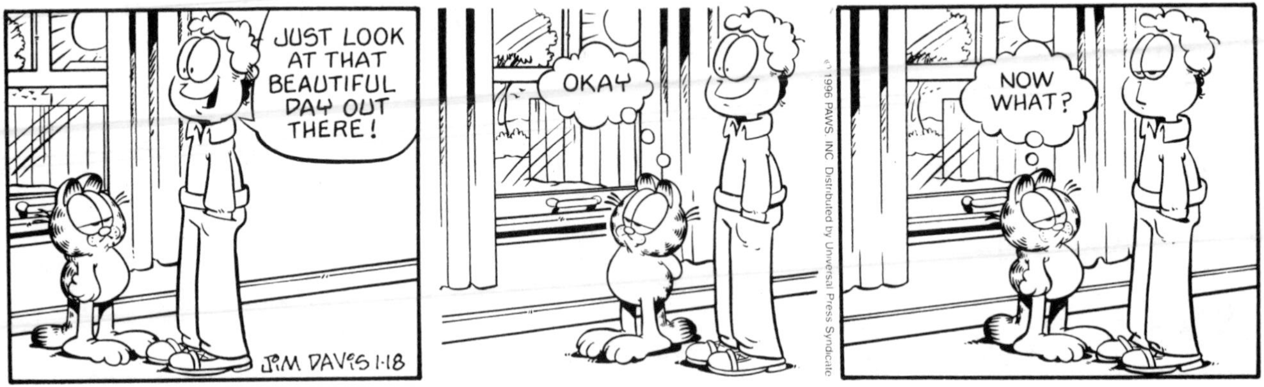
JUST LOOK AT THAT BEAUTIFUL DAY OUT THERE!
JIM DAVIS 1-18
OKAY
© 1996 PAWS, INC. Distributed by Universal Press Syndicate
NOW WHAT?

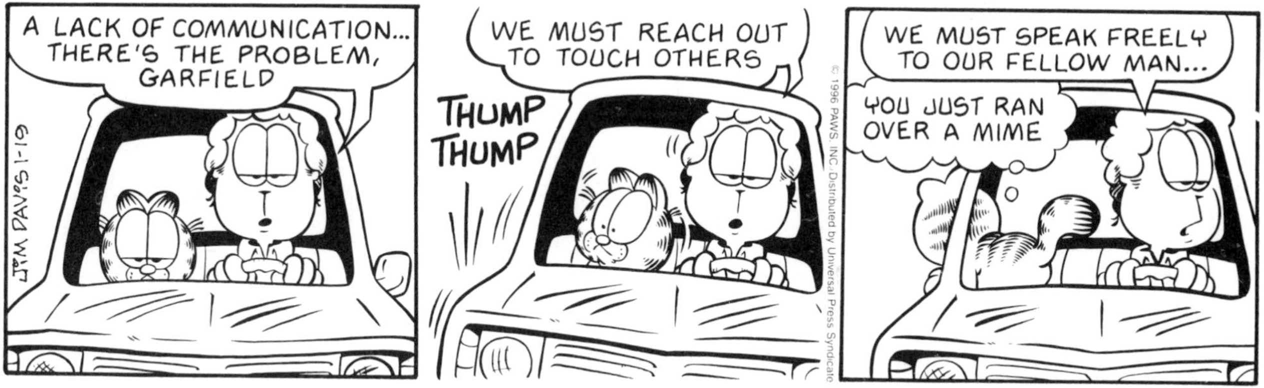
JIM DAVIS 1-19
A LACK OF COMMUNICATION... THERE'S THE PROBLEM, GARFIELD
WE MUST REACH OUT TO TOUCH OTHERS
THUMP THUMP
WE MUST SPEAK FREELY TO OUR FELLOW MAN...
YOU JUST RAN OVER A MIME

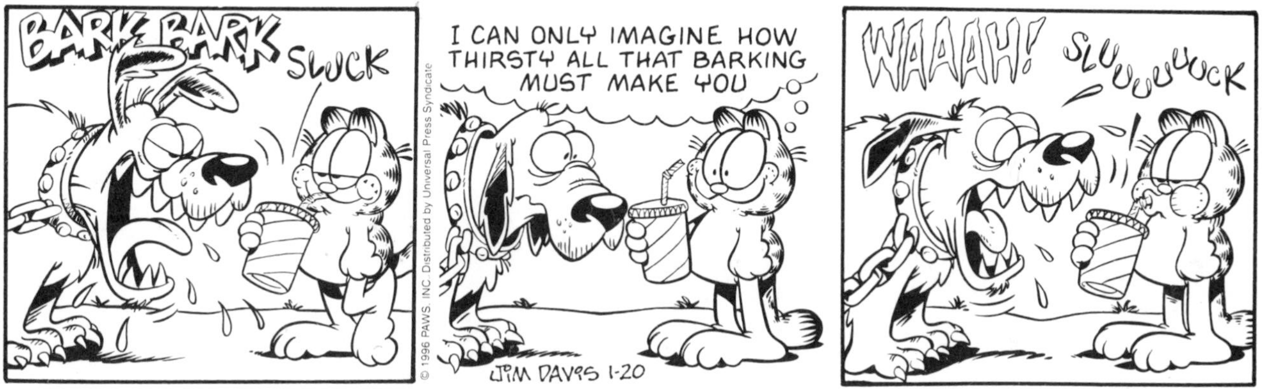
BARK BARK
SLUCK
I CAN ONLY IMAGINE HOW THIRSTY ALL THAT BARKING MUST MAKE YOU
JIM DAVIS 1-20
WAAAH!
SLUUUUUUCK

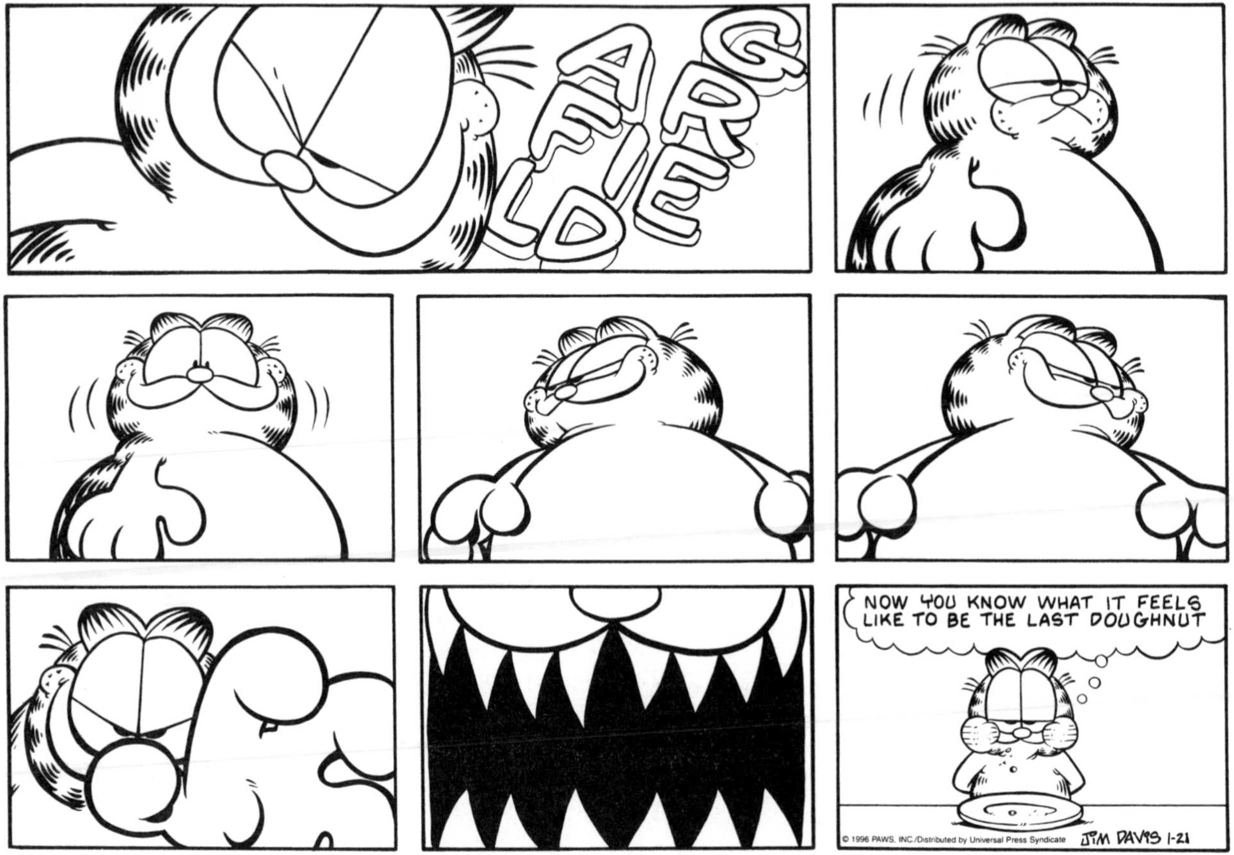
GARFIELD
NOW YOU KNOW WHAT IT FEELS LIKE TO BE THE LAST DOUGHNUT
© 1996 PAWS, INC./Distributed by Universal Press Syndicate
JIM DAVIS 1-21

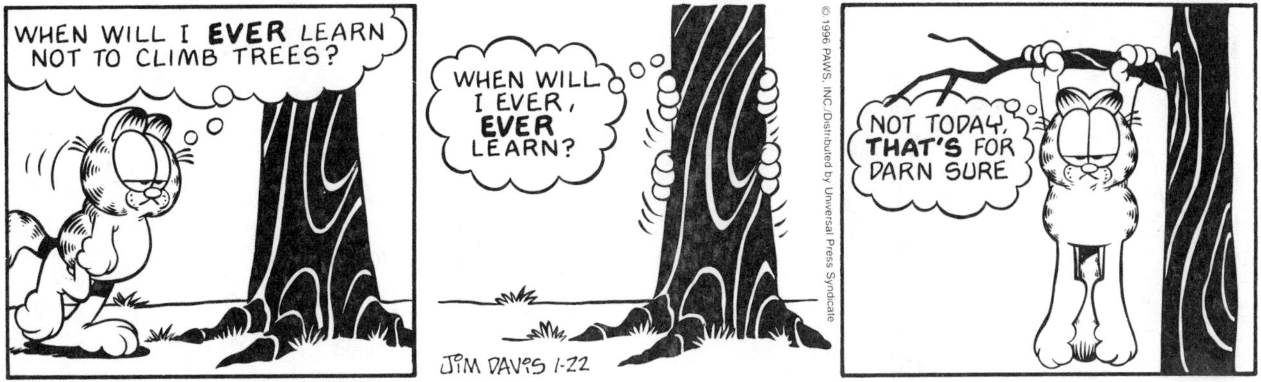
WHEN WILL I **EVER** LEARN NOT TO CLIMB TREES?
WHEN WILL I EVER, **EVER** LEARN?
JIM DAVIS 1-22
NOT TODAY, **THAT'S** FOR DARN SURE
© 1996 PAWS, INC./Distributed by Universal Press Syndicate

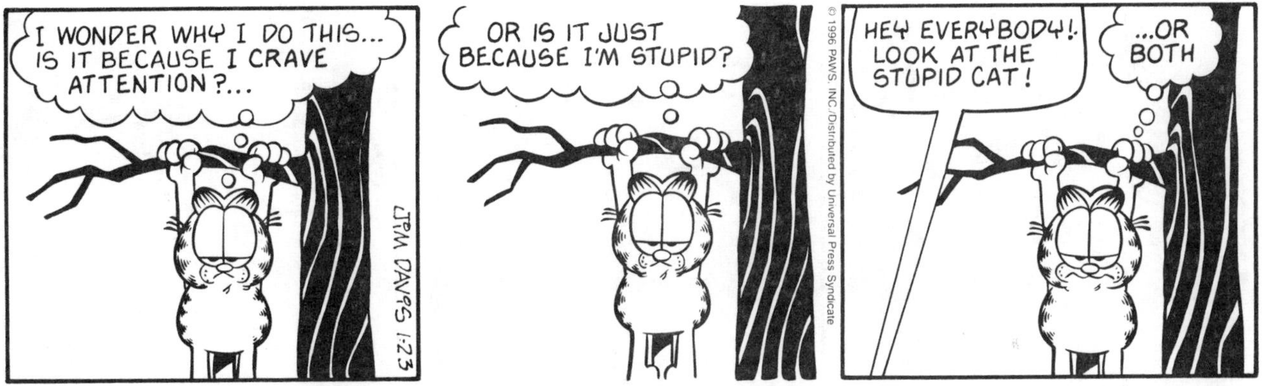
I WONDER WHY I DO THIS... IS IT BECAUSE I CRAVE ATTENTION?...
JIM DAVIS 1-23
OR IS IT JUST BECAUSE I'M STUPID?
HEY EVERYBODY! LOOK AT THE STUPID CAT!
...OR BOTH
© 1996 PAWS, INC./Distributed by Universal Press Syndicate

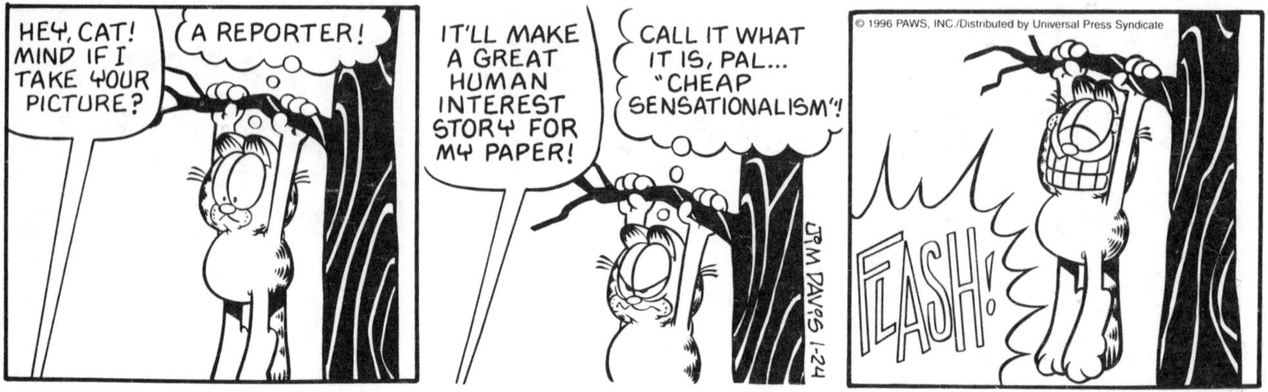
HEY, CAT! MIND IF I TAKE YOUR PICTURE?
A REPORTER!
IT'LL MAKE A GREAT HUMAN INTEREST STORY FOR MY PAPER!
CALL IT WHAT IT IS, PAL... "CHEAP SENSATIONALISM"!
JIM DAVIS 1-24
© 1996 PAWS, INC./Distributed by Universal Press Syndicate
FLASH!

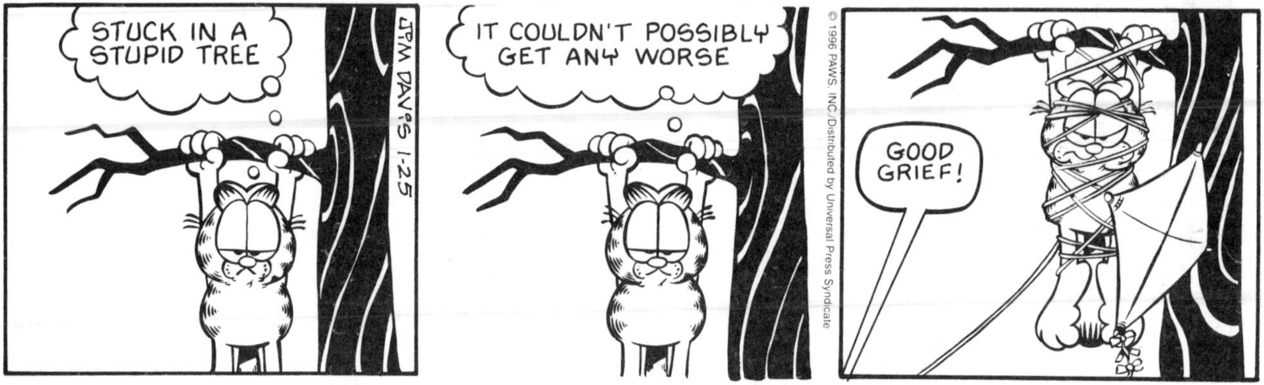
STUCK IN A STUPID TREE
JIM DAVIS 1-25
IT COULDN'T POSSIBLY GET ANY WORSE
© 1996 PAWS, INC./Distributed by Universal Press Syndicate
GOOD GRIEF!

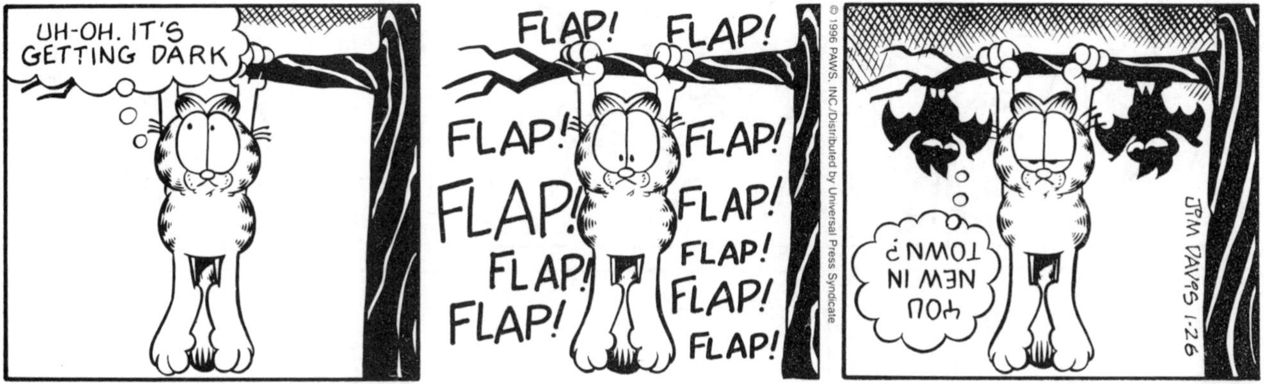
UH-OH. IT'S GETTING DARK
FLAP! FLAP!
FLAP! FLAP!
FLAP! FLAP!
FLAP! FLAP!
FLAP! FLAP!
FLAP!
© 1996 PAWS, INC./Distributed by Universal Press Syndicate
YOU NEW IN TOWN?
JIM DAVIS 1-26

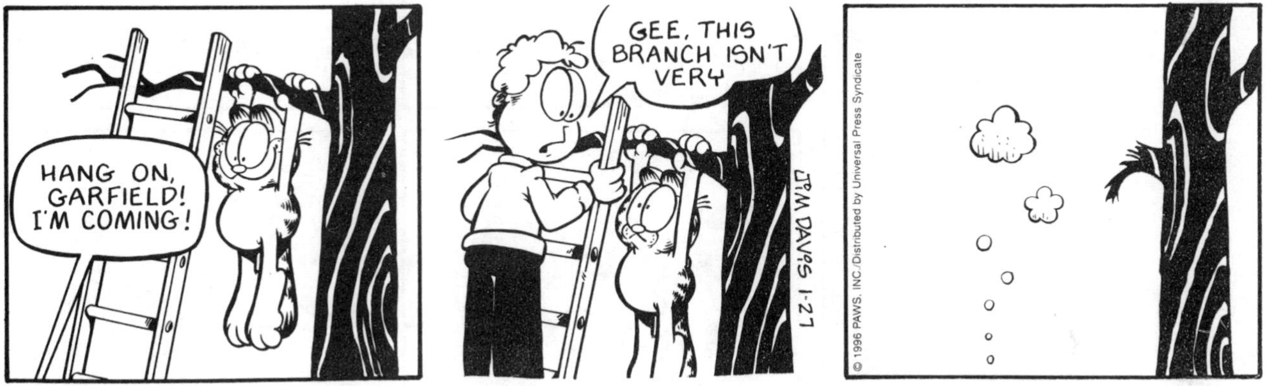
HANG ON, GARFIELD! I'M COMING!
GEE, THIS BRANCH ISN'T VERY
JIM DAVIS 1-27
© 1996 PAWS, INC./Distributed by Universal Press Syndicate

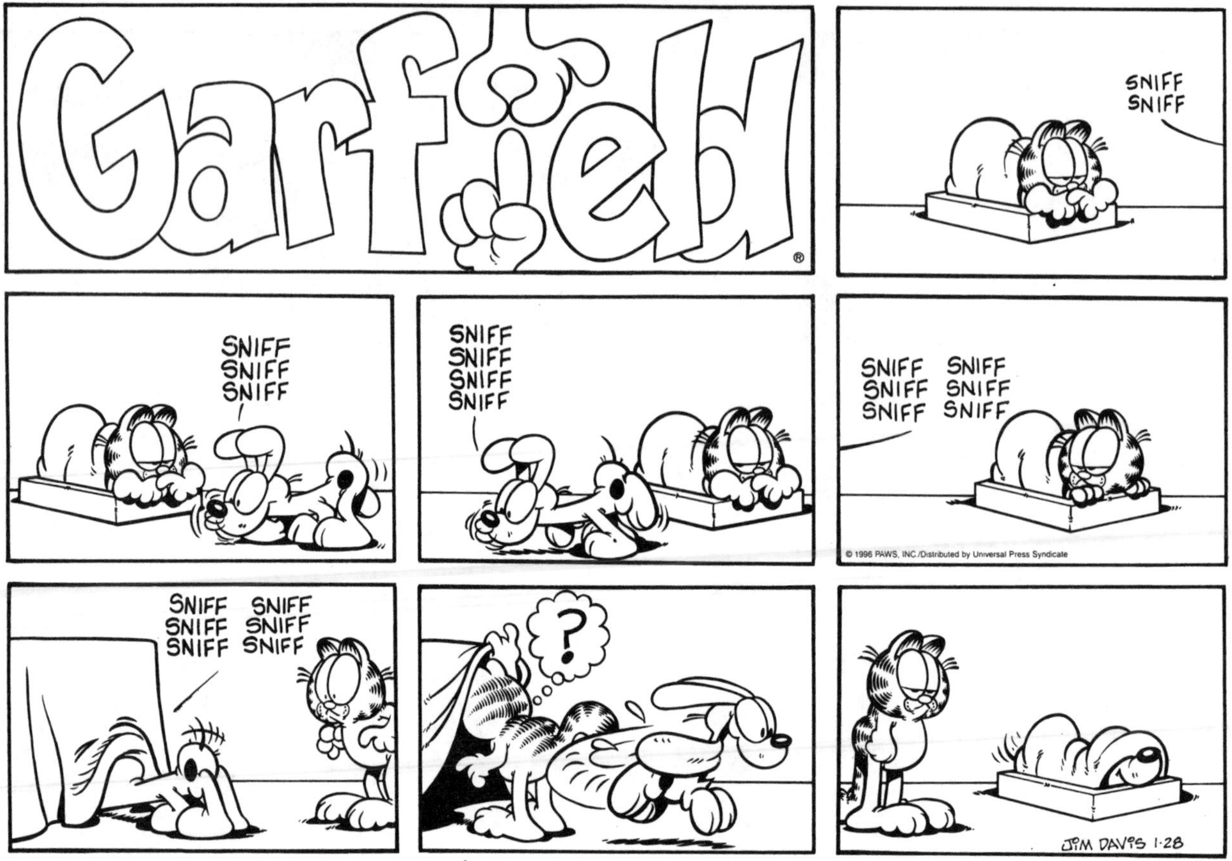
Garfield®
SNIFF
SNIFF
SNIFF
SNIFF
SNIFF
SNIFF
SNIFF
SNIFF
SNIFF
SNIFF SNIFF
SNIFF SNIFF
SNIFF SNIFF
© 1996 PAWS, INC./Distributed by Universal Press Syndicate
SNIFF SNIFF
SNIFF SNIFF
SNIFF SNIFF
?
JIM DAVIS 1·28

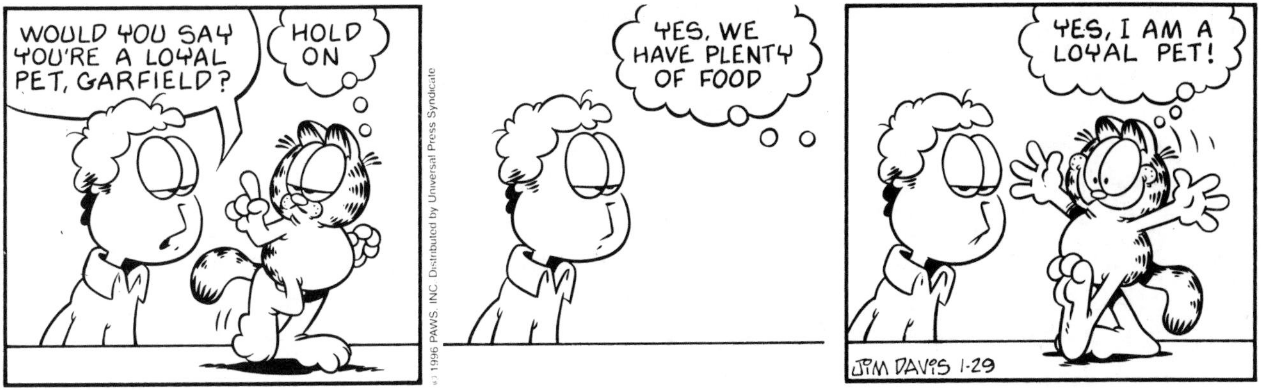
WOULD YOU SAY YOU'RE A LOYAL PET, GARFIELD?
HOLD ON
YES, WE HAVE PLENTY OF FOOD
YES, I AM A LOYAL PET!
© 1996 PAWS, INC Distributed by Universal Press Syndicate
JIM DAVIS 1-29

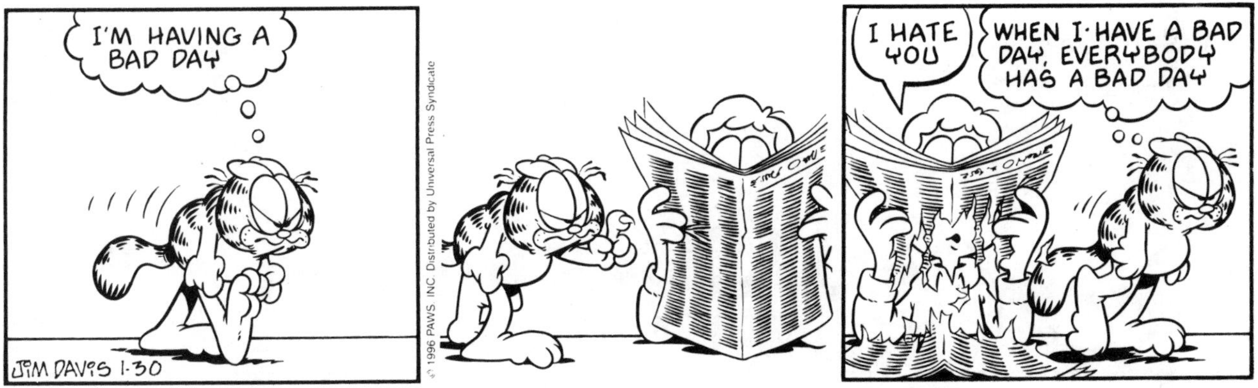
I'M HAVING A BAD DAY
JIM DAVIS 1-30
© 1996 PAWS, INC Distributed by Universal Press Syndicate
I HATE YOU
WHEN I HAVE A BAD DAY, EVERYBODY HAS A BAD DAY

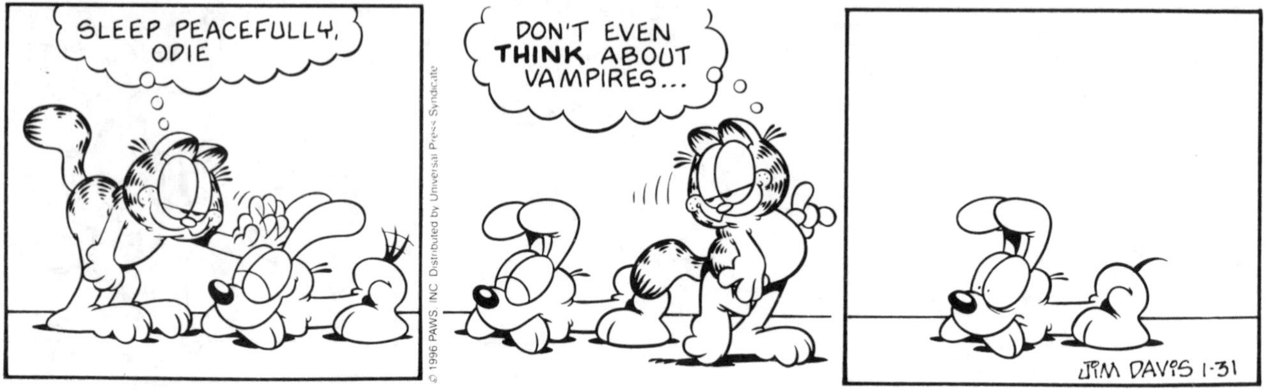
SLEEP PEACEFULLY, ODIE
© 1996 PAWS, INC Distributed by Universal Press Syndicate
DON'T EVEN **THINK** ABOUT VAMPIRES...
JIM DAVIS 1-31

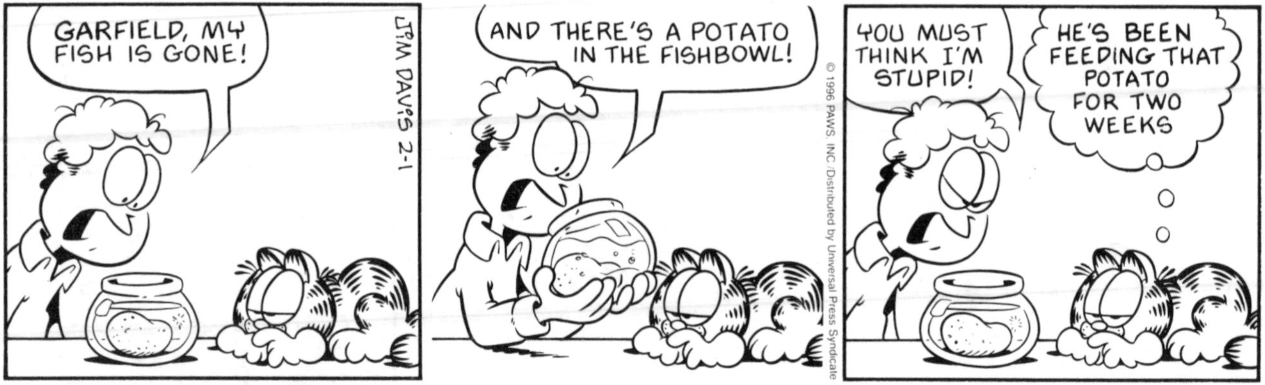
GARFIELD, MY FISH IS GONE!
JIM DAVIS 2-1
AND THERE'S A POTATO IN THE FISHBOWL!
© 1996 PAWS, INC./Distributed by Universal Press Syndicate
YOU MUST THINK I'M STUPID!
HE'S BEEN FEEDING THAT POTATO FOR TWO WEEKS

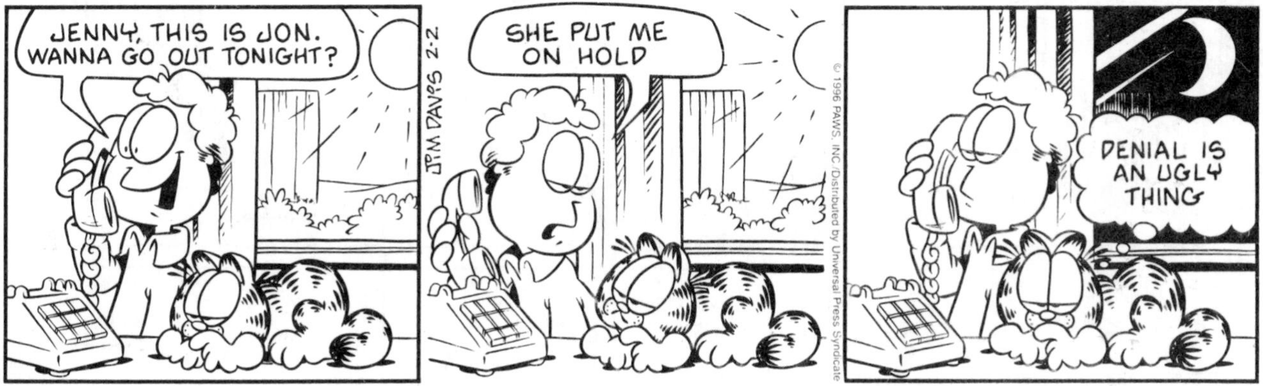
JENNY, THIS IS JON. WANNA GO OUT TONIGHT?
JIM DAVIS 2-2
SHE PUT ME ON HOLD
© 1996 PAWS, INC./Distributed by Universal Press Syndicate
DENIAL IS AN UGLY THING

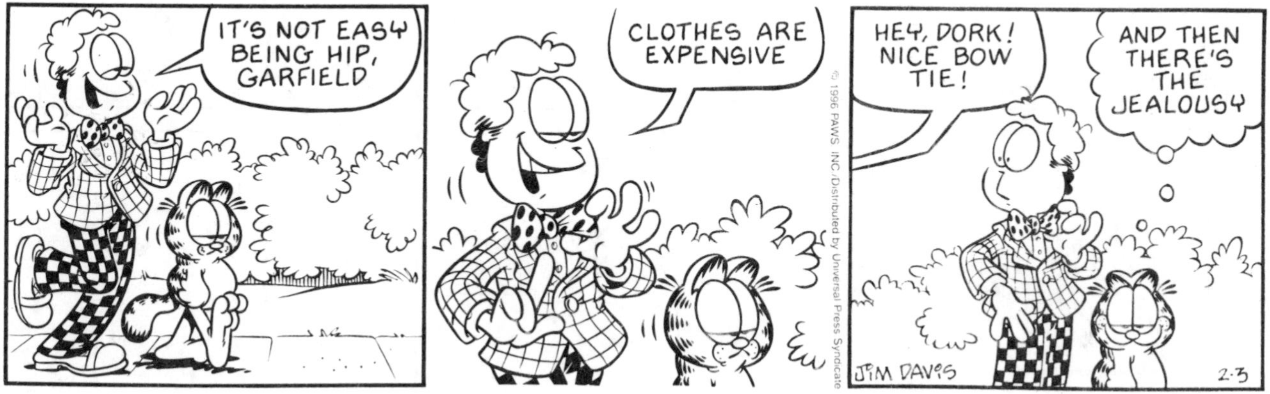
IT'S NOT EASY BEING HIP, GARFIELD
CLOTHES ARE EXPENSIVE
© 1996 PAWS, INC./Distributed by Universal Press Syndicate
HEY, DORK! NICE BOW TIE!
AND THEN THERE'S THE JEALOUSY
JIM DAVIS
2-3

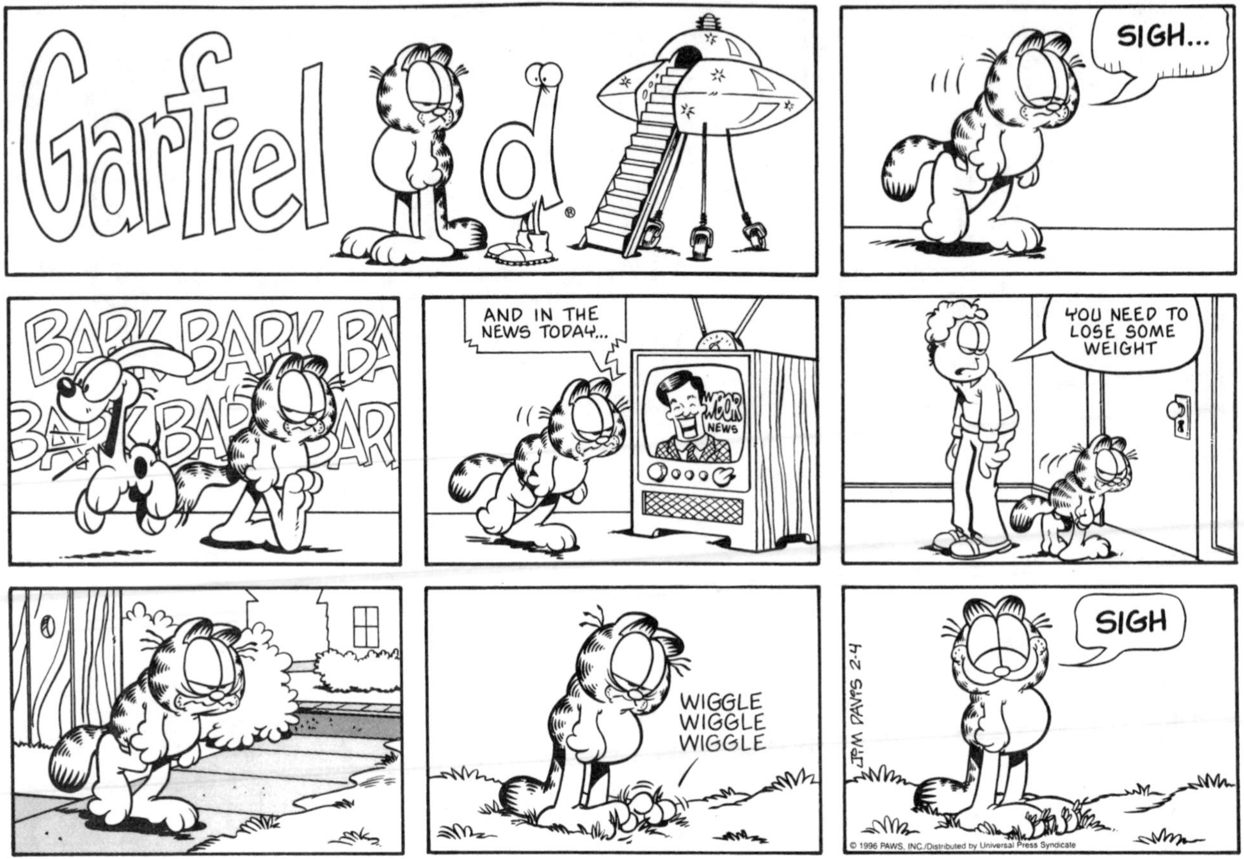
Garfield®
SIGH...
BARK BARK BARK BARK BARK BARK
AND IN THE NEWS TODAY...
WBOR NEWS
YOU NEED TO LOSE SOME WEIGHT
WIGGLE WIGGLE WIGGLE
SIGH
JPM DAVPS 2-4
© 1996 PAWS, INC./Distributed by Universal Press Syndicate

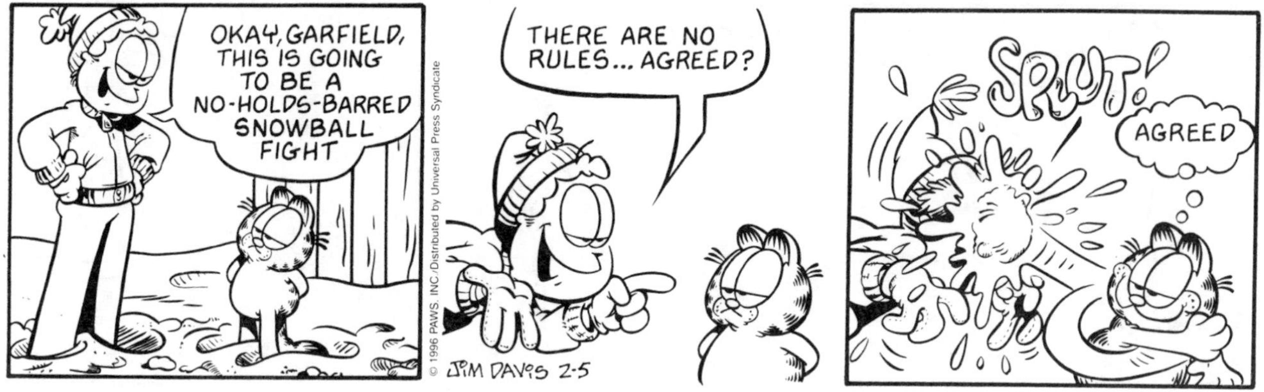
OKAY, GARFIELD, THIS IS GOING TO BE A NO-HOLDS-BARRED SNOWBALL FIGHT
© 1996 PAWS, INC./Distributed by Universal Press Syndicate
JIM DAVIS 2-5
THERE ARE NO RULES... AGREED?
SPLUT!
AGREED

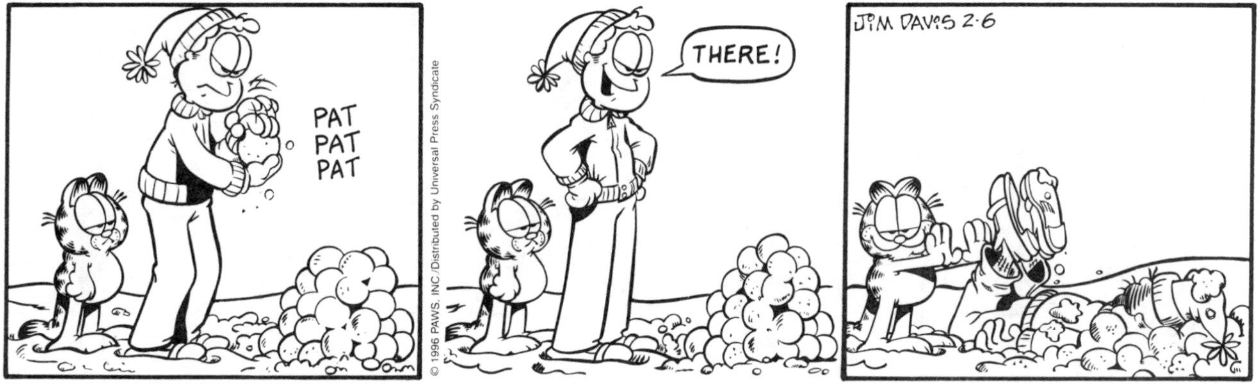
PAT
PAT
PAT
© 1996 PAWS, INC./Distributed by Universal Press Syndicate
THERE!
JIM DAVIS 2-6

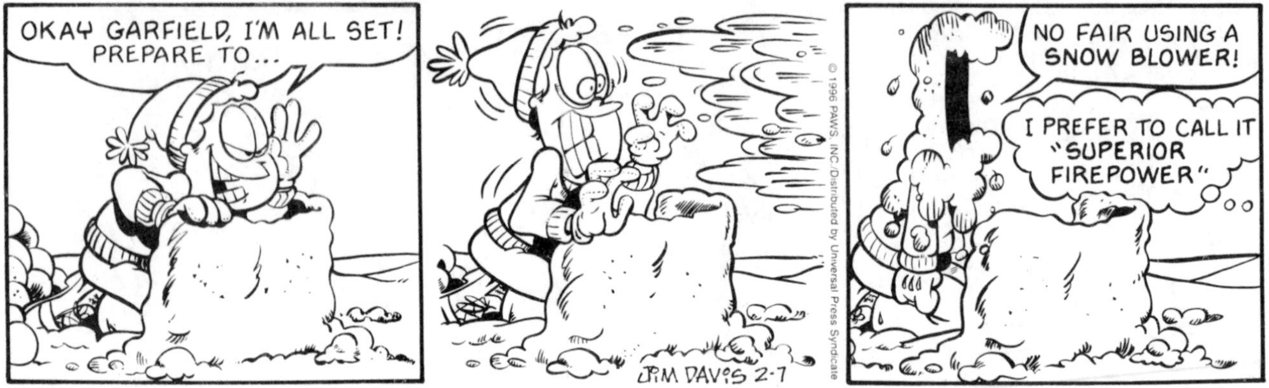
OKAY GARFIELD, I'M ALL SET! PREPARE TO...
JIM DAVIS 2-7
© 1996 PAWS, INC./Distributed by Universal Press Syndicate
NO FAIR USING A SNOW BLOWER!
I PREFER TO CALL IT "SUPERIOR FIREPOWER"

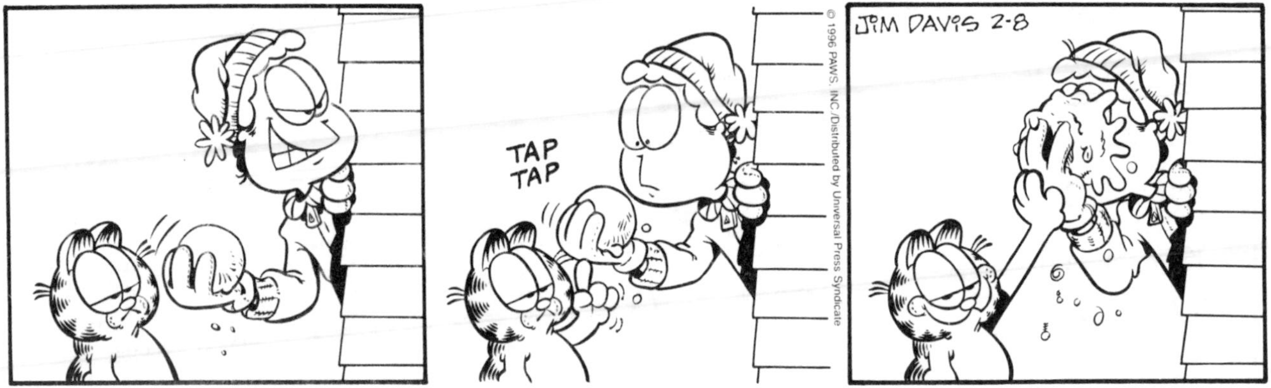
TAP TAP
© 1996 PAWS, INC./Distributed by Universal Press Syndicate
JIM DAVIS 2-8

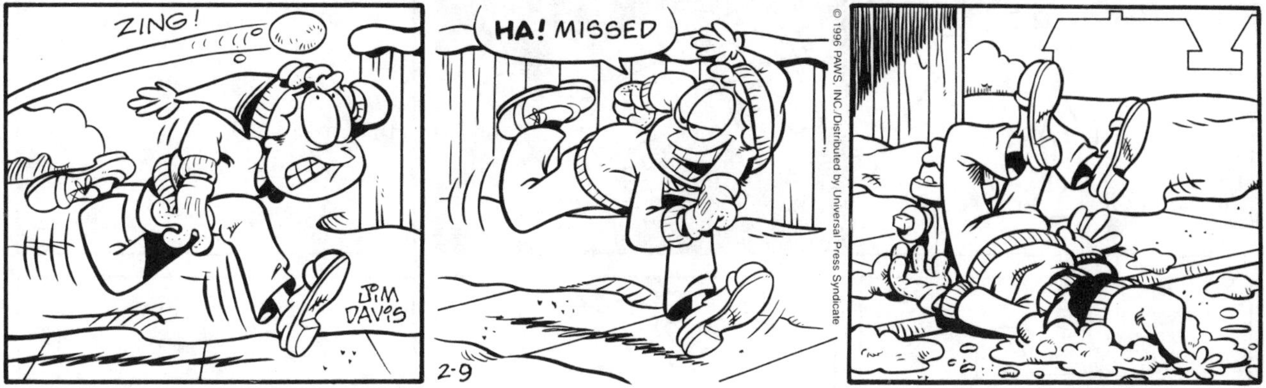
ZING!
JIM DAVIS
HA! MISSED
2-9
© 1996 PAWS, INC./Distributed by Universal Press Syndicate

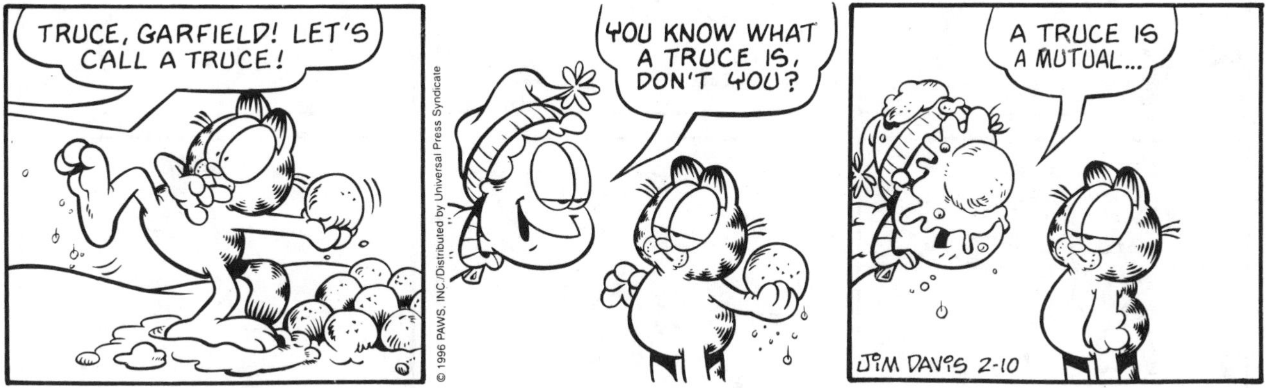
TRUCE, GARFIELD! LET'S CALL A TRUCE!
© 1996 PAWS, INC./Distributed by Universal Press Syndicate
YOU KNOW WHAT A TRUCE IS, DON'T YOU?
A TRUCE IS A MUTUAL...
JIM DAVIS 2-10

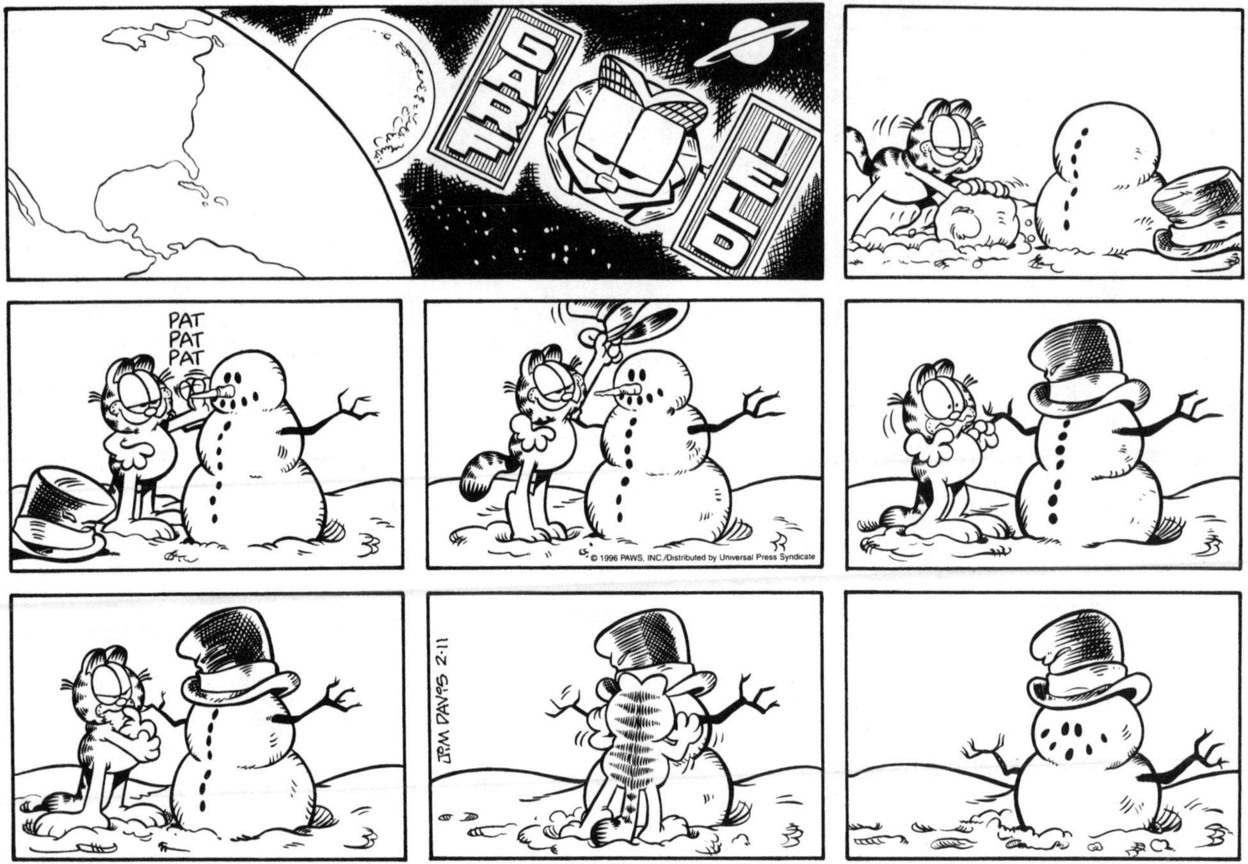
GARFIELD
PAT
PAT
PAT
© 1996 PAWS, INC./Distributed by Universal Press Syndicate
JIM DAVIS 2-11

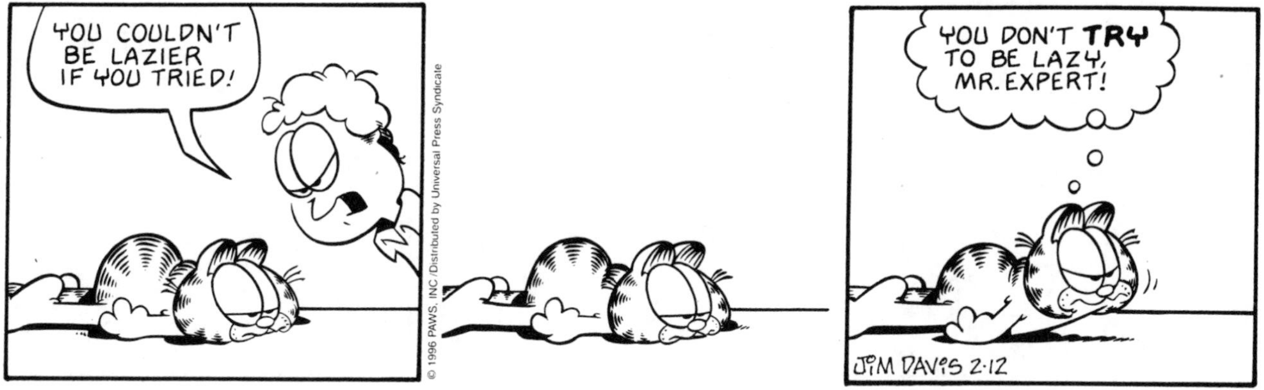
YOU COULDN'T BE LAZIER IF YOU TRIED!
YOU DON'T **TRY** TO BE LAZY, MR. EXPERT!
JIM DAVIS 2-12

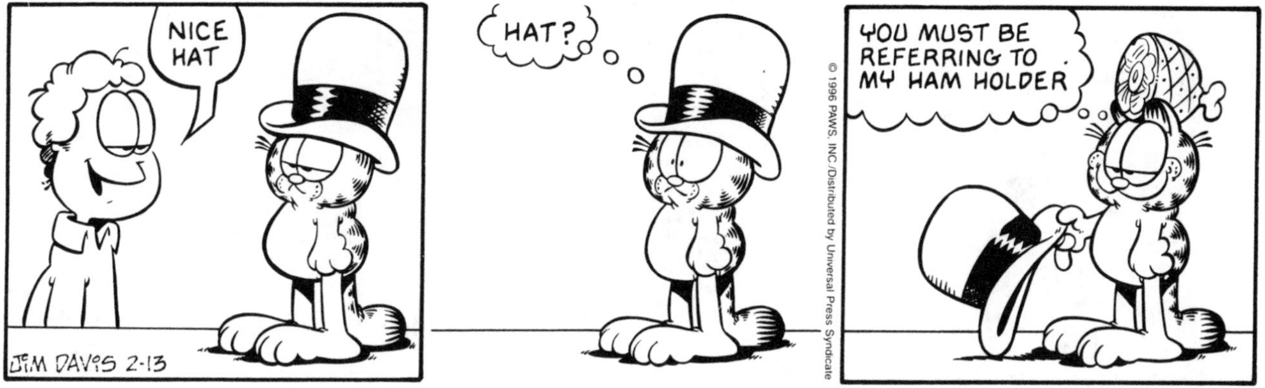
NICE HAT
HAT?
YOU MUST BE REFERRING TO MY HAM HOLDER
JIM DAVIS 2-13

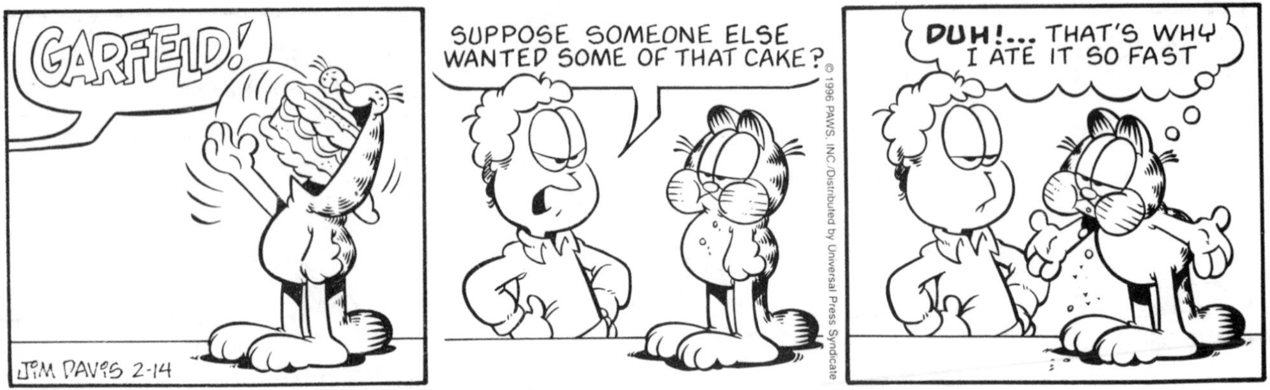
GARFIELD!
JIM DAVIS 2-14
SUPPOSE SOMEONE ELSE WANTED SOME OF THAT CAKE?
© 1996 PAWS, INC./Distributed by Universal Press Syndicate
DUH!... THAT'S WHY I ATE IT SO FAST

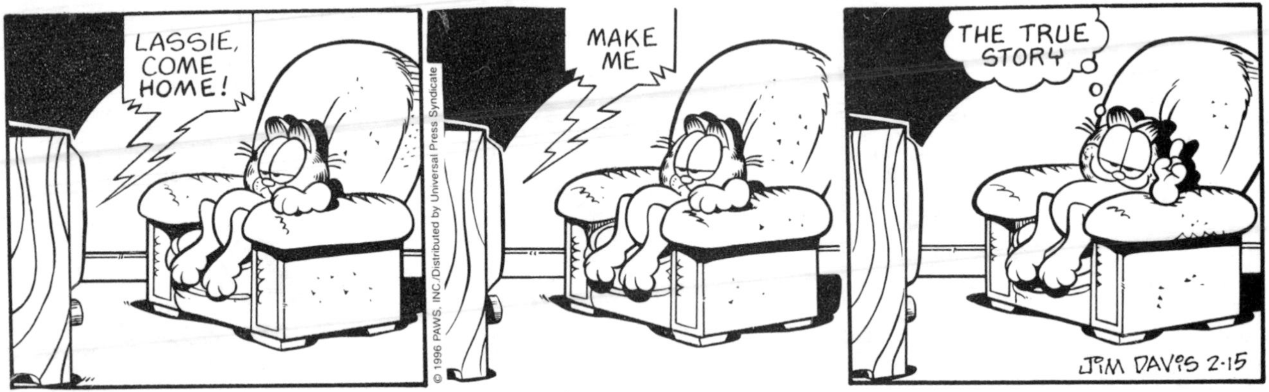
LASSIE, COME HOME!
© 1996 PAWS, INC./Distributed by Universal Press Syndicate
MAKE ME
THE TRUE STORY
JIM DAVIS 2-15

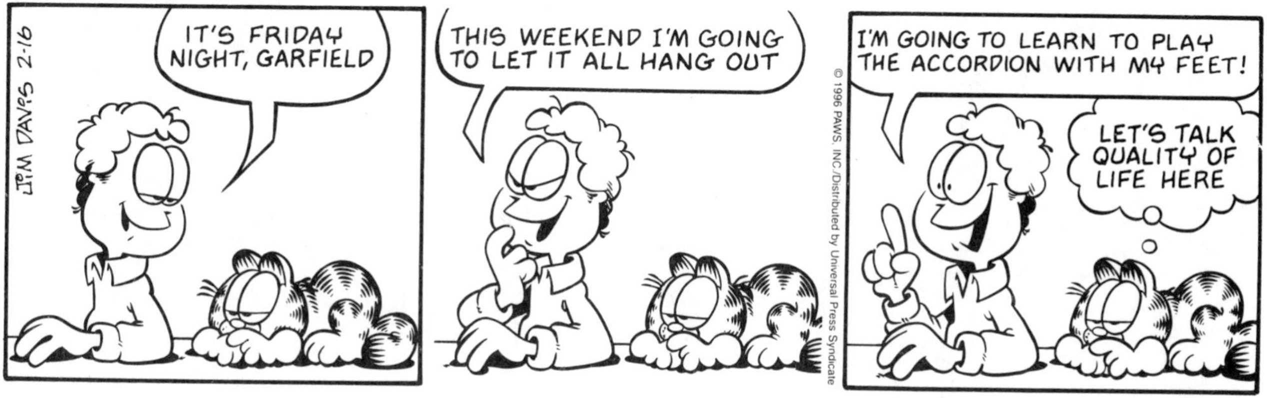
JIM DAVIS 2-16
IT'S FRIDAY NIGHT, GARFIELD
THIS WEEKEND I'M GOING TO LET IT ALL HANG OUT
I'M GOING TO LEARN TO PLAY THE ACCORDION WITH MY FEET!
LET'S TALK QUALITY OF LIFE HERE

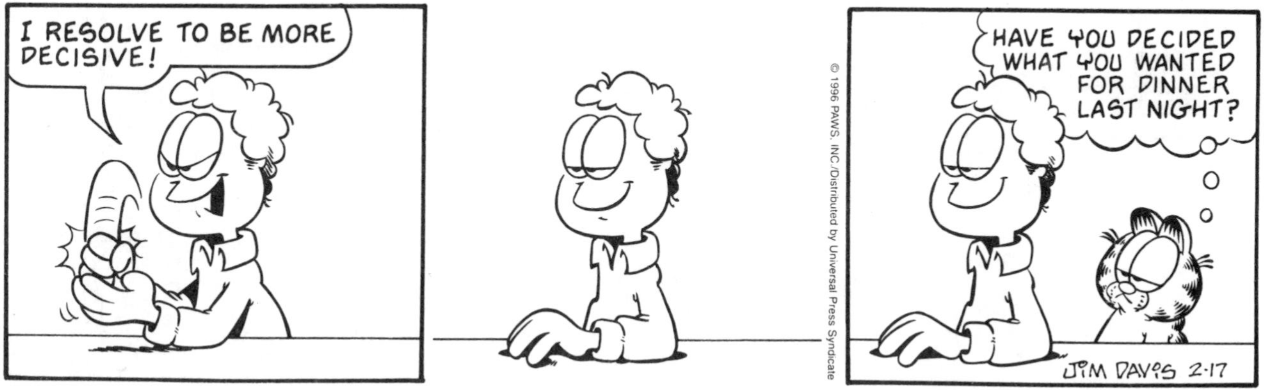
I RESOLVE TO BE MORE DECISIVE!
HAVE YOU DECIDED WHAT YOU WANTED FOR DINNER LAST NIGHT?
JIM DAVIS 2-17

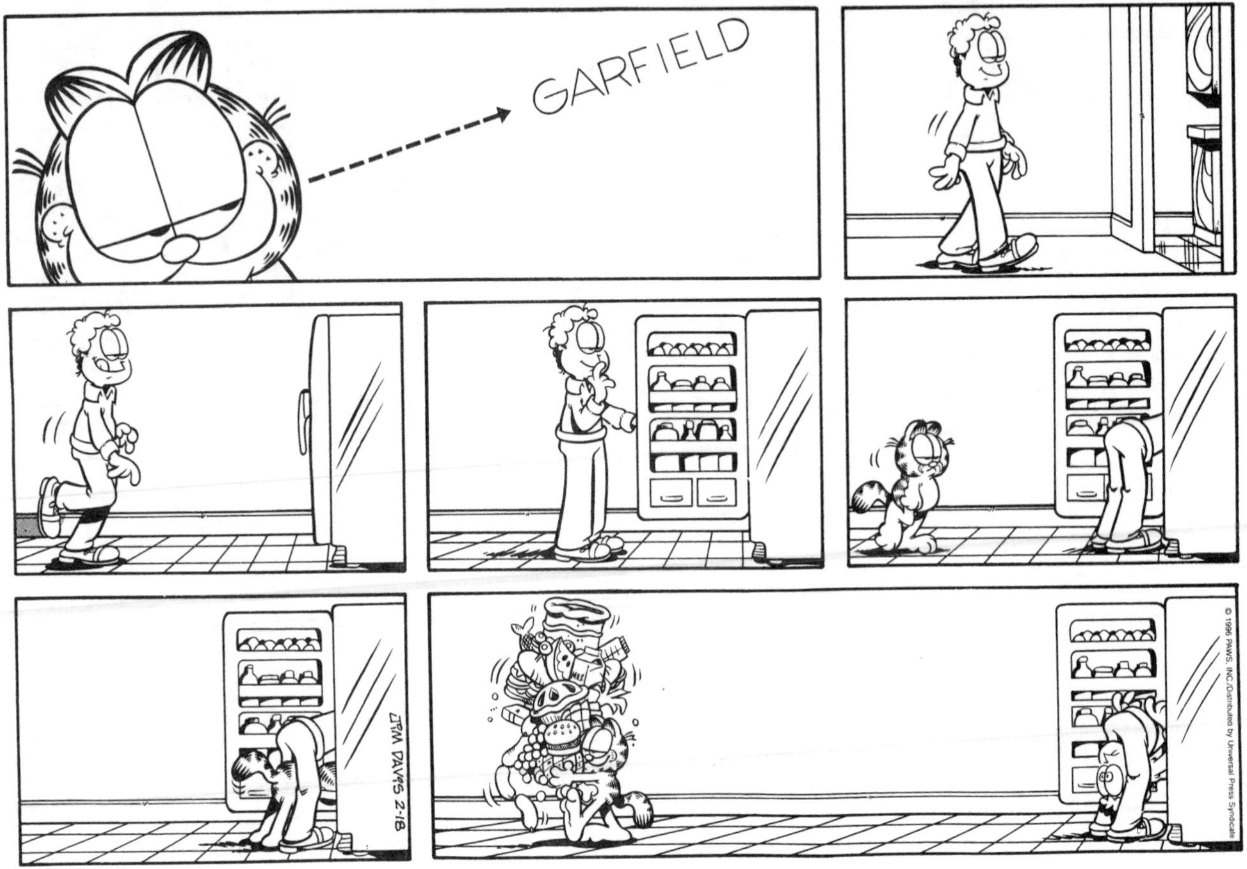
GARFIELD
JIM DAVIS 2-18
© 1996 PAWS, INC./Distributed by Universal Press Syndicate

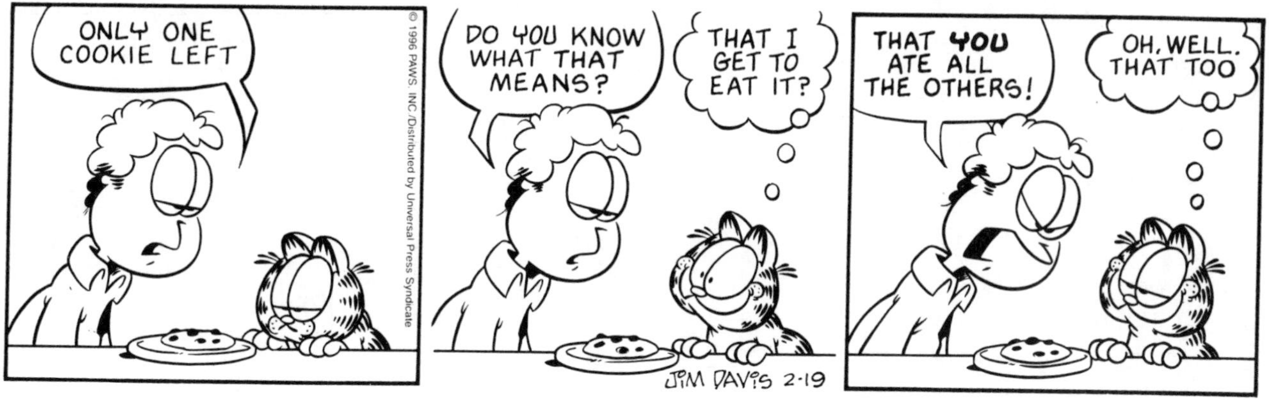
ONLY ONE COOKIE LEFT
© 1996 PAWS, INC./Distributed by Universal Press Syndicate
DO YOU KNOW WHAT THAT MEANS?
THAT I GET TO EAT IT?
JIM DAVIS 2-19
THAT YOU ATE ALL THE OTHERS!
OH, WELL. THAT TOO

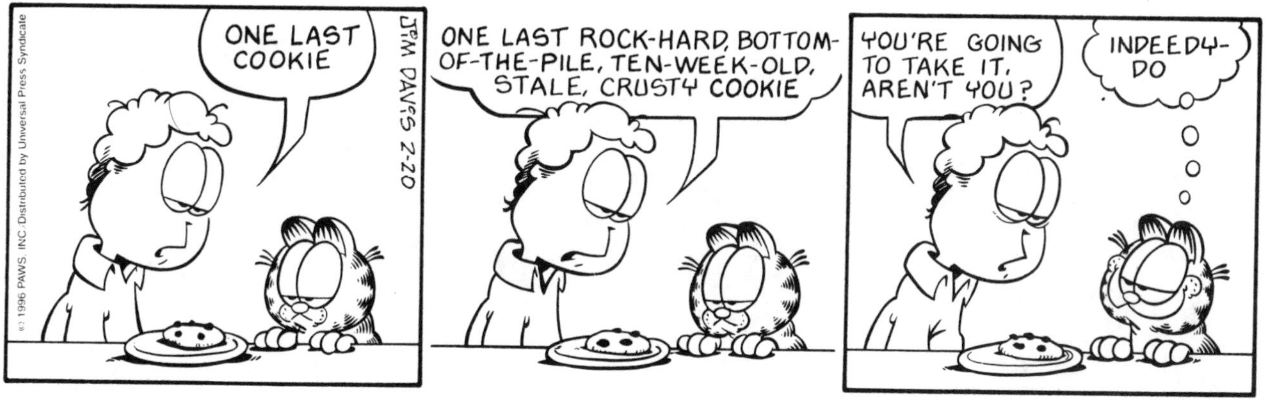
© 1996 PAWS, INC./Distributed by Universal Press Syndicate
ONE LAST COOKIE
JIM DAVIS 2-20
ONE LAST ROCK-HARD, BOTTOM-OF-THE-PILE, TEN-WEEK-OLD, STALE, CRUSTY COOKIE
YOU'RE GOING TO TAKE IT, AREN'T YOU?
INDEEDY-DO

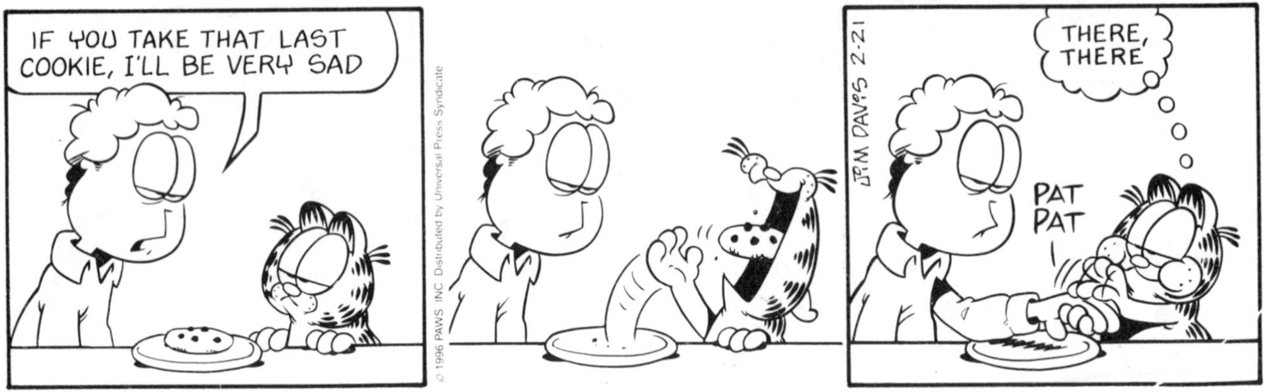
IF YOU TAKE THAT LAST COOKIE, I'LL BE VERY SAD
© 1996 PAWS, INC Distributed by Universal Press Syndicate
JIM DAVIS 2·21
THERE, THERE
PAT PAT

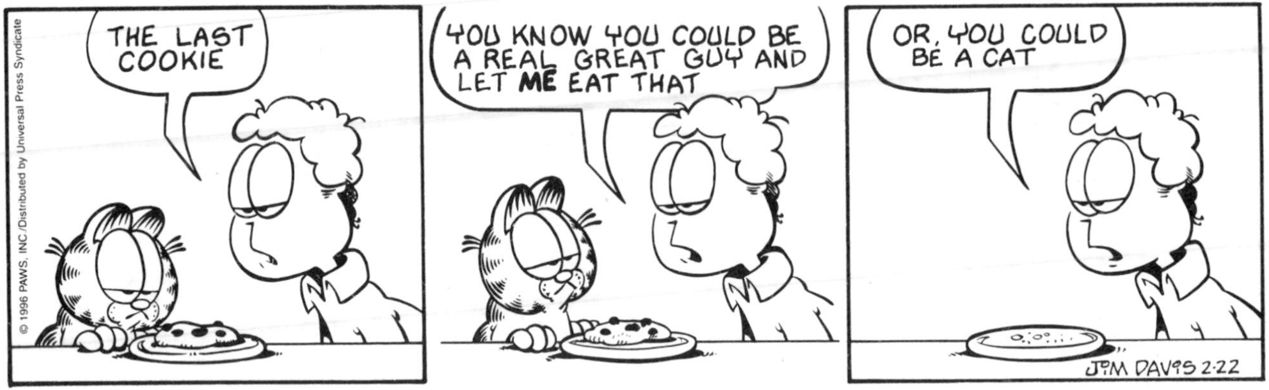
© 1996 PAWS, INC./Distributed by Universal Press Syndicate
THE LAST COOKIE
YOU KNOW YOU COULD BE A REAL GREAT GUY AND LET **ME** EAT THAT
OR, YOU COULD BE A CAT
JIM DAVIS 2·22

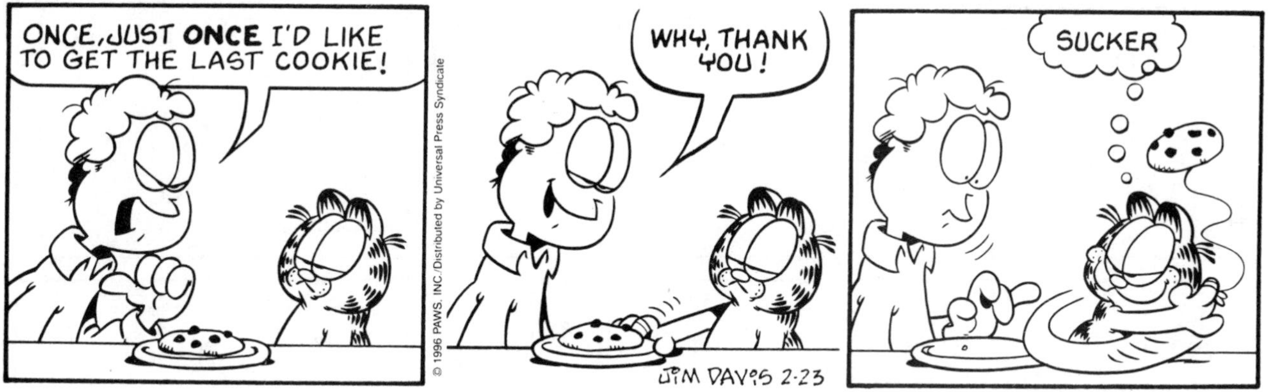
ONCE, JUST **ONCE** I'D LIKE TO GET THE LAST COOKIE!
WHY, THANK YOU!
SUCKER
JIM DAVIS 2-23

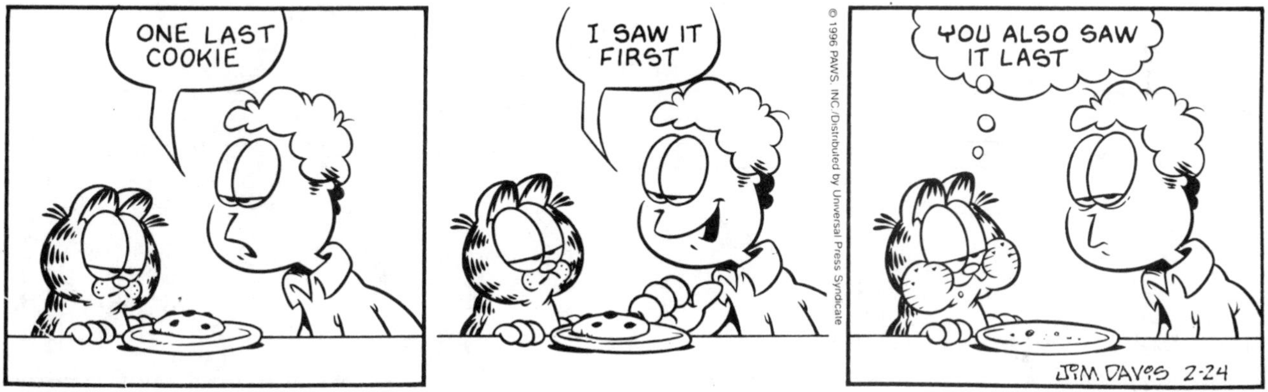
ONE LAST COOKIE
I SAW IT FIRST
YOU ALSO SAW IT LAST
JIM DAVIS 2-24

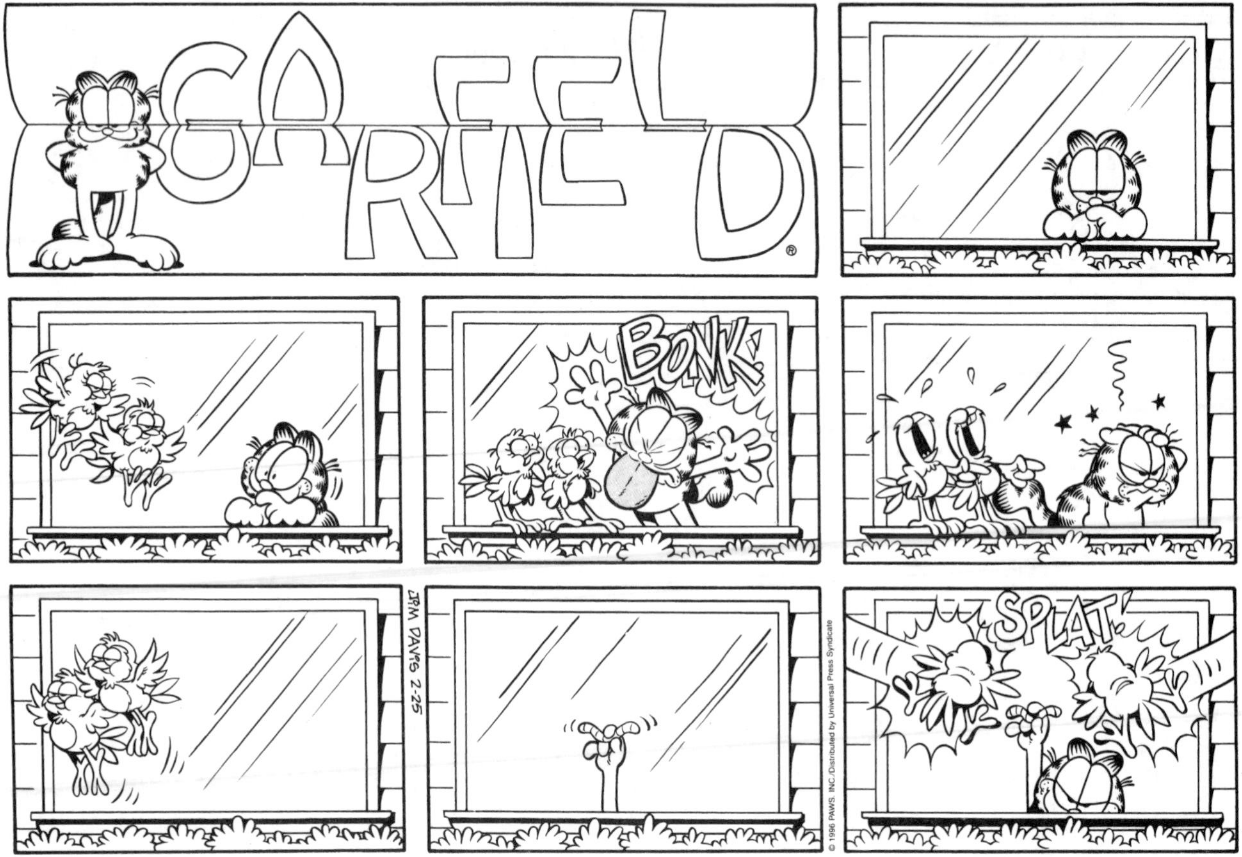
GARFIELD®
BONK!
JIM DAVIS 2-25
SPLAT!

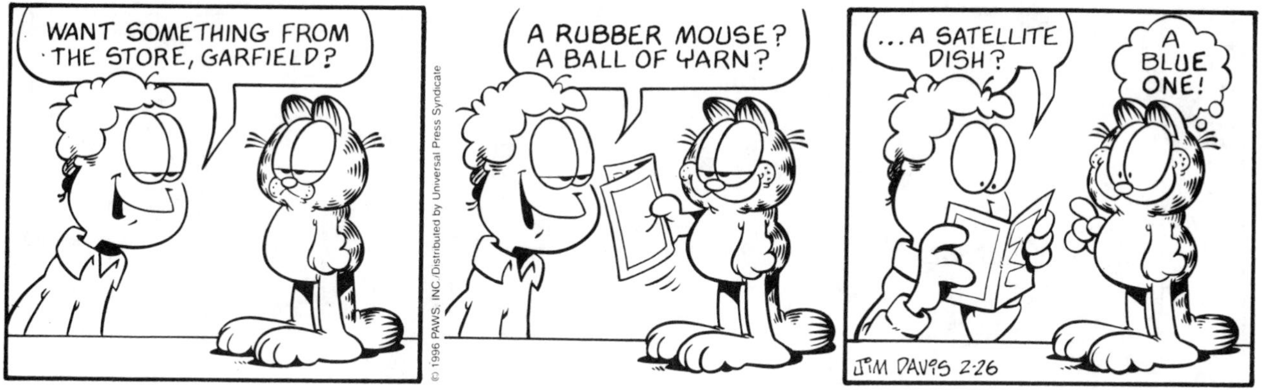
WANT SOMETHING FROM THE STORE, GARFIELD?
A RUBBER MOUSE? A BALL OF YARN?
...A SATELLITE DISH?
A BLUE ONE!
JIM DAVIS 2-26

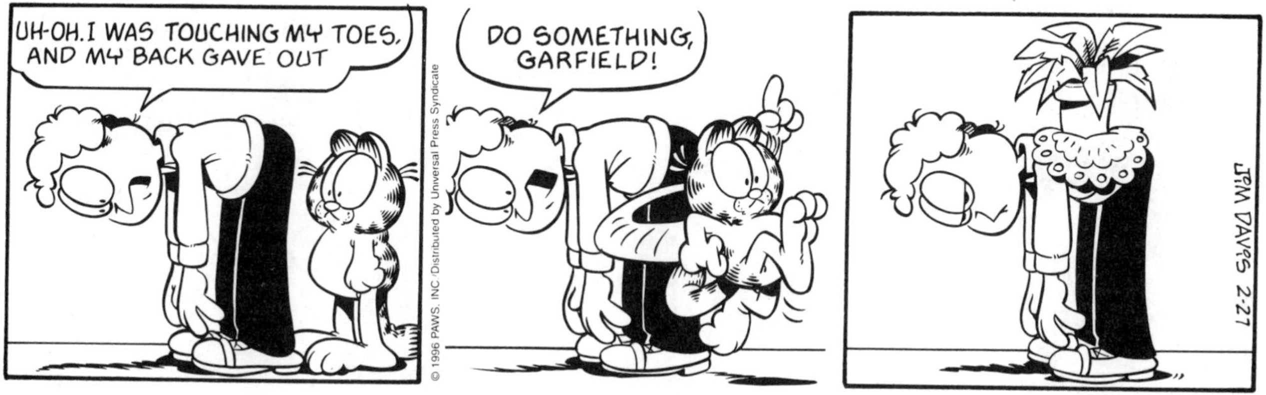
UH-OH. I WAS TOUCHING MY TOES, AND MY BACK GAVE OUT
DO SOMETHING, GARFIELD!
JIM DAVIS 2-27

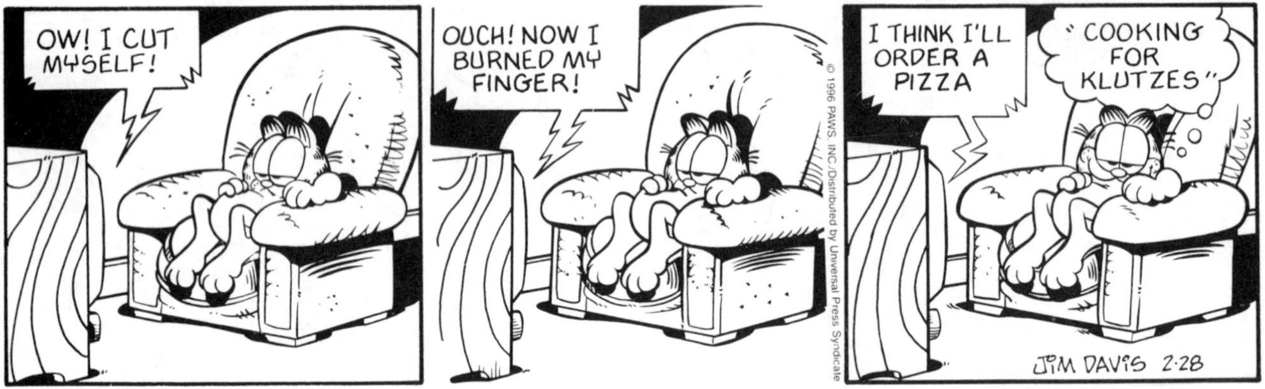
OW! I CUT MYSELF!
OUCH! NOW I BURNED MY FINGER!
© 1996 PAWS, INC./Distributed by Universal Press Syndicate
I THINK I'LL ORDER A PIZZA
"COOKING FOR KLUTZES"
JIM DAVIS 2·28

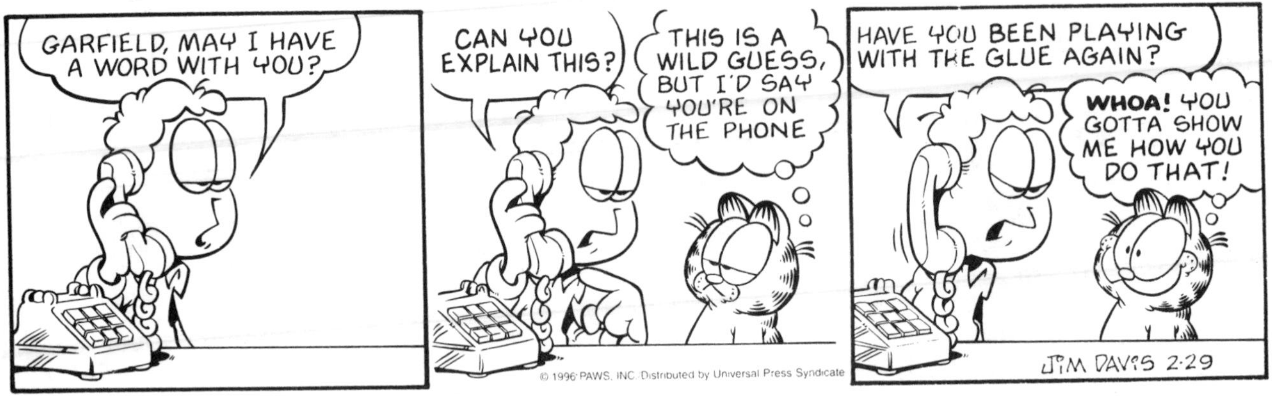
GARFIELD, MAY I HAVE A WORD WITH YOU?
CAN YOU EXPLAIN THIS?
THIS IS A WILD GUESS, BUT I'D SAY YOU'RE ON THE PHONE
© 1996 PAWS, INC. Distributed by Universal Press Syndicate
HAVE YOU BEEN PLAYING WITH THE GLUE AGAIN?
WHOA! YOU GOTTA SHOW ME HOW YOU DO THAT!
JIM DAVIS 2·29

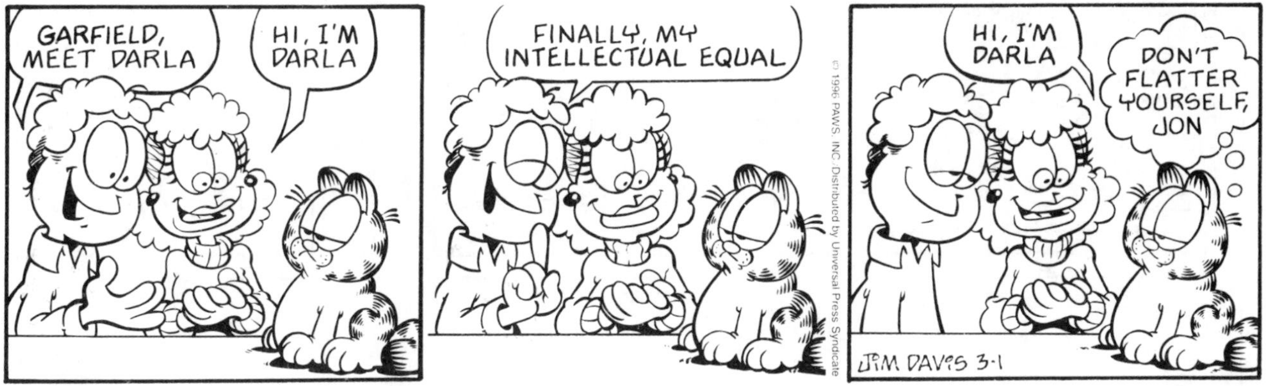
GARFIELD, MEET DARLA
HI, I'M DARLA
FINALLY, MY INTELLECTUAL EQUAL
HI, I'M DARLA
DON'T FLATTER YOURSELF, JON
JIM DAVIS 3-1
© 1996 PAWS, INC./Distributed by Universal Press Syndicate

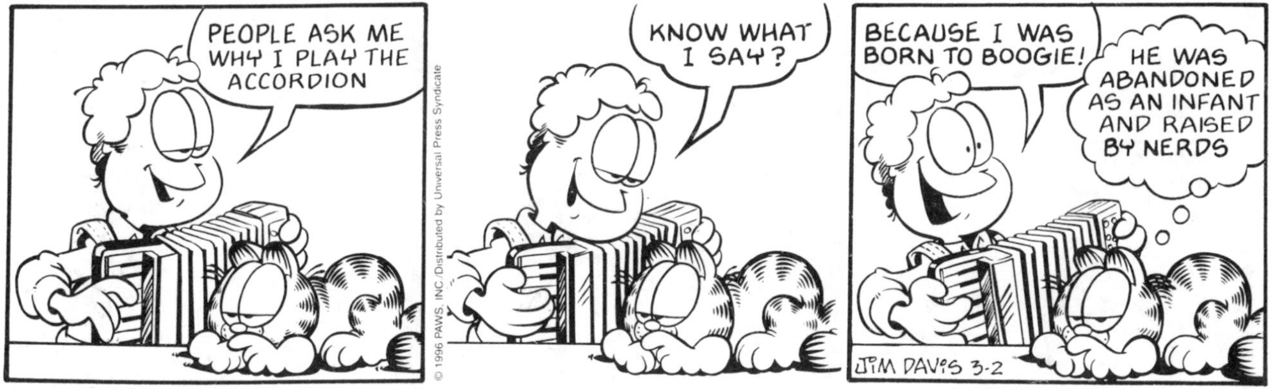
PEOPLE ASK ME WHY I PLAY THE ACCORDION
KNOW WHAT I SAY?
BECAUSE I WAS BORN TO BOOGIE!
HE WAS ABANDONED AS AN INFANT AND RAISED BY NERDS
JIM DAVIS 3-2
© 1996 PAWS, INC./Distributed by Universal Press Syndicate

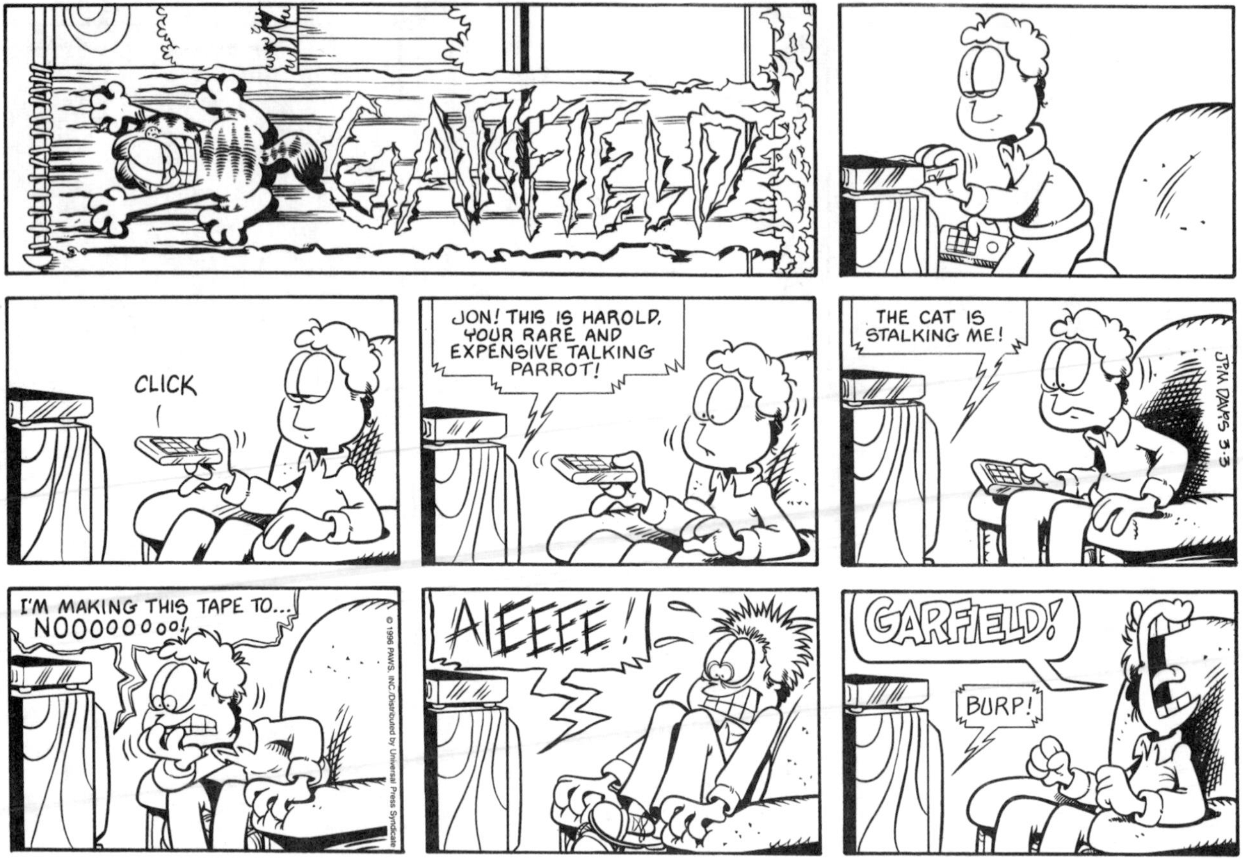
GARFIELD
CLICK
JON! THIS IS HAROLD, YOUR RARE AND EXPENSIVE TALKING PARROT!
THE CAT IS STALKING ME!
JIM DAVIS 3-3
I'M MAKING THIS TAPE TO... NOOOOOOoo!
© 1996 PAWS, INC./Distributed by Universal Press Syndicate
AIEEEE!
GARFIELD!
BURP!

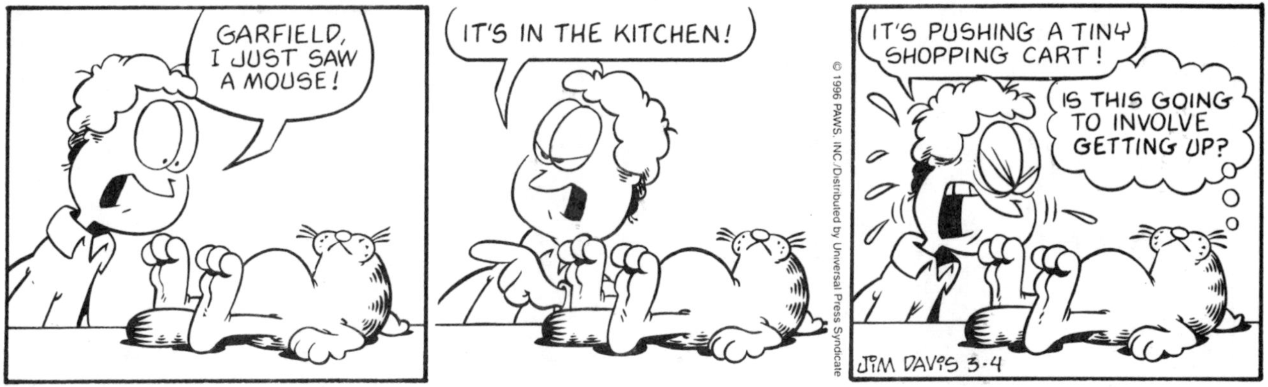
GARFIELD, I JUST SAW A MOUSE!
IT'S IN THE KITCHEN!
IT'S PUSHING A TINY SHOPPING CART!
IS THIS GOING TO INVOLVE GETTING UP?
JIM DAVIS 3-4
© 1996 PAWS, INC./Distributed by Universal Press Syndicate

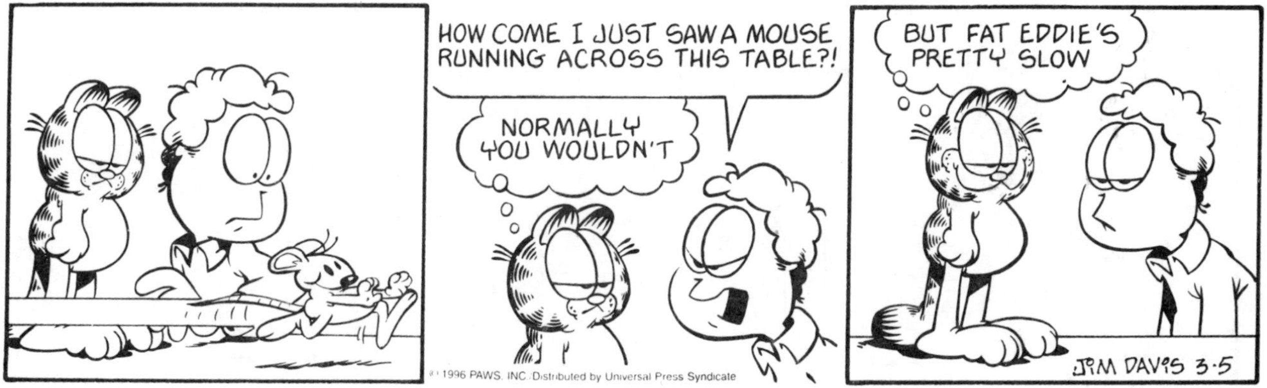
HOW COME I JUST SAW A MOUSE RUNNING ACROSS THIS TABLE?!
NORMALLY YOU WOULDN'T
BUT FAT EDDIE'S PRETTY SLOW
JIM DAVIS 3-5
© 1996 PAWS, INC./Distributed by Universal Press Syndicate

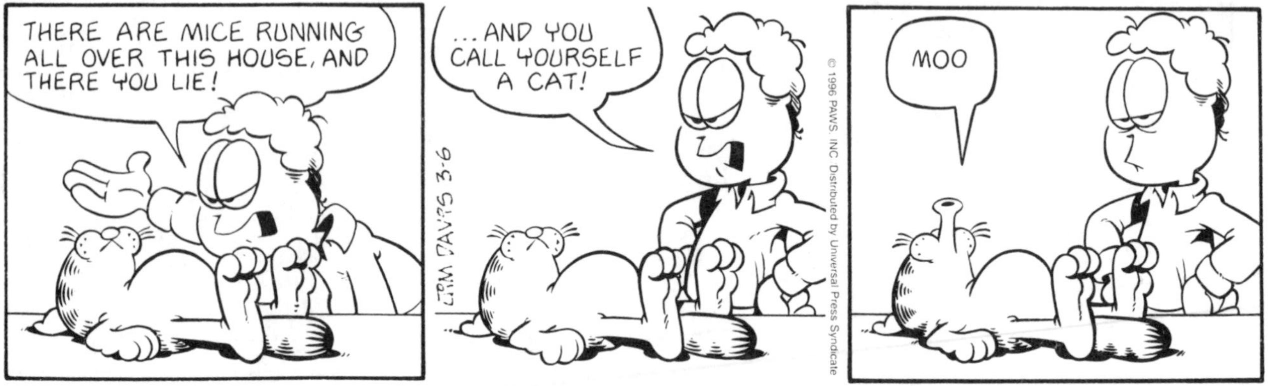
THERE ARE MICE RUNNING ALL OVER THIS HOUSE, AND THERE YOU LIE!
...AND YOU CALL YOURSELF A CAT!
JIM DAVIS 3-6
MOO
© 1996 PAWS, INC Distributed by Universal Press Syndicate

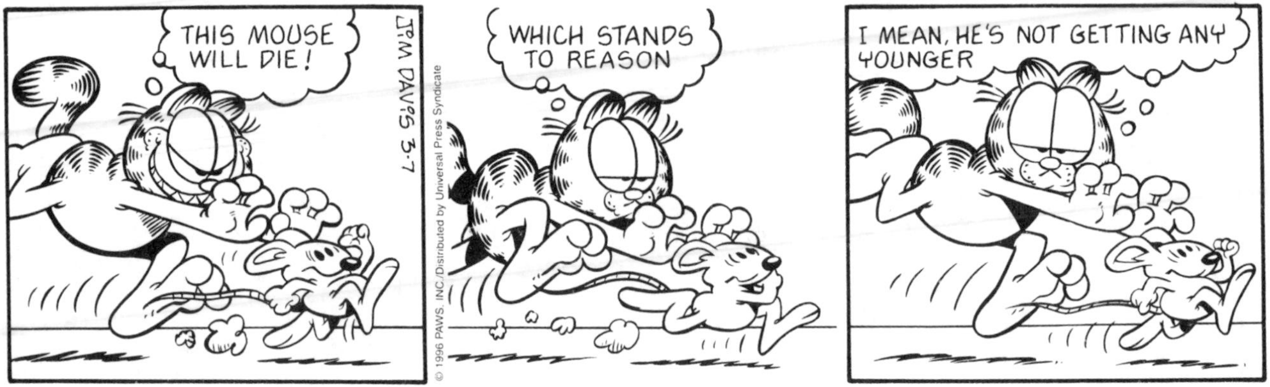
THIS MOUSE WILL DIE!
JIM DAVIS 3-7
© 1996 PAWS, INC./Distributed by Universal Press Syndicate
WHICH STANDS TO REASON
I MEAN, HE'S NOT GETTING ANY YOUNGER

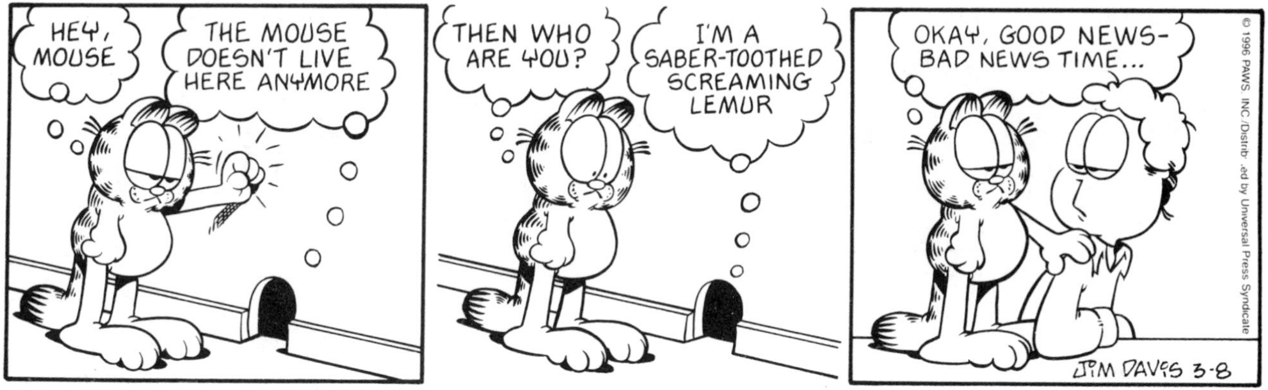
HEY, MOUSE
THE MOUSE DOESN'T LIVE HERE ANYMORE
THEN WHO ARE YOU?
I'M A SABER-TOOTHED SCREAMING LEMUR
OKAY, GOOD NEWS-BAD NEWS TIME...
JIM DAVIS 3-8
© 1996 PAWS. INC./Distributed by Universal Press Syndicate

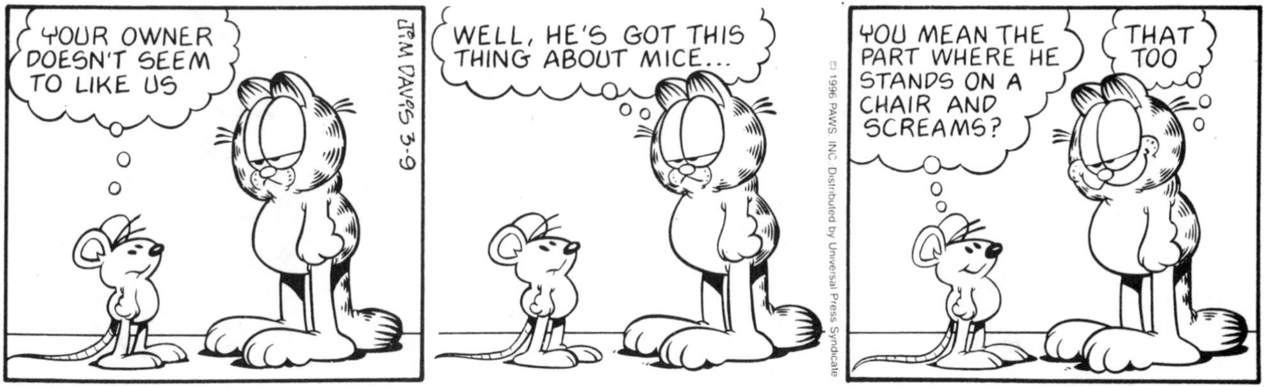
YOUR OWNER DOESN'T SEEM TO LIKE US
JIM DAVIS 3-9
WELL, HE'S GOT THIS THING ABOUT MICE...
© 1996 PAWS. INC. Distributed by Universal Press Syndicate
YOU MEAN THE PART WHERE HE STANDS ON A CHAIR AND SCREAMS?
THAT TOO

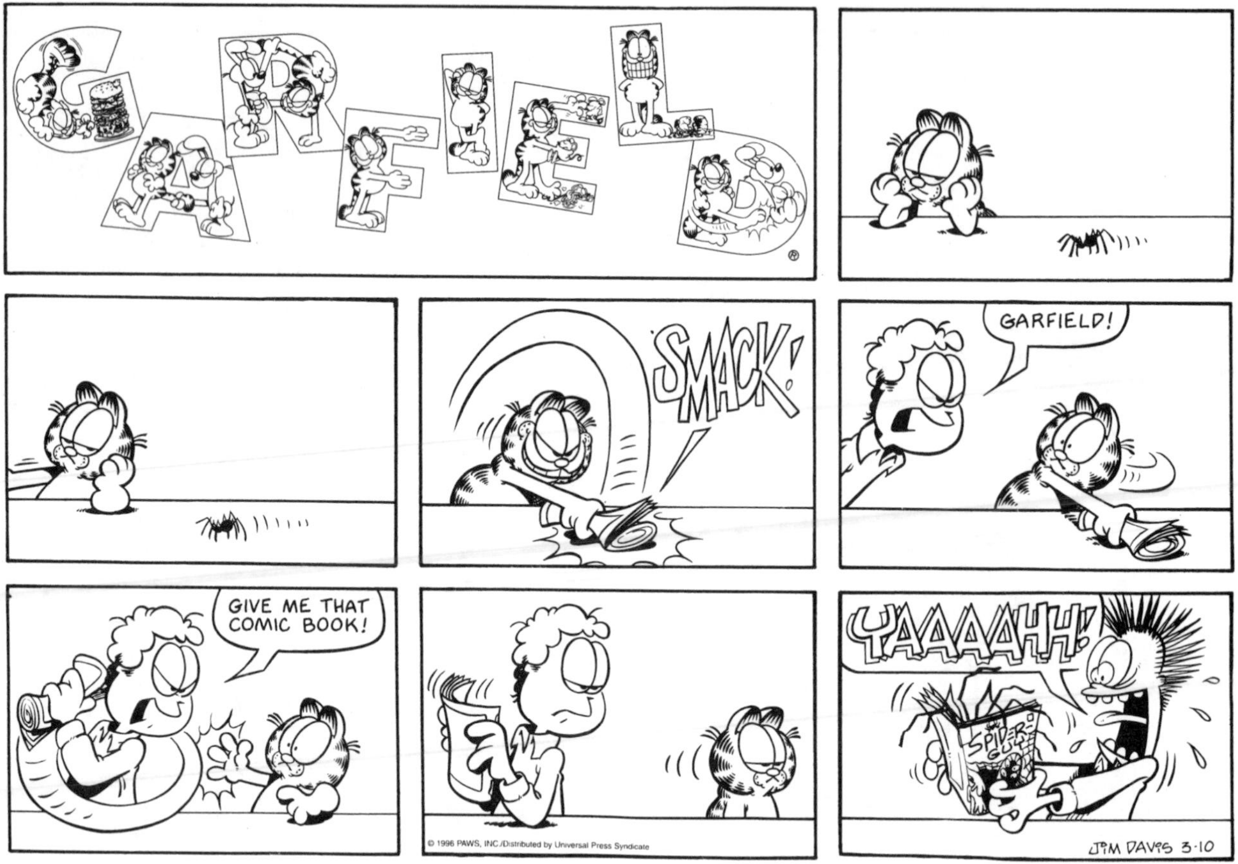
GARFIELD
SMACK!
GARFIELD!
GIVE ME THAT COMIC BOOK!
© 1996 PAWS, INC./Distributed by Universal Press Syndicate
YAAAAHH!
SPIDER-GUY
JIM DAVIS 3-10

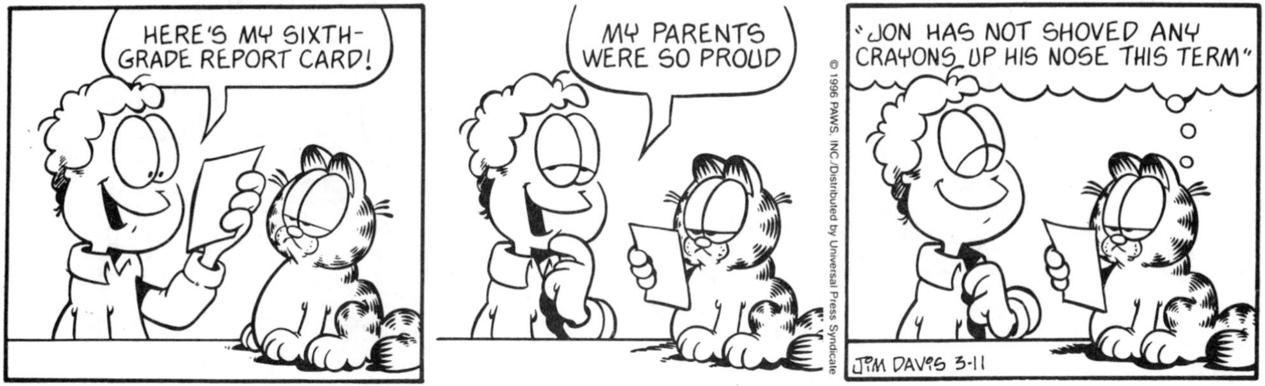
HERE'S MY SIXTH-GRADE REPORT CARD!
MY PARENTS WERE SO PROUD
"JON HAS NOT SHOVED ANY CRAYONS UP HIS NOSE THIS TERM"
JIM DAVIS 3-11

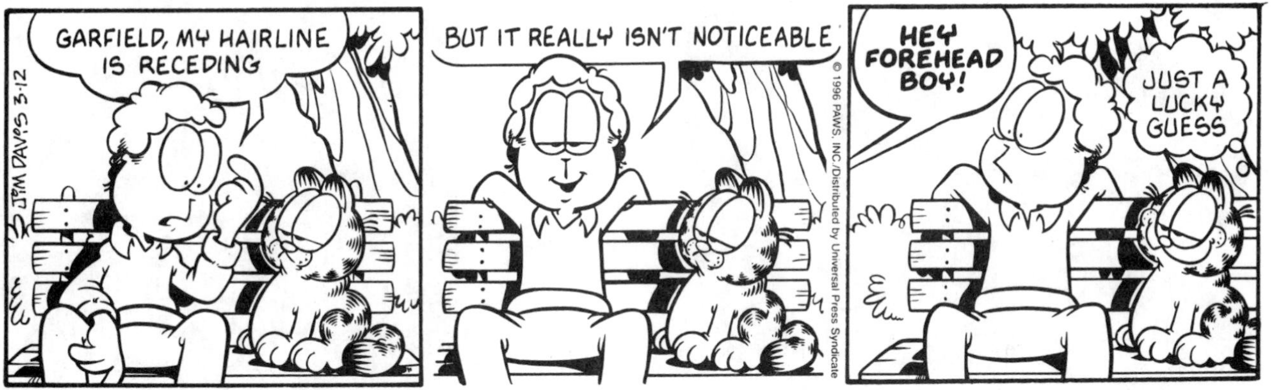
JIM DAVIS 3-12
GARFIELD, MY HAIRLINE IS RECEDING
BUT IT REALLY ISN'T NOTICEABLE
HEY FOREHEAD BOY!
JUST A LUCKY GUESS

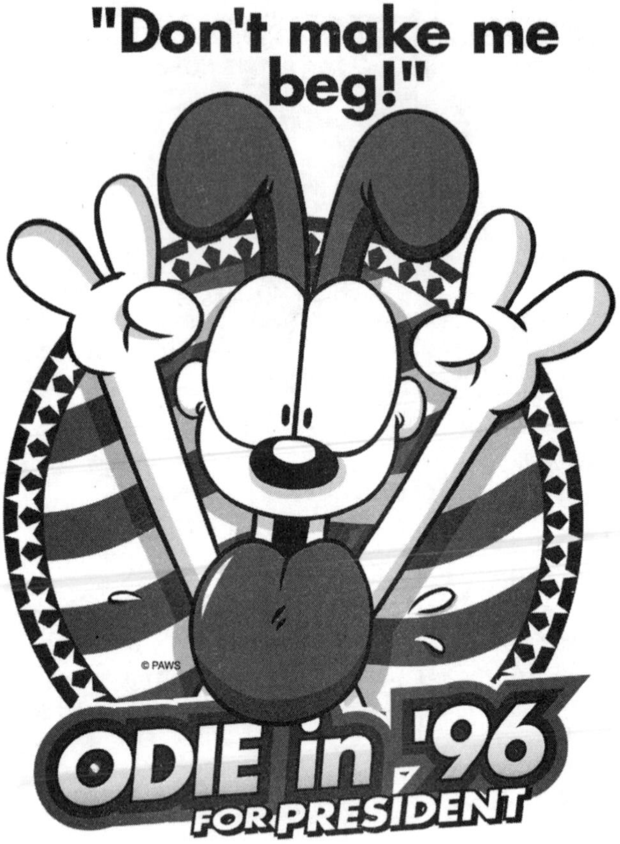
"Don't make me beg!"
© PAWS
ODIE in '96
FOR PRESIDENT

IF ODIE WERE PRESIDENT, HE WOULD...

- Replace Washington Monument with giant fire hydrant
- Start every press conference with an Underdog cartoon
- Repeal oppressive leash laws
- Have all cats de-clawed
- Require mailmen to wear short pants
- Be the first chief executive to lick himself in public!

STRIPS, SPECIALS, OR BESTSELLING BOOKS . . .
GARFIELD'S ON EVERYONE'S MENU
Don't miss even one episode in the Tubby Tabby's hilarious series!

__GARFIELD AT LARGE (#1) 32013/$6.95
__GARFIELD GAINS WEIGHT (#2) 32008/$6.95
__GARFIELD BIGGER THAN LIFE (#3) 32007/$6.95
__GARFIELD WEIGHS IN (#4) 32010/$6.95
__GARFIELD TAKES THE CAKE (#5) 32009/$6.95
__GARFIELD EATS HIS HEART OUT (#6) 32018/$6.95
__GARFIELD SITS AROUND THE HOUSE (#7) 32011/$6.95
__GARFIELD TIPS THE SCALES (#8) 33580/$6.95
__GARFIELD LOSES HIS FEET (#9) 31805/$6.95
__GARFIELD MAKES IT BIG (#10) 31928/$6.95
__GARFIELD ROLLS ON (#11) 32634/$6.95
__GARFIELD OUT TO LUNCH (#12) 33118/$6.95
__GARFIELD FOOD FOR THOUGHT (#13) 34129/$6.95
__GARFIELD SWALLOWS HIS PRIDE (#14) 34725/$6.95
__GARFIELD WORLDWIDE (#15) 35158/$6.95
__GARFIELD ROUNDS OUT (#16) 35388/$6.95

__GARFIELD CHEWS THE FAT (#17) 35956/$6.95
__GARFIELD GOES TO WAIST (#18) 36430/$6.95
__GARFIELD HANGS OUT (#19) 36835/$6.95
__GARFIELD TAKES UP SPACE (#20) 37029/$6.95
__GARFIELD SAYS A MOUTHFUL (#21) 37368/$6.95
__GARFIELD BY THE POUND (#22) 37579/$6.95
__GARFIELD KEEPS HIS CHINS UP (#23) 37959/$6.95
__GARFIELD TAKES HIS LICKS (#24) 38170/$6.95
__GARFIELD HITS THE BIG TIME (#25) 38332/$6.95
__GARFIELD PULLS HIS WEIGHT (#26) 38666/$6.95
__GARFIELD DISHES IT OUT (#27) 39287/$6.95
__GARFIELD LIFE IN THE FAT LANE (#28) 39776/$6.95
__GARFIELD TONS OF FUN (#29) 40386/$6.95

GARFIELD AT HIS SUNDAY BEST!
__GARFIELD TREASURY 32106/$11.95
__THE SECOND GARFIELD TREASURY 33276/$10.95
__THE THIRD GARFIELD TREASURY 32635/$11.00
__THE FOURTH GARFIELD TREASURY 34726/$10.95
__THE FIFTH GARFIELD TREASURY 36268/$12.00
__THE SIXTH GARFIELD TREASURY 37367/$10.95
__THE SEVENTH GARFIELD TREASURY 38427/$10.95
__THE EIGHTH GARFIELD TREASURY 39778/$12.00

Please send me the BALLANTINE BOOKS I have checked above. I am enclosing $_____. (Please add $2.00 for the first book and $.50 for each additional book for postage and handling and include the appropriate state sales tax.) Send check or money order (no cash or C.O.D.'s) to Ballantine Mail Sales Dept. TA, 400 Hahn Road, Westminster, MD 21157.

To order by phone, call 1-800-733-3000 and use your major credit card.

Prices and numbers are subject to change without notice. Valid in the U.S. only. All orders are subject to availability.

Name_____

Address_____

City_____ State_____ Zip_____

Allow at least 4 weeks for delivery 7/93

BIRTHDAYS, HOLIDAYS, OR ANY DAY . . .

Keep GARFIELD on your calendar all year 'round!

GARFIELD TV SPECIALS

__BABES & BULLETS   36339/$5.95
__GARFIELD GOES HOLLYWOOD   34580/$6.95
__GARFIELD'S HALLOWEEN ADVENTURE   33045/$6.95
  (formerly GARFIELD IN DISGUISE)
__GARFIELD'S FELINE FANTASY   36902/$6.95
__GARFIELD IN PARADISE   33796/$6.95
__GARFIELD IN THE ROUGH   32242/$6.95
__GARFIELD ON THE TOWN   31542/$6.95
__GARFIELD'S THANKSGIVING   35650/$6.95
__HERE COMES GARFIELD   32021/$6.95
__GARFIELD GETS A LIFE   37375/$6.95
__A GARFIELD CHRISTMAS   35368/$5.95

Please send me the BALLANTINE BOOKS I have checked above. I am enclosing $_____. (Please add $2.00 for the first book and $.50 for each additional book for postage and handling and include the appropriate state sales tax.) Send check or money order (no cash or C.O.D.'s) to Ballantine Mail Sales Dept. TA, 400 Hahn Road, Westminster, MD 21157.

To order by phone, call 1-800-733-3000 and use your major credit card.

Prices and numbers are subject to change without notice. Valid in the U.S. only. All orders are subject to availability.

GREETINGS FROM GARFIELD!

GARFIELD POSTCARD BOOKS FOR ALL OCCASIONS.
__GARFIELD THINKING OF YOU   36516/$6.95
__GARFIELD WORDS TO LIVE BY   36679/$6.95
__GARFIELD BIRTHDAY GREETINGS   36771/$7.95
__GARFIELD BE MY VALENTINE   37121/$7.95
__GARFIELD SEASON'S GREETINGS   37435/$8.95
__GARFIELD VACATION GREETINGS   37774/$10.00
__GARFIELD'S THANK YOU POSTCARD BOOK   37893/$10.00

ALSO FROM GARFIELD:

__GARFIELD: HIS NINE LIVES   32061/$9.95
__THE GARFIELD BOOK OF CAT NAMES   35082/$5.95
__THE GARFIELD TRIVIA BOOK   33771/$6.95
__THE UNABRIDGED UNCENSORED
  UNBELIEVABLE GARFIELD   33772/$5.95
__GARFIELD: THE ME BOOK   36545/$7.95
__GARFIELD'S JUDGMENT DAY   36755/$6.95
__THE TRUTH ABOUT CATS   37226/$6.95

Name_____

Address_____

City_____ State_____ Zip_____
30   Allow at least 4 weeks for delivery   7/93 TA-267